Praise for

UNHINGED

"Juicy."
—*New York Times*

"This entertaining, gossipy memoir of White House dysfunction will be catnip to scandal lovers."
—*Publishers Weekly*

"Omarosa Manigault Newman sashays in for the kill in *Unhinged.* . . . Deftly executed."
—*The Guardian*

"The impress of Omarosa's personality on the page is indelible and mesmerizing. . . . *Unhinged* is such a pleasure to read because it is unashamedly, thrillingly vindictive."
—*The Weekly Standard*

"Fascinating."
—*Slate*

"Manigault Newman has unleashed Trump's own tricks and tactics against him."
—*The Washington Post*

"A deeply critical portrait of the president."
—*Time*

"Explosive."
—*The Boston Globe*

"Omarosa titled her kiss-and-tell *Unhinged*. Trump seems intent on proving her right."
—*The New Yorker*

"Newman has written a revealing book. . . . Her accounts of trying to connect Trump with black voters during the 2016 presidential campaign are priceless."
—*Financial Times*

UNHINGED

An Insider's Account of
the Trump White House

OMAROSA MANIGAULT NEWMAN

GALLERY BOOKS

New York   London   Toronto   Sydney   New Delhi

To my loving mother

Theresa Manigault

G

Gallery Books
An Imprint of Simon & Schuster, Inc.
1230 Avenue of the Americas
New York, NY 10020

First Gallery Books trade paperback edition April 2019

GALLERY BOOKS and colophon are registered trademarks of Simon & Schuster, Inc.

For information about special discounts for bulk purchases, please contact Simon & Schuster Special Sales at 1-866-506-1949 or business@simonandschuster.com.

The Simon & Schuster Speakers Bureau can bring authors to your live event. For more information or to book an event, contact the Simon & Schuster Speakers Bureau at 1-866-248-3049 or visit our website at www.simonspeakers.com.

Interior design by Jaime Putorti

Manufactured in the United States of America

10 9 8 7 6 5 4 3 2 1

Library of Congress Cataloging-in-Publication Data

Names: Omarosa, author.
Title: Unhinged : an insider's account of the Trump White House / Omarosa Manigault Newman.
Description: New York : Gallery Books, [2018]
Identifiers: LCCN 2018038565 (print) | LCCN 2018042010 (ebook) | ISBN 9781982109721 (ebook) | ISBN 9781982109707(hardcover :alk. paper)
Subjects: LCSH: Omarosa. | Trump, Donald, 1946- | Television personalities--United States--Biography. | United States. White House Office of Public Liaison--Officials and employees--Biography. | Presidents--United States--Staff--Biography. | Press and politics--United States--History--21st century. | United States--Politics and government--2009-2017. | United States--Politics and government--2017- | LCGFT: Autobiographies.
Classification: LCC E912 (ebook) | LCC E912 .O47 2018 (print) | DDC 973.933092--dc23
LC record available at https://urldefense.proofpoint.com/v2/url?u=https-3A__lccn.loc.gov_2018038 565&d=DwIFAg&c=jGUuvAdBXp_VqQ6t0yah2g&r=iIS9Ehmtagfv2Wod-0c9o3NpXCQFPE6T0 4ElRYMIB6ZGQlDIQOdN8iBmw5zUQie0&m=aAQ3uhd0WEleHdmV5CYHwMRyd5ZjGdi-uk 0cilwuRGw&s=m7EFsRRXeQ_q_lHDP9aiR1LsPR4q-Eg4102rAJpBs-U&e=

ISBN 978-1-9821-0970-7
ISBN 978-1-9821-0971-4 (pbk)
ISBN 978-1-9821-0972-1 (ebook)

Contents

CONTENTS

Part Three: The White House

Foreword

Even before *Unhinged* was published in summer 2018, my book made headlines around the world. Nearly two weeks before the book's release date, London's *Daily Mail* obtained an excerpt that focused on my observations about the sharp decline in President Donald Trump's mental health over the fifteen years I'd known him.

I showed how he repeatedly contradicted himself leading up to and during the now-famous May 2017 interview between Trump and NBC News's Lester Holt about his reason for firing former FBI Director James Comey. As part of the White House communications team, I regularly had to prepare Trump for speeches and interviews. He'd often forget the bullet points and go off script, even after multiple briefings. Many pundits had commented on Trump's lack of discipline during interviews. I witnessed it firsthand. I was the first high-level White House staffer to show exactly how the president was experiencing rapid cognitive decline.

That was just the first major revelation in *Unhinged* to dominate the news cycle. Many more would come, and the book seemed like all anyone was talking about for weeks.

I wondered how President Trump would react to the news of the book's existence, and to the many revelations I shared in it. Despite that *Daily Mail* piece, he stayed quiet. He is not known for his restraint, so that surprised me.

On August 12, I began my press tour to discuss the book with an interview with *Meet the Press*'s Chuck Todd. I told him exactly what General John Kelly said to me when he locked me in the Situation Room in the White House and forced me to resign. Trump couldn't stay quiet any longer. In a pair of tweets he wrote, "Wacky Omarosa, who got fired 3 times on the Apprentice, now got fired for the last time. She never made it, never will. She begged me for a job, tears in her eyes, I said Ok. People in the White House hated her. She was vicious, but not smart. I would rarely see her but heard really bad things. Nasty to people & would constantly miss meetings & work. When Gen. Kelly came on board he told me she was a loser & nothing but problems. I told him to try working it out, if possible, because she only said GREAT things about me - until she got fired!"

Typical Trump. If you praise him, he loves you. If you're critical of him, he calls you a loser. That tweet didn't upset me. It fit the pattern of how he reacts whenever anyone—especially a former staffer—comes out against him.

While speaking with Savannah Guthrie on *Today* on August 13, I shared an earlier conversation between Trump and myself, one that seemed to contradict his comments about how negatively he regarded me. In this conversation, he claimed not to have known about Kelly's treatment of me or that I'd been terminated. "I didn't know that," the president said. "I don't love you leaving at all." As I wrote in *Unhinged*, I wasn't sure at the time if Trump genuinely didn't know that Kelly intended to fire me, or if he'd lied about that. He was either clueless or a liar. Probably both. My intention in sharing this conversation was to demonstrate the constant chaos and confusion of working in the most bizarre White House in history.

In response to this revelation, the president tweeted, "When you give a crazed, crying lowlife a break, and give her a job at the White House, I guess it just didn't work out. Good work by General Kelly for quickly firing that dog!"

He called me "that dog."

Trump had accused people of acting "like a dog" before, but this was a new low. He called me an animal. The president of the United States had resorted to calling a woman, a former trusted friend, a slur with obvious racial overtones. The tweet set off another round of shock waves. Even people who'd opposed me for being part of the Trump team came to my defense and said how inappropriate it was for him to attack me this way.

Instead of acknowledging the shady way he and Kelly handled my departure, Trump kept attacking me and contradicting himself. He now claimed he knew that Kelly intended to fire me, and that he'd directed it. But Kelly himself had told me that Trump didn't know. Trump had told me he didn't know. His tweeting continued: "While I know it's 'not presidential' to take on a lowlife like Omarosa, and while I would rather not be doing so, this is a modern day form of communication and I know the Fake News Media will be working overtime to make even Wacky Omarosa look legitimate as possible. Sorry!"

Mind you, this was all just the Monday and Tuesday of the book's release week. It was all very insane.

My former colleagues shared with me that Trump was livid that I'd exposed him and Kelly, and that he'd lobbied then–Attorney General Jeff Sessions to have the Justice Department arrest me! On what charge? For having the courage to blow the whistle on all the corruption that I'd witnessed? For being honest? For telling the public what was really going on in the White House? I had exposed their thuggish ways and they were furious. Can you imagine how authoritarian it would be to arrest citizens for revealing the truth about the unethical behavior of our public servants? That's why there are whistle-blower laws to protect those who have the courage to come forward. But Trump seemed to believe that his loyal followers would do whatever he wanted in the moment, regardless of its legality.

Trump being Trump, he wasn't satisfied with bullying me on Twitter. He sent his minions out to debunk all of the forthcoming revelations in the book, the secrets and lies I would expose about him and members of his Trumpworld cult. If he really wanted my book to fail, he had a funny way of showing it. His rants made people more interested in *Unhinged*—of course!

And the attention he generated gave me an opportunity to go on television and prove that the statements I'd made in *Unhinged* were well documented, accurate, and verifiable. The fact that I had proof of my statements sent shock waves throughout the White House itself. As they said, I had "receipts." People who'd attempted to undermine and mistreat me were particularly concerned about what would come out next.

One of the biggest, most controversial subjects in the book concerned the elusive recording of Trump saying the N-word. In the book, I faithfully recounted the history of my knowledge of that tape, starting during the presidential campaign with an October 2016 tweet and subsequent NPR interview with first-season *The Apprentice* producer Bill Pruitt, who said he'd witnessed Trump use racially offensive language with his own eyes and ears and believed there was a tape of it out there somewhere. Pruitt's claims triggered my pursuit of that alleged tape so I could know the truth for myself. During that crucial period in the campaign, I had several conversations with advisers Jason Miller, Lynne Patton, and Katrina Pierson to discuss the headlines that Pruitt's tweet had triggered and the persistent rumors. Miller solicited my assistance in developing an appropriate strategy if the tape were ever made public, which I recounted in *Unhinged*.

On August 13, Pierson, the former spokesperson for the Trump campaign, told Ed Henry on Fox News that the conversation transcribed faithfully in *Unhinged* never took place. "That did not happen. It sounds like she's writing a script for a movie. I've already been out there talking about this. That is absolutely not true. I have no sources with that tape," she said. "But I will not stand by and allow her to continue to tarnish everyone's reputation and hurt the one person that helped her become who she is in that celebrity world." She also said, "[Omarosa] can't keep her lies straight."

I couldn't let that stand. Later that day, during a CBS News interview, I shared the full conversation in question, including the line of Katrina's saying, about Trump using the N-word, "No, he said it. He's embarrassed." Once the actual conversation was revealed, Pierson had to go back on Fox News and explain to Ed Henry why she lied to his face about her knowledge of the conversation and the N-word tape. She had similar humiliating interviews with Erin Burnett on CNN and other outlets on her apology tour. She made a nonsensical claim that she'd indulged me in talking about the tape in order to shut me up, saying I was "like a dog with a bone" in my efforts to uncover it. You can almost hear Trump issuing her orders: "When in doubt, attack her by calling her a 'dog.'"

When asked at a White House press briefing if she could guarantee that Donald had never used the N-word, Sarah Huckabee Sanders refused to say that Trump never said it and made this shocking statement: "I can't guarantee anything, but I can tell you that the president addressed this question directly. I can tell you that I've never heard it." She couldn't deny the possibility! A sad and profound "statement" by the White House press secretary.

As I explained in many interviews about *Unhinged*, everything I wrote in the book could be verified and documented. If I didn't have proof that such conversations took place, no one would have believed me. I had to protect myself. I knew they'd call me a liar. It's what they do. Everyone connected to Trump—and Trump himself—constantly lies about everything. The *Washington Post* had a funny term for repeated stated untruths: "bottomless Pinocchios." My recordings were my shield.

Trump, predictably, dispatched his legal team. First, they sent a cease and desist letter to my publisher, Simon & Schuster, threatening them with substantial monetary and punitive damages if they published *Unhinged* on schedule. The publisher's counsel, Elizabeth McNamara, replied, "Mr. Trump is the president of the United States, with a 'bully pulpit' at his disposal. To the extent he disputes any statements in the Book, he has the largest platform in the world to challenge them. While your letter generally claims that excerpts from the book contain 'disparaging statements,' it is quite telling that at no point do you claim that any specific statement in the book is false," McNamara wrote. "Your client does not have a viable legal claim merely because unspecified truthful statements in the Book may embarrass the president or his associates. At base, [Trump's lawyer's] letter is nothing more than an obvious attempt to silence legitimate criticism of the President. Simon & Schuster will not be intimidated by hollow legal threats and have proceeded with publication of the Book as scheduled."

Next, Trump's lawyers came after me personally. I am still in arbitration on this issue. Hopefully we will be victorious and it'll be over soon.

Another major revelation from the book came two days later, and it exposed members of the First Family. For *MSNBC Live* with Craig Melvin, I shared a conversation between Lara Trump, Donald's son Eric's wife, and myself, during which Lara offered me a fifteen-thousand-dollar-per-month job contract to work for the 2020 reelection campaign. It was an obvious bribe, an effort to silence me about the illegal, unethical, and amoral things I'd witnessed during my White House year. "It sounds a little like, obviously, that there are some things you've got in the back pocket to pull out," said Lara. "Clearly, if you come on board, like, we can't have . . . Everything, everybody positive, right?"

Sharing that conversation gave me no joy. Lara and I had been close friends for ten years. I had really come to like Eric as well. But I also realized that she had gone over to the dark side. She was no longer the Lara that I'd known. The power and corruption had seeped in and she'd become a member of the Trump cult. They were using her, intentionally, to get to me. I think they had her call me because of our close friendship, thinking, *Omarosa won't say no to Lara.*

The sad truth is, they're all being used.

Eric Trump is forced to say some of the most ridiculous things to support his father. Despite his characterization on *Saturday Night Live*, Eric had always been the sensible one. Not anymore. Now he's no better than any of the Trump attackers. When I released the tape of his wife attempting to bribe me, he wrote on Twitter, "I hate disloyal people."

To which I, and many others, replied that Eric's father was disloyal to his mother, cheated on his first stepmother, and cheated on his current wife by reportedly having unprotected sex with a *Playboy* playmate and with at least one porn star that we know of.

All of what I've been describing about the book's release happened in just one week. The first week. During my hectic media tour, my husband, John, was by my side for every interview and appearance, and I'm beyond grateful for that support.

It was all magnified when my publisher and I learned that *Unhinged* had debuted on the *New York Times* bestseller list at number one. It would remain on the list for weeks to come. The truth about the Trump White House, and how every member of his wretched crew behaved, was resonating with the public.

The reaction from readers (and from people who hadn't read it, but somehow had strong opinions about it) was first incredulity, and then amazement about the truths I revealed.

Many of the comments I received were a kind of apology from people who admitted to having formed their opinion of me based solely on how I was portrayed in the media. After reading my whole story, they had gained a new perspective on my unique journey. *Unhinged* was the first time I've opened up about who I am and what I've survived, including my childhood in extreme poverty, surviving a house fire, losing my father and brother to violence, my miscarriage, and the sudden death of my fiancé. Sharing these experiences was liberating and cathartic. Readers far and wide—from New Zealand and Australia, Gambia, Nigeria, China, Germany, and England—told me their similar stories of pain and loss and that they'd realized I wasn't just a caricature of my famous TV persona. After they read *Unhinged*, I was human to them.

MEANWHILE, BY THE end of the summer of 2018, the popularity of *Unhinged* had become a thorn in Trump's side. But he now had bigger problems to worry about.

Special counsel Robert Mueller's investigation has been a chilling undercurrent in Trumpworld for nearly his entire presidency. If the number of confessions and indictments of administration officials says anything, I was either working with some pretty corrupt people in the campaign and later in the White House, or many good people had extreme lapses of judgment under the guise of loyalty to the president. Neither is good for the country.

The public has been frustrated by the pace of the Mueller investigation, but I can tell you that he is leaving no stone unturned. There are literally millions of documents to go through, from the campaign, the transition, and the administration. I know. Mueller's folks called me, too.

Back in October, Trump tweeted, "For the record, I have no financial interests in Saudi Arabia (or Russia, for that matter)." I replied, "I wonder if #45 will ever disclose how much they contributed to his inauguration?" And now, the inauguration is being investigated. From new reports, tens of millions of dollars of donor money remains unaccounted for. The Trump Foundation, the "charity" arm of the organization, has been shuttered amid allegations of outrageous corruption.

That is just a taste of what Mueller will inevitably discover. We all have to be patient. The truth will come out, but not before Mueller is ready to show what he's got. For now, we have to content ourselves with the glimpses into his proceedings in his court documents. If you think it's agony for you to wait, imagine what it's been like for the man who sits behind the desk in the Oval Office. I still have friends in the White House, and they tell me he's become totally . . . well, unhinged.

When my book was published, longtime Trump attorney and my closest friend in the Trump Organization, Michael Cohen, was being investigated by the FBI and the Southern District of New York for various crimes, and has since pled guilty to lying to Congress and violating campaign finance laws. Like the rest of the country, I watched him walk into court with his family for his sentencing—his daughter on crutches, his father in a wheelchair, his wife and son in obvious pain. My heart went out to them. I thought, *It's all because of their association with toxic Trump.*

All fall and winter, Trump had been attacking Michael on Twitter, calling him "a weak person," calling for harsh punishment, and tweeting, "You mean [Cohen] can do all of the TERRIBLE, unrelated to Trump, things having to do with fraud, big loans, Taxis, etc., and not serve a long prison term? He makes up stories to get a GREAT & ALREADY reduced deal for himself, and get his wife and father-in-law (who has the money?) off Scott Free. He lied for this outcome and should, in my opinion, serve a full and complete sentence."

As Michael told Judge William Pauley, "Today is the day that I am getting my freedom back. . . . I have been living in a personal and mental incarceration ever since the fateful day that I accepted the offer to work for a famous real estate mogul whose business acumen I truly admired. . . . I felt it was my duty to cover up his dirty deeds rather than to listen to my own inner voice and my moral compass."

The idea of Michael Cohen going to prison makes me terribly sad for him and his family, especially his daughter, Samantha, who was my intern at the White House. At the time of this writing, Michael is cooperating with the Mueller investigation and that might result in a reassessment of his sentence, but as of now, he's facing three years and $1.9 million in fines. That's a steep price to pay for, as Michael described it in court, his "blind loyalty to this man that led me to choose a path of darkness over light."

It was Michael who initially recruited me to work on the 2016 campaign to help Trump with his "woman problem." Thank God I was snapped out of my Trump trance before it was too late. When Michael spoke out in court about "blind loyalty," he echoed the cult dynamic I explained in *Unhinged*. He'd been living with it for ten years at the Trump Organization, seeing and dealing with Donald every day.

For the majority of my "friendship" with the president, I lived in California and had geographical and emotional distance. Michael never got a break. I could always say that Donald treated me with respect and courtesy. But Trump had always treated Michael cruelly, berating him in public, going "nuclear" on him.

After the FBI raid that turned Michael's life upside down, Trump washed his hands of him, even called him a "low-level" employee who did more public relations than legal work.

Michael shared some revelations of his own about Trump's offensive, homophobic, racist language, too. In November 2018, he told *Vanity Fair* that the president called Kwame Jackson of *The Apprentice* a "black f*g," as well as other racist comments. Others did come forward to back me up. Penn Jillette, who also did time on *Celebrity Apprentice*, defended me to *Vulture*, saying he was in the room when Trump said "racially insensitive things that made me uncomfortable."

THE MIDTERM ELECTIONS in November 2018 brought in a new Democratic majority in the House of Representatives. The blue tsunami was a very clear rebuke of Trump and his policies. The country showed that it is either against his administration or against him. Or both. The House of Representatives gained forty seats, a huge number. I celebrated the many women who were elected, and love that we will have more diversity on the Hill.

For the first two years of Trump's presidency, the Republican-controlled Congress had virtually no impactful oversight of his administration. There is a litany of abuses of power and conflicts of interest this administration has participated in without any accountability. That all changed with the Democrats taking control of Congress. Now there will be congressional hearings on those issues where there has been absolutely none, from actions by the EPA to protections of our citizens from corporate greed. Rep. Richard Neal, Democratic chairman of the House Ways & Means Committee, has already indicated that he plans to ask for Trump's tax returns. And he and his committee now have the power to get them.

Simply put, there is no longer a congressional rubber stamp for this administration. And for a president who hasn't demonstrated any depth of emotional maturity, we can only assume the reaction won't be good when he is told "No!" Just imagine how he'll explode when important and revealing documents are subpoenaed. If you think you've seen tweetstorms, trust me, you haven't seen anything yet.

Some of the decisions that Trump makes and policies that he enacts completely undermine the platform of the Republican party—for example, government shutdowns and troop withdrawals. His behavior has totally and permanently damaged the party and I think they'll be feeling the effects for a very long time. Trump does not care about what he's doing to the GOP. He only cares about himself. Republican lawmakers stay loyal to him because they don't have any choice. They can't change boats in the middle of the ocean, and Trump's base is sticking with him.

For his part, Trump does not demonstrate the same loyalty to others that he demands from them. Chief of Staff General John Kelly stepped down in December 2018, almost a year to the day after he locked me in the Situation Room. I got a lot of media requests to comment on his departure. Many people on social media said things like "Omarosa is getting the last laugh." I didn't feel happy or joyful about it. It was just an exclamation point, an emphatic end to the sad saga. I knew that John Kelly was a bigot, a racist, and a misogynist. Because of my race and my gender, he treated me horribly. He called the wife-beater Rob Porter a "man of integrity," and dismissed me for fabricated "integrity issues." In *Unhinged*, I exposed him, and now he's gone. I don't think many people look at John Kelly the same way they did when he entered the White House. His true colors have now been revealed.

Mike Pence's longtime chief of staff, Nick Ayers, has also departed.

Back in September 2018, the infamous "I Am Part of the Resistance Inside the Trump Administration" was published in the *New York Times*. The op-ed validated what I'd written in *Unhinged* about the silent army of people who were working to prevent disaster in the Trump administration. I did a poll on Twitter, asking the public who might have written it. The majority of respondents said Nick Ayers, and I agreed with them. I've always been suspicious of Nick Ayers because he played the part perfectly—too perfectly. He's like Pence, just saying whatever Trump wants to hear, biding his time. But he must have sensed a change in the tide. By refusing to take Kelly's job as Trump's chief of staff, he's playing the long game. He has bigger plans for himself, whatever they might be, and he doesn't want to be stained by serving Donald Trump for two years, until the run-up to 2020. Ayers had also witnessed many of Trump's "going nuclear" outbursts, which can't be unseen. He is reported to have taken a job at America First, the Trump-supporting Super PAC he helped to form.

There have been many more casualties of this administration. Attorney General Jeff Sessions was axed the day after the midterms. General James Mattis resigned in December over Trump's decision to withdraw troops from Syria. Also in December, Ryan Zinke resigned as secretary of the interior after one too many scandals. Secretary of the treasury and Trump favorite Steve Mnuchin is currently in Trump's crosshairs over the precipitous plunge in the stock market since the midterms. By the time this paperback comes out, he might be out of a job as well.

Kellyanne Conway clings to her post, even as her husband, George Conway, seems to have made it his personal mission to embarrass Trump and question his policies on Twitter. When *Unhinged* came out, Conway said that he and Trump were friends, disagreeing with my assertion that Trump hated him. I don't think anyone, including George, would deny my take on their relationship now. Donald—and Don Jr. and Eric—are at war with George, while Kellyanne continues to serve loyally. Can you imagine their Sunday dinners?

Betsy DeVos still remains secretary of education, although she continues to be as incompetent as I described in *Unhinged*. Recently, she was sued for failing to cancel the debt for students who borrowed funds to attend shuttered for-profit colleges. Under her tenure, historically black colleges and universities—or HBCUs, which

I fought for throughout my year in the White House—have suffered. All-female Bennett College in Greensboro, North Carolina, is losing its accreditation because of financial issues. Saint Augustine's University in Raleigh is facing probation, also because of finances. Theses colleges need to receive donations to keep the doors open, exactly the situation I'd hoped to prevent.

The Trump–Fox News direct connections that I wrote about have only strengthened in the last year. Bill Shine, the White House deputy chief of staff for communications, left Fox News in the wake of the sexual harassment lawsuit against Roger Ailes. It has just been reported that his severance package with the network, $8.4 million, will be paid out to him while he is working in the White House. He is, in effect, a de facto employee of Fox News and the government at the same time. That's just wrong.

Shine replaced Hope Hicks, former director of communications. She left the White House and landed (where else?) at Fox News, as its chief communications officer. Hope and Bill basically swapped jobs. You could see it as their having the same job, actually—in a different office, but with the same objective: justify and defend Trump and rally his base.

Don Jr. left his wife, Vanessa, mother of his five children, and is now in a romantic relationship with former Fox host Kimberly Guilfoyle. Together, "Donberly" tour the country, speaking at rallies and fund-raisers on behalf of the president.

In *Unhinged*, I noted that Trump had to clean up Don Jr.'s disastrous handling of that meeting in Trump Tower with the Russian lawyer that was the trigger for the Mueller investigation and remains at the center of it. I believe Don Jr. is still trying, and will always try, to make up for that screw-up. The son's hero worship of his father knows no bounds.

Melania Trump came out of her shell in the fall of 2018 and did a few televised interviews, telling ABC News that she is the "most bullied person on the world," to the delight of Twitter commenters. Regarding the Brett Kavanaugh hearings, she said, "You cannot just say to somebody, you know, 'I was sexually assaulted' or 'You did that to me,' because sometimes the media goes too far and the way they portray some stories, it's not correct, it's not right." She might as well have been talking about the sixteen women who have accused her husband of sexual misconduct, not to mention the two—Stormy Daniels and Karen McDougal—who were paid hush money to stay silent about their affairs with the president.

Unfortunately for Melania, her favorability numbers have dropped double digits. Before she started expressing her views, people gave her the benefit of the doubt, or saw her as a sympathetic figure (#freemelania, etc.). But now they realize that she's a co-signer of Trump's agenda. She's defending sexual harassers. She asks people not to bully, while ignoring her own husband's aggressive tactics. When the Trump administration started to separate mothers from their children, she had an opportunity to speak out against it, but she wore the "I don't really care, do you?" jacket. On her visit to Africa, she dressed in a costume of European colonizers and oppressors. As I wrote in *Unhinged*, none of her fashion choices are accidental. She knew what she was doing, and how it would look.

I have watched Melania over the last sixteen years, and I firmly believe she knew about Donald's affairs. He didn't hide them. He chased woman openly, right in front of her. She accepted him for who he is. Like Republicans in Congress, she's stuck with him, like it or not.

By any measure, Trumpworld is considerably smaller and less tenable than it was when I left it a year ago, and it will only get worse in coming days. Right now, in the West Wing, Trump is probably sitting in his private chambers, in front of his wall of televisions, with a can of Diet Coke and a plate of fried chicken, screaming at whoever happens to be nearby, blaming the media for all his problems, and feeling the squeeze. As the walls close in, as the firings continue and the stock market plummets, he will become more and more unhinged, bracing for more hearings, investigations, and possible impeachment.

I don't think we've hit bottom, though. It will likely get worse. Much worse.

When the investigations start focusing on his family, particularly zeroing in on Ivanka, he will completely unravel.

It's very interesting that Ivanka and her husband, Jared Kushner, have not been interviewed by the Mueller team—yet. That means they might be at the center of the whole thing. It's been reported that Ivanka's role in negotiating inflated contracts to vendors at the Trump International Hotel in Washington, DC, for the inauguration is being investigated. Jared has been involved with the Saudi royal family, way before the savage murder in Turkey of an American resident, journalist Jamal Khashoggi, in October 2018. Jared is still operating in the White House and around the world with limited security clearance. I predict that, very soon, the Mueller investigation will close in on the Kushners.

Donald will be apoplectic when it does. He'll be frustrated by his limitations, because the office of the presidency does not allow him to fight back against a special prosecutor's investigation. He's spent his whole life bullying and buying his way out of trouble. But this time, threats of violence and an envelope full of cash won't help. He has no recourse for the Mueller attacks, and so he has to use the only weapon he has—Twitter.

I strongly believe Trump will face impeachment proceedings before the 2020 election. He might be found guilty of obstruction or collusion. Don't think for a second that means he will resign or choose not to seek reelection in 2020. He'll do what he always does, deflect and demean, lie and deny—and thousands of his Trumpworld cult followers will believe him. He has no shame, no dignity, no concern for uniting the nation. He will run on outrage, aggression, and ego, just as he did in 2016.

And sadly, it just might work again.

In the meantime, his rivals will wait for their opening. Mike Pence will bide his time. He won't say or do anything to rock the boat, even if he is mocked for being human wallpaper. Why didn't he comment on the Stormy Daniels payoff? Why is he silent? Where's his moral compass? No matter how awful Trump's lies and behavior are, Pence will smile and enable. He can feel the presidency in his grasp, so close. He is only a heartbeat away, and it's not like Trump is getting healthier.

On December 22, 2018, the second shutdown of the US federal government under Donald Trump began. The shutdown started when Donald and the soon-to-be Democratic-controlled US Congress could not agree on how to fund the government for fiscal year 2019, specifically, whether Trump could include $5.7 billion in the budget to build a wall across the southern border. As a result, nine agencies and 800,000 employees went without pay.

Under the guise of national security, Trump used almost a million government workers as bargaining chips. In a clear attempt to solidify his base, he jeopardized aviation security, food safety, and a host of other critical areas of government just so he could build his wall, which even experts say won't deter illegal immigration as he claims it will. What's most insulting is that he showed no empathy for the families wounded in the process of this farce. It was not until we began seeing images of Americans stranded at airports with countless delays that threatened commerce that the president found a way to reopen the government. And he put Americans at risk while claiming he was trying to protect us.

The shutdown lasted almost six weeks. While the number of federal workers affected was 800,000, that doesn't take into account the loss of income to families connected to those federal workers. In reality, millions of Americans were directly affected by what was essentially a political stunt using federal employees as pawns.

As of this writing, the latest government shutdown has been temporarily resolved. As you notice, I said "temporarily." There are new negotiations taking place to find a more permanent solution to this ongoing problem. We can only hope that our federal workers won't be used again as political fodder. One can only hope.

As for me, I'm finally free, and it feels great. *Unhinged* has been an incredible journey for me, and helped heal many wounds. I'm humbled that the book has been a success and grateful to every person who heard me out, supported me, and gave me a chance to share how I got into Trumpworld, and how I escaped. I will use this second chance to do what I can to bring dignity back to the country I love. Thanks again, for everything. The best is yet to come.

Omarosa Manigault Newman,
February 2019

Prologue

"The Staff Works for Me, Not the President."

On Tuesday, December 12, 2017, I was sitting at my desk in the Eisenhower Executive Office Building (EEOB) in the White House complex, when my assistant, Alexa Pursley, walked in looking perplexed.

"I just got an email from General Kelly's executive assistant," she said. "He wants to meet you in the Situation Room at five."

"Really," I said. Ever since General John Kelly had become chief of staff at the end of July, replacing Reince Priebus, he rarely had two minutes for me. And now, suddenly, he wanted a meeting? It was highly unusual to be called to the Situation Room in the West Wing—where former president Barack Obama plotted the strategy to kill Osama bin Laden; where President Donald Trump planned the attack on Syria to retaliate for their use of chemical weapons; where every president since John F. Kennedy had top-secret conversations with world leaders. Why didn't Kelly want to meet in his office?

At the appropriate time, Alexa and I walked over to the Situation Room. We sat down at the large boardroom table. Next to arrive were several White House lawyers, including Uttam Dhillon, deputy counsel to the president, and Stefan Passantino, deputy White House counsel in charge of compliance and ethics. Finally, General Kelly walked in.

A brusque man, Kelly looked at Alexa and asked, "Who are you?"

She said, "Omarosa's assistant."

He said, "Could you leave us alone?"

Alexa gathered her things and left.

General Kelly sat down and said, "We're going to talk to you about leaving the White House. It's come to my attention there have been significant integrity issues related to you. The integrity issues are very serious. If this were the military, this would be a pretty high level of accountability, meaning a court-martial. We're not suggesting any legal action here. It's a pretty serious offense. I'd like to see this be a friendly departure. There are pretty significant legal issues that we hope won't make it ugly for you. If we make this a friendly departure, you can look at your time here in the White House as a year of service to the nation. You can go on without any type of difficulty in the future relative to your reputation. But it's very important that you understand there are serious legal issues that have been violated and you are open to some legal action that we hope we can control."

I asked whether the president was aware of this.

"This is a nonnegotiable discussion."

"I'd like the opportunity to understand," I said.

"There are serious integrity violations," he said.

Why was he being so vague? What violations?

"The staff works for me, not the president. So after your departure, I'll inform him. With that, I'll let you go."

What is he talking about? Where is this coming from?

Quickly, I connected the dots.

This had to be about the N-word tape.

THE FIRST TIME I heard about the N-word tape was during the campaign. The day after the infamous *Access Hollywood* tape came out, a former *Apprentice* producer named Bill Pruitt sent a tantalizing tweet that "there are far worse" tapes of Donald Trump captured on set; in October 2017, Pruitt told NPR the tapes contained unfathomably despicable words about African Americans, Jewish people, all of the above. At that time, Pruitt had reached out to several people in Trumpworld, including Lynne Patton, then Eric Trump's longtime personal assistant who was running HUD's programs in New York and New Jersey, to try to raise awareness about this tape. Jason Miller, the campaign's communications director, had also received a heads-up call that the N-word tape was about to drop. On a four-way conference call with Jason, Lynne, spokesperson Katrina Pierson, and myself, we discussed whether it was possible Trump really had said those things and, if so, how it would be handled. But the tape never came out. I had to assume something or someone stopped it from happening. We got through the election and hadn't heard a peep about it again.

Until now.

Speculation about the N-word tape had become intense again, and I was determined to get to the bottom of it. When I'd first heard about the possibility of a tape of Trump using the N-word a year ago, I was highly doubtful that it existed. My first thought was to protect the candidate about something false. But in the year since, my mind was turning about the man I'd called a friend for almost fifteen years. I'd been loyal to him all this time, but if I had any proof that this tape was real, I would pack up my office and submit my resignation immediately.

I'd had one foot out the door since the mishandling of the Unite the Right rally in Charlottesville, Virginia, in August 2017. And, in October, there was Trump's insensitive condolence call with the widow of an Army Special Forces soldier killed in Niger, followed by Trump and Kelly's racially charged attack on Representative Frederica Wilson who heard the call and told the press about it. Trump's endorsement of Alabama Senate candidate Roy Moore, a man who'd been accused of sexual misconduct by multiple women, only added insult to injury.

The N-word tape would be the last "last straw" for me. With so much speculation, I had to assume that its release was imminent, and I did *not* want to be sitting at 1600 Pennsylvania Avenue if and when the story broke, with Trump's scrambles to defend his usage of *that word* played repeatedly on every news channel for weeks.

I'd informed Hope Hicks, the White House director of communications at the time, that chatter about the N-word tape was heating up. The very existence of it fell squarely in my portfolio since it centered on race relations. I'd emailed before one of our daily comms meetings that a source from *The Apprentice* days had contacted me and claimed to be in possession of the tape.

By that point, three sources in three separate conversations had described the contents of this tape. They all told me that President Trump hadn't just dropped a single N-word bomb. He'd said it *multiple times* throughout the show's taping during off-camera outtakes, particularly during the first season of *The Apprentice*.

I appeared on the first season. I was the only African American woman, and Kwame Jackson was the only black man, in a cast of sixteen. I had to wonder, if Trump used the N-word so frequently during that season of the show, had he ever used it to refer to either Kwame or myself? I would look like the biggest imbecile alive for supporting a man who used that word. And if he'd used it about me, the betrayal would be devastating. I'd known him since the first day of shooting *The Apprentic*e in September 2003, and we'd grown closer ever since. If he'd spewed that hateful word about me or anyone, I had to know.

"I *need* to hear it for myself," I told Hope.

"What's the plan?" she asked. "What are you going to do?" Ever since that meeting, she'd been eager and asking frequently about my progress on the matter.

What I suspect happened: Hope Hicks had told John Kelly that I was *this close* to getting my hands on the tape. As had been widely reported, Kelly had been dying to get rid of me since his first day. Now he had cause. I wasn't sure how he'd justify it, but I was sure it all led back to that tape.

In the Situation Room, with Kelly now gone, I turned to the lawyers, dying to hear what my significant infractions were. One of them said, "We found out that you abused the car service."

"The car service?" As a commissioned officer, I had the use of the car service for official business. Additionally, I lived in Penn Quarter, which was a ten- to fifteen-minute walk from my office. I mostly Ubered or walked back and forth between home and work nearly every day—and I had the daily Uber and Fitbit logs to prove it.

"We understand that you took the car service to a Washington Nationals game for personal use," said one of the lawyers, looking smug, like I was busted.

"What was the date of that?"

"June fifteenth," he said.

I checked my calendar. "That was the Congressional Baseball Game. That was certainly official business." The game was an annual charity event, of particular importance that year, because House Majority Whip Steve Scalise and three others had been shot by a deranged man at a practice the day before, and we wanted to come out in force in honor of him and to show unity between the parties. Half the White House had taken government cars there! Kellyanne Conway, Steve Mnuchin, Gary Cohn, and Ivanka Trump and her kids were there, too. I hadn't been to a Nationals game since I'd been back in Washington, and the only time I went to Nationals Park was on that day.

The White House lawyers looked back and forth at one another cluelessly, like the Three Stooges.

"It's the first time I'm hearing about this." It just didn't make sense. I'd never received a warning or notification. During my entire tenure in the Trump White House, I'd never heard of anyone taken to task over car-service trips, and certainly not in the Situation Room with the chief of staff!

"I have a running list of every time I used the car service for official business; I can give it to you, and we can compare notes," I said. You better believe I kept vigilant records of everything. As the only African American senior staffer, I crossed every *t*, dotted every *i*. I shook my head in disbelief, thinking, *This can't be the only thing you could come up with to justify getting rid of me.*

But they had nothing else! We went back and forth. They kept saying things like, "We know about some serious violations!"

"Just tell me what they are!"

"Well, you had your husband ride in the car with you."

"We're allowed to bring our spouse in the car if we're attending the same official event." The guidelines were clear; I knew them by heart. This was my second tour of duty working in the White House, after all. I'd worked for a year in Al Gore's office when he was vice president, and then in Bill Clinton's presidential personnel office during the last year of his presidency.

Stefan shrugged and gave me a look that said, *Yeah, we're just grasping at straws.*

Were they really coming after me about a totally legitimate car ride? Mind you, Secretary Steven Mnuchin's use of private jets—to the tune of nearly one million dollars of taxpayer money—had just been given the "okay" by the inspector general for the Treasury Department. Scott Pruitt, the head of the Environmental Protection Agency (EPA), spent upward of $3 million on a nineteen-man security team, and he still has his job. Several months after I left, Ben Carson got to keep his job after ordering a $31,000 dining set.

"I see a long line of White House appointees' official vehicles at the same events, and I'm in violation, not anyone else? This is why

I kept records of every trip and meeting and asked for guidance on travel. I want to go one by one through this. I keep detailed logs. I'm ready for it. I'm prepared."

"We're not going through this one by one," said Uttam Dhillon, the same lawyer who reportedly misled Trump about FBI Director James Comey's firing. "It's not a fight that's winnable."

My temper flared. "I'm being railroaded," I said.

"This discussion is over. Let's bring in HR," said Dhillon.

Irene Porada, who has worked in White House HR for twenty years, handed me a water and said, "I know this is a bad day."

We discussed my departure, and I had to negotiate how I was going to leave the White House. Eventually, they said I had to resign immediately but would be paid through January 20. They insisted on packing my office for me and sending the contents to me, but I pushed back on that. I asked for a statement to be released from the president immediately. I asked what would happen to my assistant. They said they'd get answers to all these questions.

All they cared about was a quiet, calm exit so that they could "control the message in the media" about it, as if social media didn't exist, as if people wouldn't hash over it on every news channel for days or weeks.

They were delusional.

I'm an asthma sufferer, and I began to feel a tightness in my chest. I had to calm myself down or I could have had a full-blown asthma attack. I asked if I could go get my purse, where I had stashed my inhaler, and they wouldn't let me leave the room. I asked why I was not allowed to leave, and they said this is how Kelly had set up the meeting. They let my assistant, who was seated outside, go get my purse. My asthma is triggered by stressful situations, and this was definitely one. I asked again if I was allowed to leave the room or speak to my husband, and they refused. I was being held against my will in a secure room guarded by men with guns.

Irene told me that she'd never been in the Situation Room in her entire career in HR at the White House and certainly never to facilitate a separation.

After a considerable amount of time, they allowed me to leave and agreed to let me pick up some things in my office, but only after they checked to make sure the path to my office in the EEOB was cleared so people wouldn't see what was happening. Everyone had already gone to the Christmas party in the West Wing, which they knew would be the case.

I stood up, my legs surprisingly steady, and walked straight back to my office, Stefan and Irene in tow.

The only people in sight were my husband, John, who'd come to accompany me to the Christmas party, Alexa, and my intern, Dexter Taylor. As soon as I saw my husband, I quickly told him what had happened.

He said, "Honey, you don't look well."

Stefan and Irene were hovering behind me.

I said, "Let's get my things and go. We can talk at home."

He nodded, sizing up the situation and my mood instantly.

We quickly packed up my briefcase, my coat, and a couple of boxes with personal items. Irene asked me to hand her my badge and my laptop. John, Alexa, and Dexter loaded the boxes into Alexa's SUV, and we left the premises.

• • •

THE NIGHT OF my departure, we drove straight home from the White House. My husband and I unloaded my things from Alexa's SUV. She was shaking and clearly upset about the situation. I told her that we would talk the next day and not to worry, everything would be cleared up once I spoke to the president. John asked me if he should cancel our dinner plans for that evening. We had friends in from Jacksonville whom I'd invited to attend the White House Christmas party that evening, and we agreed that we should go to dinner with them. My breathing now under control, we headed out to see our friends. At dinner they asked why I missed the party. I told them I had gotten tied up at work. My head was spinning, and we left early.

My dominant emotion? Relief. I was *out*. No more fighting an uphill battle, day in, day out. No more scrambling to do damage control over tweets. No more N-word tape haunting me every day.

I assumed the White House would issue a statement in the morning thanking me for my service, etcetera, and that would be that. I certainly wasn't the first to leave, and I hoped that the announcement would be no big deal.

"Omarosa Manigault Newman resigned yesterday to pursue other opportunities," announced White House Press Secretary Sarah Huckabee Sanders the next day from the podium at the press briefing room. "We wish her the best in future endeavors and are grateful for her service."

Exactly as I expected.

What I didn't expect: *Within hours*, a completely fabricated and over-the-top, insane narrative about my departure was reported on social media by a White House reporter. Soon news outlets started to pick it up. According to these tweets, John Kelly and I had gotten in a big fight at the Christmas party in front of the six hundred invited guests and he'd yelled, "You're fired!" I apparently proceeded to have a complete meltdown; hurled obscenities; tried to fight my way past security to get into the residence, triggering alarms; and had to be dragged away physically by the Secret Service, screaming that I wanted to talk to Donald.

I never imagined that this ludicrous story—pure gossip—would blow up like it did. It dominated the news cycle for days.

During a taping of *Nightline*, a producer at ABC told me to my face that she had multiple sources confirm the Christmas party meltdown. And yet . . . no one in attendance took a picture? I haven't walked into an event in fifteen years without *someone* snapping my picture. Thousands of photos and videos of the event were posted on social media and news outlets, but not a single person in attendance took a photo of me flipping tables and shouting curses? Someone would have tweeted. A video or photo would have been worth serious money. But it didn't exist. It didn't happen. I wasn't there.

All day long, I texted Hope Hicks and Sarah Huckabee Sanders, asking, "Where's the statement?" When were they going to say what really happened?

At 3:08 on December 13, the Secret Service tweeted the truth. It. Did. Not. Happen. "Reporting regarding Secret Service personnel physically removing Omarosa Manigault Newman from the @WhiteHouse complex is incorrect." A follow-up tweet four hours later said, "The Secret Service was not involved in the termination process of Ms Manigault Newman or the escort off of the complex. Our only involvement in this matter was to deactivate the individual's pass which grants access to the complex."

I'm eternally grateful that the Secret Service had my back. Thank God they issued that statement, because things were getting crazy!

The president, a.k.a. Twitter Fingers, didn't tweet until nearly an hour after the Secret Service, and nearly a full day after my meeting with Kelly. At 3:58, he posted, "Thank you Omarosa for your service! I wish you continued success."

The tweet was weak. When the press shouted a question to him about me a couple of days later, he said, "I like Omarosa." Vague. Faint praise. He didn't defend me at all. He didn't refute the "fake news" stories. After fourteen years, this was the best he could do for me?

Where did the hysterical rant story come from? Someone had to have leaked this fiction.

I suspect that it came from the chief of staff's office. He'd threatened me in the Situation Room that it might get ugly and there could be "difficulty" to my reputation, and there was. That would explain the clandestine meeting, so no one else would see how it had really been handled. In their effort to discredit, distract, and deny—their usual pattern—they had the added bonus of making me look crazy to frighten away the anonymous N-word tape source.

John Kelly attempted to assassinate my character. He displayed his disdain for black women. I asked myself, *Why?* Given the circumstances and timing, I had to believe that the purpose was to prevent me from getting the N-word tape, which, by logic, I was now convinced had to be real.

While all this was going on, I called my sources about the tape and couldn't reach any of them. As soon as the fiction hit the news, the trail went cold. Ice cold.

I tried to set the record straight on *Good Morning America* on Thursday morning. Michael Strahan and I had a very polite conversation. I made my points, asking why there were no photos of my being dragged away, and discussing the absurdity of a raving woman barging into the residence of the most secure building in the world. Michael reminded me of something I once said about the reason I worked at the Trump White House: "If you're not at the table, you're on the menu." Then he asked me where that left me now that I was no longer at the table.

Considering what was going on, I'd say my place on the plate was fairly obvious. I couldn't speak out against the White House while I was still on its payroll, so I was intentionally vague about what happened and didn't volunteer new information.

That Saturday, Leslie Jones played me on *Saturday Night Live*, standing outside the White House, ranting at Alec Baldwin as Trump to let me back in. The narrative of the blinded Trump worshipper was good for laughs, but it couldn't have been further from the truth.

I GOT MANY offers after leaving the White House, but I chose *Celebrity Big Brother* because it has always been one of my favorite shows, it started right away, and I knew the spotlight would be on me. I figured that if anyone threatened to hurt me, the world would be watching. Bad things can happen to you in the shadows, in the dark, especially when you're threatened in the Situation Room by one of the most ominous figures in US government. But on *Big Brother*, I'd be on three live TV shows a week. Twenty-four-hour live feeds. Anything they tried to do would be litigated in the court of public opinion.

On the show, I said some things that were not flattering to the president.

The day after that episode aired, Raj Shah, the deputy press secretary, stood up and contradicted what Sarah Sanders had previously said—that I had resigned. "Omarosa was fired three times on *The Apprentice*, and this is the fourth time we let her go. She had limited contact with the president while here; she has no contact now."

So which is it? Did I resign or was I fired? Had I exploited my walk-in privileges and spent too much time with the president (the predominant complaint of other advisers for the first six months of my tenure), or did I have no access and never spend any time with him at all, contrary to the hundreds of videos and photos of our often daily White House meetings?

This White House has a problem with the truth. But at least they are consistent—and only too predictable—with the lies they tell.

I left the White House to a barrage of threats from John Kelly's staff. They accused me of keeping my White House computer. Mind you, when Stefan and Irene oversaw my packing, they provided me with a checklist that I signed, turning over all my technology and my ID. It's standard protocol for departures. I wouldn't have been able to leave the complex with any of it.

My assistant, Alexa, was barred from communicating with me

and was effectively banned from all department meetings and correspondence after I left. They tormented her daily, until she got out several months later and moved to a new job.

In the rush to get out of the White House after my meeting with Kelly, I left behind some very personal items: financial documents, a drive containing my wedding proofs, photos, gifts, cards, and most important, my commission certificate. According to an email from the White House counsel's office, if I wanted to see my personal items again, I would have to sign a draconian departure nondisclosure agreement (NDA) about my time at the White House.

I'd read that White House counsel tried to make other appointees sign NDAs during and after their tenure at the White House (some were forced to), but I refused.

At the time of this writing, General John Kelly is still holding my personal items hostage at 1600 Pennsylvania Avenue and advising the counsel's office to harass me constantly.

A normal person would have crumbled under the kind of scare tactics and pressure they put me under. But I'm not your average person. And I'm not easily intimidated. In my previous experience in the White House, with the Clinton administration, I saw what happened when people abused power and how that ultimately led to their downfall.

That experience of being locked up in the Situation Room was extremely traumatic, but it was not the worst situation I had ever faced in my tumultuous life.

Believe me, I am the ultimate survivor.

Loyalty Over Logic

Since driving out of the gates of West Executive Drive on that night of my separation from the White House, I've had a lot of time to reflect. The months that followed were very emotional and exhausting, but also cathartic.

In hindsight, I can see that there were so many times I could have—and perhaps should have—left Trumpworld. But at every single juncture, I stayed. Many have wondered why I stood by President Trump for nearly fifteen years. The simple answer to this very complex question: I stayed because of loyalty.

Loyalty is a loaded topic when it comes to Donald Trump. His moblike loyalty requirements are exacting, imperishable, and sometimes unethical (as in James Comey's case). But for the people in

Trumpworld, loyalty to him is an absolute and unyielding necessity, akin to followers' devotion to a cult leader.

My membership in Trumpworld began when I was in my twenties, in 2003. He was one of the most famous men in America, a businessman I admired and wanted to emulate. I grew up poor and on public assistance, and I looked up to affluent figures like him. I desired to experience his extraordinary success for myself, to have a life of wealth and luxury. Donald Trump was uncannily intuitive and extremely perceptive. He seemed to be able to sense when certain individuals were susceptible to being influenced by his power and abiding by his loyalty demands—as was seen later with people like his longtime lawyer Michael Cohen, his first campaign manager Corey Lewandowski, and Hope Hicks. His demands increased over time, as did the loyalty of his followers.

Even if people are banished from Trumpworld, it's usually only temporary. No one can ever leave for good. As soon as you get out, they reel you back in, like ousted adviser Steve Bannon (now back on in an unofficial capacity), fired campaign manager Lewandowski (now working at Mike Pence's PAC, or political action committee), and personal aide John McEntee (now on the Trump reelection campaign).

Just a few days after my departure from the White House, I received a call from Eric Trump and his wife, Lara Trump. They were calling me together, prior to their yearly trip to Mar-a-Lago, to check on me. Lara said, "You know how much we love you, how much DJT loves you. The first thing he said to me on Thursday night was, 'Where is Omarosa? Is she okay?' He wants to make sure you're okay and taken care of. I'd love to have you on board the campaign."

She was calling on behalf of the president to offer me a senior position on his 2020 reelection campaign. I expressed my gratitude to Lara and asked her to send the details of the offer over in an email, which I received soon after. I called to share the news with my husband, who expressed incredulity.

Treating someone with love and kindness after abuse is a classic cult tactic. I felt myself being manipulated, but refused to allow that to happen.

Before ending the call, Lara mentioned a recent article about my departure in the *New York Times* by Katie Rogers and Maggie Haberman, where they reported, "Mrs. Newman said in the *Good Morning America* interview, 'I have seen things that have made me uncomfortable, that have upset me, that have affected me deeply and emotionally, that have affected my community and my people. It is a profound story that I know the world will want to hear.' . . . [Mrs. Newman] had been trying to raise 'grave concerns' about an issue that would 'affect the president in a big way.' Former and current White House officials said they were uncertain what she was referring to. . . . The woman who cultivated a reputation as the ultimate TV villain is urging viewers to stay tuned to find out why she really left."

Lara continued, "That's something you can't tell people about," she said. "If you come on board, we can't have you mention that stuff."

In the moment, I believed she was referring most specifically to *The Apprentice*–era N-word tape. Or was it the nearly fifteen years of Trumpworld insider information I was privy to?

I turned down the president's offer to work for the 2020 campaign. In my response declining the position, I explained that I was not interested in working for his campaign, his company, his family, or for him directly in *any* capacity. My break with Donald Trump was not just a matter of resentment over how my separation was mishandled by John Kelly and the team of lawyers who locked me in the Situation Room that night. The change in my mind and heart was due to a combination of factors, but mainly, my growing realization that Donald Trump was indeed a racist, a bigot, and a misogynist. My certainty about the N-word tape and his frequent uses of that word were the top of a high mountain of truly appalling things I'd experienced with him, during the last two years in particular. It had finally sunk in that the person I thought I'd known so well for so long was actually a racist. Using the N-word was not just the way he talks, but, more disturbing, it was how he thought of me and African Americans as a whole.

SOME PEOPLE MIGHT say they knew his true colors all along, so why didn't I? I'm not sure that I could have, given our long history and the slow evolution of our connection.

Among all *The Apprentice* alumni, I was the first contestant Donald Trump singled out, whom he had invested in professionally, who he'd brought onto his campaign and into the White House. When we first met, he needed his show to have big ratings and to be a resounding success. I sought to win the job, lead one of his companies, and learn valuable business lessons from "one of the most successful businessmen of all time," as he described himself. If I gained fame and fortune along the way, that would not be a problem for me.

We were repeatedly told how lucky we were to have been selected from 215,000 applicants for the first season of the show. I did feel very fortunate to have been chosen, as it changed the trajectory of my career and my life. Our relationship was symbiotic; we exploited each other. Trump and NBC used me to promote the show, lobby for an Emmy, and bring in diverse viewers. I used the success of the first season to catapult my Hollywood career on multiple shows, movies, a book deal, and celebrity appearances. Back then, being in Trumpworld was lucrative.

It paid social dividends as well. People thought it was so cool to know Donald Trump personally. Very frequently, people came up to me and said, "Wow, you know him! What's he really like? Is his hair real?" They were fascinated by him, and by me for knowing him.

The Donald Trump of 2018 is not the same man he was in 2003. When I met him, many of our beliefs were aligned. He identified with Democrats and supported commonsense gun control, like banning assault weapons; legalizing marijuana; universal health care; and even a tax hike on the wealthy. He thought Hillary Clinton was a "great" senator and donated money to her campaigns and at least $100,000 to the Clinton Foundation. Between then and his run for the White House, he changed his party affiliation several times, landing on Republican. When he announced on CNN's *Larry King Live* his exploratory committee with possible intent to run for president, he said, "I'm a registered Republican. I'm a pretty conservative guy. I'm somewhat liberal on social issues, especially health care, etcetera. . . . I think that nobody is really hitting it right. The Democrats are too far left. . . . The Republicans are too far right."

I couldn't say I disagreed. When his campaign began, I received calls and notes from friends and confidants warning me to be careful not to get used or exploited. I was confused about their concern. I would reply, "Donald and I have known each other for years, and I'm loyal to him." My loyalty was baked in by then. And remember, in the summer of 2015, no one took his campaign seriously, or thought he was ever going to win. What harm was there in helping out my old pal, especially in light of my having been betrayed by the Clinton campaign a month earlier? (We will get to that a little later.)

That fateful evening when I was locked in the Situation Room was one of the most pivotal moments in my adult life. The next day, when people laughed with glee about my departure, I wasn't surprised. They thought I had it coming, and that might have been fair. I'm famous for dishing it out, and I can take my lumps, too. I also believe that mocking me was their way of belittling Trump. Donald Trump, the president of the United States, was unreachable to them, but I was low-hanging fruit, an easy target to swing at. If the story that was being reported was true, it confirmed their suspicions, that Trump was just using me and would discard me the first chance he got. Having been in politics for twenty years, I've seen this type of bad behavior on both sides of the aisle. I worked in the

Clinton White House *and* the Trump White House. I worked with the Democratic Party *and* the Republican Party. I've observed the media and voter manipulation, lies, corruption, and scandals from both parties. Considering that acrimony in politics touches everyone, I never took it personally. I used their mockery and meanness to fuel my comeback plans.

Leaving this job or being mocked in the media are hardly the worst things I've faced. I am tough because of the extraordinarily difficult things I have been through in life. As hard as times have been, my life is an example of how great and powerful the American dream is. A girl from the Westlake Terrace housing project in Youngstown, Ohio, can grow up in abject poverty and rise—not once, but twice—to work as a political appointee to two US presidents. I accomplished this despite preexisting racial biases toward strong black women. Say what you will about my standing by Trump for way too long (which I agree with!), I was the only African American woman in the room, the only one speaking up for a community that, in the Trump White House, had not one other voice.

I've been cast as the villain since my first day on television, and I nurtured that persona because it worked for my Hollywood career. That was fine for a reality TV star. But people didn't want to see a reality star in the White House—I mean, other than Trump himself.

It's time to tell my story.

It's a good one.

No doubt, you've come here with prejudice about who you think I am. But all I'm asking is that you hear me out.

Part One

The Apprentice Years

Chapter One

"Make Us Proud"

In the moments leading up to my first face-to-face meeting with Donald Trump, I was certain that the next twenty-four hours would change my life. I stood in Trump Tower and looked around to take in the scene. It was warm there, with all the production lights beaming down on each of us, sixteen in total. Sitting behind the big reception desk was Robin Himmler, one of Trump's executive assistants. Robin's voice broke my reverie. "Mr. Trump will see you now. You can go in over there."

By "over there," she meant *The Apprentice* boardroom, where Donald Trump was sitting with his two advisers, George Ross and Carolyn Kepcher. Once we walked through those doors, the adventure of a lifetime would truly begin.

The sixteen cast members of the first season of *The Apprentice*, including myself, had been sequestered for a week before we began taping the show. We weren't allowed to meet or speak with one another and were kept in different hotels. When we were finally brought to 725 Fifth Avenue, Trump Tower, it was the first time we'd been able to assess the competition.

Donald asked us to go around the table and introduce ourselves, a scripted repetition of our show intros: "My name is Omarosa Manigault Stallworth. I grew up in the projects but I am now a PhD candidate and work as a political consultant. Four years ago, I worked at the White House for the president of the United States."

I didn't know if Trump had been briefed with a deeper biography. I assumed he knew something about my background but not the whole story.

WHEN MY MOTHER, Theresa Walker, met my father, Jack Manigault, a long-distance truck driver, they fell in love, got married, and in quick succession, they had my brother Jack Jr., followed by my sister, Gladys, and, finally, me. I was born in 1974, the year of the tornado outbreak. Ohio was hit with the most violent tornado outbreak ever recorded until then, thirty-one—including me.

We lived in Westlake Terrace, a four-hundred-unit barracks-style apartment complex in Youngstown, Ohio. Built in the 1940s, Westlake was one of the first public housing projects in the nation, situated near the Mahoning River, a highway, and a US Steel Ohio Works mill. At its peak, Youngstown was a bustling steel manufacturer, and when the steel industry collapsed, the city was devastated. As work became scarce, gangs and violence flooded the community. One of my earliest memories is of an afternoon when my sister Gladys and I were playing on the playground swings, when, all of a sudden, we heard gunshots. A man came tearing through the playground and ran between two of the projects' buildings. A policeman was chasing him, firing rounds every few seconds.

My mother dashed for us from the back door of our unit. "Get down, get down!" she screamed.

Mother grabbed both of us and ran back through the door, making us crouch down on the floor between the refrigerator and the stove until the commotion subsided. If we hadn't made it to the door in time, we might have been trampled or killed. Scenes like this became common in Westlake, and my family was determined to get out.

One evening, my siblings and I were sleeping at my grandparents' house at 1050½ Wilson Avenue when an electrical fire swept through. There were five adults (my grandmother Betty, my grandfather Robert, my aunts Mary and Evelyn, and my uncle Carl) and nine kids (Gladys; Lester, my older half brother; and Jack Jr.; and my cousins Belinda, James, Gerald, Lydia, and Tanressa).

I remembered being awakened by the dogs barking loudly and the adults yelling, "Fire!" and being taken by my grandma to the flat roof of the porch. My aunt Evelyn picked me up and threw me off the second-story back porch. My uncle Carl caught me with no problem, put me down into the snow, and told me to run in the direction that the others were headed. But my feet were cold and wet. The snow seemed so deep. Probably driven by comfort and curiosity, I tried to run back toward the burning building. My uncle grabbed me and pulled me away. (That's so indicative of my life. I'm always running toward the fire, unafraid of anything.)

My three-year-old cousin, Tanressa, was sleeping on the far side of the house, and, try as he might, my uncle couldn't reach her. The firefighters arrived and carried her out of the house. They performed mouth-to-mouth on her but were unable to resuscitate her. She hadn't been burned at all, but the smoke overcame her and she died. Tanressa's mother, Brenda, was not at the house at the time of her death; in fact, she was at the hospital giving birth that morning to a healthy baby girl named Mildred. My mother had to go with her sisters to the hospital to deliver the news that Tanressa had been lost in the fire.

At that tender age, I learned this bittersweet complexity of life, that joy and pain are two sides of the same coin.

Picking up the pieces after the fire and the devastating loss of Tanressa, our family grew closer and stronger. We spent most weekends together and did not miss a chance to celebrate life's milestones, like birthdays and graduations. My mother and father smothered us with attention and love to help us through our grief. As a truck driver, my father was on the road a lot, but when he was home, we would go to Mill Creek Park or fishing at Lake Erie. He loved to take us driving around town to visit friends and family in his prized Cadillac.

Several years later, my father got into an argument with a friend over property that the man had stolen from my dad. The argument escalated into a fight, and my father was badly beaten and left for dead. He was found and taken to a hospital, where he lingered for two weeks before he died from his injuries. The perpetrator was caught and charged with murder.

I remember going to the wake, walking up to the casket, and looking at my father's body, with my sister and a cousin at my side.

My cousin said, "He's sleeping."

I said, "No, he's not going to wake up. Mommy said he's going to heaven now."

At seven, I understood the finality of death, that I'd never see my father again.

My mom went to work at a plastics factory, and we didn't get to see her much anymore. She worked from three to eleven o'clock at night, would take a short break, and then work a second shift until seven in the morning. She'd come home to help us get dressed and off to school, and then she'd sleep until her next shift started in the afternoon. My oldest brother, Lester, was responsible for feeding us dinner, helping us with homework, and getting us ready for bed. Most often we'd go to Grandma's new house on the north side, or to the homes of other members of our huge family. I had six aunts and three uncles, two sets of grandparents and sixty-two first cousins.

We all attended the same church, New Grace Missionary Baptist Church, where we made up half of the congregation. New Grace was like a second home for me, a safe, happy place, with a wonderful pastor, Reverend Albert Ross Sr.

As you can imagine, after my father's death, our single-minimum-wage-income family of five struggled to make ends meet, and we relied on public assistance like food stamps and Section Eight, a program where the government subsidizes rent in public housing.

Nowadays when you receive government assistance for food, you are given an electronics benefits transfer (EBT) card. But when I was growing up, food stamps were actual colored stamps in multiple denominations. I remember circling the store and trying to wait until the other shoppers cleared out of the grocery store so they wouldn't see me putting the stamps on the counter to pay. The looks were withering, and the stigma was real. To my knowledge, the United States is the only country in the world that has created a separate currency for its poor. To me, it seems to be a form of intentionally shaming those in need. After my father died, we wouldn't have had enough to eat without that aid. That was the new reality of my mom as a widow and having to raise four kids the best way she knew how. She did what she had to do to make the most out of the difficult situation we found ourselves in back then.

Ohio was, and still is, a political battleground state, and many politicians made their way through the state every four years. In 1984, Reverend Jesse Jackson made several trips to Ohio, and I remember our pastor, Reverend Ross, taking a small group of us to listen to Reverend Jackson speak. I was only ten years old, but the presidential candidate and preacher made a huge impression on me. I remember his powerful words: "I am somebody, I may be poor, but I am somebody! I may be on welfare, but I am somebody! I must be, because I am God's child! I must be respected and protected! I am beautiful and black and I am somebody!"

I hung on his every word. I felt like he was speaking directly to me and speaking specifically to my situation. It was a pivotal moment in my life and I believed every word he said!

Afterward, I stood in the rope line with everybody else and got to shake his hand. He was the first famous person I'd ever met. It was like meeting a big movie star or a famous athlete. Reverend Jackson's first presidential campaign as one of the first black men to run for president was historic. My pastor pledged that he and the entire congregation would do everything they could to help him win. We made signs at the church and passed them out in the neighborhood. I remember asking Reverend Ross if he thought Reverend Jackson could really become the first black president. Reverend Ross looked me squarely in the eye and said, "With God, all things are possible!" To say the experience made an impression on me would be a huge understatement.* Up to that point my life hadn't been full of hope and dreams. But when I heard Reverend Jackson speak, a little light came on.

Around this same time, I became interested in politics and public speaking, especially after hearing an inspiring speech given by Ohio State Representative Les Brown in the early eighties. I also became fixated on newscasters. There was a newscaster on the local news named Ode Aduma, who was my absolute favorite. He was dynamic on camera and had a melodic voice and an African name like mine. I admired the authority the newscasters had, and the way they spoke and sat tall with dignity. I started modeling my own pos-

---

* I was fortunate to be able to meet Reverend Jackson again years later while at Howard University, and once more in the Clinton White House, and I told him how much his speech meant to me.

ture and speech after them. Watching women like Barbara Walters and Connie Chung was formative for me. When Oprah Winfrey's show debuted on national TV in 1986 when I was twelve, I was in absolute awe. I never imagined that years later I would be interviewed by Barbara Walters on the Emmys red carpet or sit on the famous yellow couch with Oprah and Donald Trump for an interview about being the breakout star of *The Apprentice*.

As I grew up, I sought any opportunity to stand out and make a name for myself. My junior high and high school years were defined by competition and performance. I played volleyball for coach Paul Oakes. I was on the debate team and chess team with Jocelyn Dabney and on the track team with Henrietta Williams. And also in the marching band with six of my cousins.

Thanks to my amazing mentor Ms. Dabney, who was also our school's librarian, I started competing in beauty pageants. My first title I won was the Miss Buckeye Elk pageant. Later that same year I was crowned Miss Youngstown and missed my high school graduation to attend the Miss Ohio pageant, a preliminary for the Miss America pageant. It was a very exciting time. I started to feel more confident about myself and my ability to make something out of my life.

The news of my becoming Miss Youngstown was covered by the local TV news and dailies. I was famous in my hometown that day. Making my family and my community proud made me feel really good. I'd grown up with a lot of labels—poor, welfare kid, a projects kid. That night, I was referred to by a new label: beauty queen.

Receiving accolades and scholarships for college gave me hope and helped to erase some of the negative labels I'd carried.

Finally, I *was* somebody.

While life for me was generally looking up, things for my brother Jack Jr. were going in the opposite direction. Jack had started hanging out with gangs and getting into trouble. One night during my senior year in high school, someone shot at our house. A bullet came through the front window, through the back of the couch, and hit the fireplace. Thank God no one was hurt. I had to get out of Youngstown.

The late eighties was a deadly time to be in Youngstown. Street violence took the lives of many of my classmates. The threat wasn't just close to home for us. It was impacting my family directly. My brother had been in and out of the juvenile detention system for years, including a stint at the Cuyahoga Hills Juvenile Correctional Facility outside Cleveland. Two weekends a month, we'd drive an hour each way to visit him there. I loved my brother and worried about him. Our family had suffered enough violence already. My father had been taken by it. I was determined not to let that happen to me.

Sports saved me. Volleyball brought me a full scholarship to Central State University (CSU), a historically black college in Wilberforce, Ohio.

My paternal grandparents drove me the 230 miles to Wilberforce from Youngstown. My grandmother hugged me goodbye warmly, handed me a little note, and then they left. Standing among my suitcases, I realized that I had never been alone before. I opened Grandmother's note and read it out loud. "We love you, Onee, we believe in you. Don't forget to read your Bible and make us proud!" Tears ran down my cheeks as I watched their car pull away. I was determined to do exactly that, to make my family very proud.

After a rocky few days, I befriended my teammates, also housed in my dorm, and we became a tight unit. I also bonded with our team's coach, Rosie Turner. She taught me that nothing matters more than winning. Her coaching style was the reason I chose Central State over other schools that offered packages. I had to overcome too many losses in my life already. I would never get tired of winning.

Wanting to attend a historically black college was instilled in me by watching two of my favorite shows of all time, *The Cosby Show* and *A Different World*. Like the fictional Hillman College (based on Stillman College) from the shows, CSU was an empowering environment that celebrated African American culture and excellence. There was so much cultural pride and opportunity for leadership and advancement there. Finally armed with the tools I needed to be successful inside the classroom, I had a whole new concept of what my life could be.

I'd lost my father very young, but I bonded with three mentors at college I called my CSU dads. Donald K. Anthony was the head of alumni affairs and connected me to people and opportunities that would help advance my education and career in Cincinnati, where he lived. Dr. Emil Dansker was my journalism professor and helped me develop my strong writing skills. Dr. John "Turk" Logan was the head of the campus radio station and the TV station. Dr. Logan helped me develop my own on-air personality and understand "show business." Dr. Logan chose me to host an early-morning-time-slot show on WCSU 88.9 that I titled *Jazz Awakening*, where I honed my newscaster voice.

Dr. Dansker ran a program he called the National Conventions Project to give student journalists the chance to cover political conventions and presidential inaugurations. I applied for the program and was thrilled to be selected to cover the Summer Olympics in Atlanta in the office of press operations for the *Atlanta Journal-Constitution*. Later that summer, I covered the Republican National Convention in San Diego and then the Democratic National Convention in Chicago for the *Dayton Daily News*. I did double duty working for the Associated Press as a film runner, literally grabbing footage shot on the floor of the RNC convention and running it to the editing room. I also got to work the inauguration of President Bill Clinton in January 1997.

Working at these high-profile political events, I was even more committed to pursuing a career in media. After I graduated from Central State University with a bachelor's degree in broadcast journalism, I continued my education at Howard University, the prestigious historically black college in the nation's capital, to get a master's in mass communication with a focus on telecommunication and policy.

Howard University is a special place. It is one of the largest producers of black professionals in the country, graduating more African American PhDs, MBAs, lawyers, doctors, and dentists than any traditional university. The school has an incredible legacy, so just being accepted was an honor.

Perhaps the best thing about Howard for me was its location—

Washington, DC. Working at the 1996 conventions and 1997 inauguration exposed me to the world of politics and political journalism, and I appreciated the role journalists played in keeping politicians honest.

I learned in a heartbeat that politics was all about connections. During my graduate studies at Howard University, I took a job at a luxury apartment building called the Lansburgh. There, I met a lot of powerful people including Janet Reno, Mary Landrieu, and, most important, Doris Crenshaw, a lobbyist who'd hired me to do part-time clerical work and knew everyone in DC. After I got my master's in May 1998, she made introductions that helped me land a job in then Vice President Al Gore's White House office. As a scheduling and advance coordinator, I assisted in processing all the correspondence and requests that came in, and coordinating the logistics in advance of his travel.

In Gore's office—a progressive, liberal, allegedly diverse administration—I was one of just a few African Americans.

It was a turbulent time to work in the White House. Then President Bill Clinton had been under investigation by special prosecutor Kenneth Starr over the Monica Lewinsky scandal for some time. When the allegations first started to come out, no one in the administration thought they would amount to much. But every day brought a new revelation. Recorded conversations between Lewinsky and her colleague at the Pentagon Linda Tripp. The blue dress. Photos. Denials. Depositions before Senate committees. I watched as his people denied, distracted, and deflected the allegations. And then, when that didn't work, they attacked and vilified his investigators. I didn't know it at the time, but I would see the same tactics twenty years later from a different man sitting in the Oval office.

Gore and his people were focused on his upcoming presidential race. The big question was, should he put some distance between himself and Clinton, or should he stay loyal to the president? I'd heard about a position opening up in Bill Clinton's office for the final year of his second term, and I took it, even though my family wanted me to leave because of all of the investigations and the toxic environment in the administration at that time. As soon as I arrived there, I was labeled a "Gore person" because I continued to support him by volunteering for his campaign at night.

I was thrilled when Gore selected Donna Brazile as his campaign manager. Donna was smart, powerful, self-possessed, self-aware. I loved working with her. And, above all, she was an unapologetically strong black woman. Many black political people tried to refine themselves by losing their accents and culture signifiers. But Donna wore her Louisiana roots like a badge of honor.

I continued to do logistics work for the advance office and had an opportunity to do advance work for Hillary Clinton as well. Before the investigation, I was absolutely captivated by Mrs. Clinton. She was remarkable. A strong woman with her own voice, she had a clear vision for our country and the direction she wanted to take it. She was the first First Lady since Eleanor Roosevelt to have a hand with setting domestic policy.

My feelings about her changed somewhat, however, after her husband's imbroglio came to light.

The president was not the first political husband to be caught in a similar drama. It had played out countless times before, and has since. The husband confesses to making a mistake; the good wife stands next to him and forgives him. The man seldomly experiences the consequences of his behavior.

For once, I thought the scene would have a different ending. Surely Hillary Clinton would not stand to be humiliated in public. She was too strong and too brilliant, an independent woman, a lawyer. So many women inside the White House and around the globe hoped that Mrs. Clinton would not tolerate her husband's chronic cheating. Women were coming out of the woodwork to accuse Bill Clinton of a full spectrum of sexual abuses. Not only did Mrs. Clinton stand by him, but she attacked the women, calling it a bimbo explosion. I remember feeling extremely disappointed. It seemed like she really wanted to help people, but she was incapable of helping herself. When I shared my feeling with Doris, she said, "Omarosa, politicians are just human. You have to separate their good works from their personal flaws."

I left the White House with the Clintons, and took a job working with my Howard classmate Cleve Mesidor in the CNN newsroom. As a newsroom assistant, I delivered scripts, researched archived footage, and performed any task that Greta Van Susteren, Judy Woodruff, and Bernard Shaw put before me. It was an action-packed job during a terrible time for CNN. They were laying many employees off, and getting a permanent job was too difficult at that time. I went to the career-services office at Howard University School of Communications for assistance. The director, Ms. Dudley, told me about a job posting for a director of research and development at the National Visionary Leadership Program, a foundation for historically black colleges. I was surprised to discover that the foundation was founded by none other than Bill Cosby and his wife, Camille.

I interviewed and got the job. I reported to his wife. I only interacted with Mr. Cosby a handful of times in my entire year at the foundation.

As the director of research and development, I was tasked with identifying programs and individuals at historically black colleges and universities to receive scholarships and grants. It was a perfect job for me! I served as a liaison to the school for the Cosby Foundation. While there, I helped to compile a tremendous video archive of civil rights leaders, community activists, and other remarkable people.

During my year at the foundation, I took a week off to compete in the Mrs. United States pageant in Hawaii. (I was married to my Howard University sweetheart at the time and was the reigning Mrs. DC.) One morning during the competition, we all woke up to the news that planes had flown into the Twin Towers in New York City and the Pentagon in Washington, and another plane had gone down in Pennsylvania. Flights to DC were canceled for a week. I was stuck in paradise . . . and miserable. I remember aching to grieve and mourn with my family and friends in my adoptive hometown, and reflecting on what really mattered in life, as we all did. I was proud of my work at NVLP and was eager to get back into politics.

One of my closest friends in Washington was Kevin L. Jefferson, who was working at the Democratic National Committee (DNC).

When he needed help with the African American Leadership finance council, he called me, and I saw this as my chance to get back into the political arena and to make a difference.

I became one of the vice chairs of the council along with my dear friend Ervin Bernard Reid. The chairman of the DNC then was Terry McAuliffe. McAuliffe had deep ties to the Clintons, having been Bill Clinton's chief fund-raiser for many years. I was reunited at the DNC with Donna Brazile, who landed there after Gore's 2000 electoral-college loss to George W. Bush. The defeat had been devastating, and the DNC was trying to rebuild and figure out what went wrong. One of McAuliffe's initiatives during my two years at the DNC was to compile a database of 170 million people who were likely to vote Democratic in upcoming elections, a.k.a. "Demzilla."

Kevin Jefferson, Ervin Bernard Reid, a political operative in DC, and I traveled the country doing fund-raisers for the DNC. One memorable event that I helped organize was at a private home on the South Side of Chicago: Maurice and Vietta Johnson hosted two hundred people in their backyard, including a young state senator by the name of Barack Hussein Obama. I noticed him as soon as he walked in the door with one of my Howard University classmates, Vera Baker. As Obama worked the crowd, she told me he was an up-and-coming political star and that we needed to support him. In his book *What a Party! My Life Among Democrats*, Terry McAuliffe recalled how Obama came up to him at the event, shook his hand, and said: "I'm going to be the next United States senator from Illinois." McAuliffe was impressed with the young politician's poise and intelligence and remembered thinking, *Why not?* Although he wasn't yet the Barack Obama we know now—he wore a rumpled suit and seemed very eager to talk to the DNC heavy hitters—he had presence.

By 2003, after five years in politics, I was disillusioned. My White House stint had ended with Clinton's impeachment and Gore's heartbreaking election loss. My DNC experience showed me just how dependent politics were on fund-raising, which made the entire enterprise suspect. I saw little but corruption, bad behavior, backstabbing, and abuses of power. I was ready to make another move, but I didn't know what or where.

I was ripe for suggestion when Kevin came into the office one day and asked me if I'd seen the casting notice soliciting contestants for a reality TV show called *The Apprentice*, hosted by his business hero, Donald Trump. "You should apply and try to win so you can go work for Trump," Kevin insisted.

Everyone in DC was talking about it. The show was going to be produced by Mark Burnett, the man behind *Survivor*, a true cultural phenomenon. We lived in a divided nation even then, but it seemed like everyone in America cared about who was voted off the island at tribal council each week.

While my male colleagues talked about what they'd do with *The Apprentice* $250,000 prize money, I went online and researched the show. I'd studied Donald Trump while I was in business classes at Central and was vaguely interested in him because as an avid golfer, I knew he owned a handful of luxury golf courses; and as a former beauty queen, I knew he owned the Miss USA pageant.

The application deadline was coming up in one week, on a Friday, but because of all my obligations—marriage, job, church—I waited until Thursday to make my audition tape. A classmate, Sasiya Songhai, from Howard helped me shoot it. I overnighted it just in time to make the deadline.

My audition tape touted my career in politics. I said something like, "Government is the biggest business of them all. Nobody comes to the table with more business acumen than someone who's worked for the biggest employer in the country!" Emphasizing my political résumé was strategic. How many of the other applicants had White House experience? I assumed that the majority of contestants would be Ivy Leaguers, Wall Streeters, in real estate, or PR people.

The more I learned about the show, the more confident I felt about applying. I had the newscaster voice and beauty queen posture I'd cultivated since childhood, discipline from ROTC, good timing from acting in high school and college. From sports, I'd learned to be a fierce competitor. I had a solid career at that point in my life and had absorbed lessons from each job about the dangers of office politics, difficult colleagues, and logistic and organizational skills.

From the moment I sent in my tape, I felt certain I'd get picked for an audition. So when I got the call that I'd made the first cut, I almost said, "What took you so long?"

Chapter Two

Winning Bigly

Donald Trump has spoken about the selection process, how he and Mark Burnett Productions cast the sixteen candidates to appear on season one of *The Apprentice*. He claimed there were 215,000 applicants, killers, Ivy Leaguers, all of them "terrific," the best, the smartest, etcetera. My first meeting with the casting directors of *The Apprentice* took place in Washington, DC. The casting team was scouring the country in search of the perfect candidates for the show. I chose to wear one of my power suits from my White House days to the downtown hotel where they were set up. After sending in my audition tape a couple of weeks prior, I received a call saying that I would be given a specific interview time and that

I would need to be there early. When I arrived at the hotel, I was surprised to see the line wrapped around the block with thousands of hopeful walk-ins, all also in suits.

I went into the bustling lobby to find the check-in table and was relieved to see a sign for slotted interview sign-ins. I gave my name and was escorted to another hold room and waited for my appointed time. When I walked in to the room, a geeky-looking guy with glasses introduced himself. "Hi, I'm Rob LaPlante," he said.

"Hi, I'm Omarosa."

"Omarosa what?" he asked.

"Just *Omarosa*!" I delivered the line with precision and sass.

During my interview (which was supposed to be only ten minutes), I talked about everything, from working in the White House to the scars and stab wounds on my arms and scalp from fights I'd survived while growing up in the hood. The casting team looked captivated. When I left the interview almost an hour later, a girl escorted me out and said, "Definitely stand by for a callback!"

The call came the next week. The casting team invited me to Los Angeles for additional screening. I had made the cut.

Trump told Oprah on her show that, because of the huge number of applicants, his team had to rely, in part, on the luck of the draw. Oprah described what she looked for when she screened audition tapes: "There's an energy, there's a spark, there's an essence, there's a life that comes through in a matter of seconds," she said. "And in five seconds, they decide if you even have anything worth listening to . . . There's an indescribable 'it factor' that, you know, I don't think you can teach. They don't teach it in the Wharton School of Business." *

Apparently, I had what Oprah would call "it."

The cut of one hundred people was flown to Los Angeles for a round of interviews.

The first step was an extremely exhausting criminal background check that was on par with the one the FBI had conducted on me to work at the White House! Next, we were subjected to a physical checkup, which included a humiliating vaginal examination and Pap smear, as well as testing for sexually transmitted diseases. We then went through a series of psychological exams, which included an IQ test and personality assessments.

I asked the doctor about all the testing, and she stated that they were looking for red flags like depression or vulnerability, how someone might react under extreme conditions, and how they would deal with the pressure and demands of a round-the-clock twenty-four-hour intense production schedule. In one session, the psychologist asked me some additional questions because of the contradictory results of several tests. I asked her to elaborate. She explained that I had an unusual balance of femininity and masculinity in my outlook on the workplace. I was extremely feminine in my style, but my test scores showed that I strategized like the men and that my com-

---

* Mr. Trump then went on to say, "And I will tell you, I went to the Wharton School of Finance, and I will say that I am sitting next to 'it,'" and then pointed at Oprah. "There is nobody ever—ever—that has had 'it' more [than Oprah]." Perhaps back then, he didn't think she was "insecure," as he called her when #Oprah2020 was trending last year.

petitive nature was more aligned with traditional male perspectives. Think like a man, act like a woman!

They kept us locked in our hotel rooms for hours at a time, with no phones, computers, or contact with the outside world. I welcomed the time in LA as a much-needed break. While I was there for those interviews, I'd planned to size up the competition, but the producers made sure that none of the candidates ever saw one another. There was a veil of secrecy around the entire process, which I understood was part of the winning reality TV formula.

A few weeks later, the production company called to say I'd made the cast but swore me to secrecy about my participation. They supplied me with logistical info—dates, a packing list—but I only half listened. I was too excited; I believed this moment was the start of something monumental in my life. This could be my entrée to the New York business and entertainment worlds. The Donald Trump of 2003 was presented as the real estate maverick, the mogul. I thought I could learn so much from him. Of course, if I won, there'd also be that $250,000 prize. No matter what, appearing on the first season of *The Apprentice* would be a life-changing opportunity. Back then, it never occurred to me that doing a reality show would lead to my being the highest-ranking African American senior adviser in the White House to the president, Donald Trump, another fellow reality star. I don't think anyone could have imagined that.

I had a short time to prepare before the show started taping in New York. Kevin and Ervin were so excited for me! They became my two drill sergeants and helped prepare me for the competition by buying me books and researching everything they could find about

Donald Trump. I read Trump's *The Art of the Deal* and *The Art of the Comeback* several times. I read every Trump magazine profile and interview. I watched videos of his TV interviews. The winner would be the person who understood Trump's business style, his negotiation style, his machismo, his boldness, his brashness. To do that, I would need to become a mirror and reflect a female version of him. Imitation is the sincerest form of flattery, after all.

A friend who worked in production for several reality shows gave me some incredible advice before taping began. First, he said, "You can win without winning just by making sure no one forgets your name." My father had done me the favor of giving me the unique Nigerian name Omarosaonee (I shortened it to Omarosa in school), which means "my beautiful child desired." Sure, it wasn't easy to pronounce, like Jill or Becky, but it was memorable.

Second, my friend said, "Reality TV is about conflict and tension." He suggested that I should either be (1) starting a fight, (2) stirring one, or (3) breaking one up. "Whatever you do, be where the action is."

Last, and the most important, he encouraged me to establish a television persona and own it. I intended to be confident and decisive, like Trump himself, but I would represent my community well as a strong black woman, proud of where she came from. I would be dignified and confident and execute my vision of success.

The promotion for *The Apprentice* was spectacular and started shortly after we wrapped shooting. The production and network spared no expense to make sure that every American knew about the show—and about the sixteen of us. Since my strategy was to emulate

Trump, when they shot a promo of me and asked, "Do you think you'll win?" I said, "Of course! I'm going to destroy the competition!" My transformation into the lady version of Trump was well under way.

Realistically, I knew that the very first *Apprentice* winner would not be a black woman. It was not that I lacked the confidence to win; I just understood the way things worked. But even with the odds against me, I still wanted to win. The question was, could I win the show without being the actual winner?

We were told to bring only a limited number of suitcases of clothes for a forty-day shoot. I'd competed in pageants my whole life, and I knew that would not be enough. Since most people were coming to New York City by plane, they had no choice but to deal with a two-bag limit. I was coming from DC on Amtrak, a train with no baggage restrictions. I showed up with seven bulging suitcases. No one said a word about it. They just hauled my stuff to the hotel and put it in my room.

All of the female contestants were young, slim, attractive, with long hair and/or blonde. I was the only African American among them, of course. The men were more diverse in terms of body type, but not race. Kwame Jackson was the only male African American, with an African name as well. In my first interactions, whenever people pronounced my name incorrectly, I said dramatically, "It's Oh-mah-roe-sah," embedding the sound in viewers' minds.

I could mirror Trump's attitude but I couldn't copy his personal aesthetic. Amy Henry and Bill Rancic were my biggest competition, as I surmised, because they were cut from the same cloth as Trump, who was always using the term "central casting." Amy was his type of woman, and Bill was his type of handsome man.

I had many famous lines to come out of the first season. For instance, I was the first person to say on a reality TV show the now-famous phrase "I'm not here to make friends." My objective was to methodically eliminate each contestant, one by one, so why would I want an emotional attachment to any of them? How could you lobby Trump to fire your "friend" on national TV with millions of people watching?

Early on in the competition, I had a puzzling conversation with Katrina Campins, my roommate, when she kept insisting that she was going to be successful by making people like her and by being a nice person. I just looked at her, thinking, *Good luck with that.* But it wasn't my job to teach her a better strategy.

I was at the center of most of the conflict on the show, by design, but I never raised my voice or called people names. I never got physical or aggressive, unlike some who called me everything in the book. I stayed cool, calm, and collected. And yet, the other women felt threatened by me. When a man is confident and stands up for himself, he's called tough and strong. He's a good businessman. When a woman plays to win, she's labeled a villain or worse. I *was* playing to win. I wanted the job running a Trump company (in reality, the winner would never run a Trump company; they would just be a project manager of a small deal) and I wanted the accolades that came with it. I needed to win, and I'm not ashamed to say it. A lot of the other candidates acted as if they were on an *Apprentice* missionary trip. I was straightforward about my stance, and it intimidated people.

Being provocative was good TV and led to huge ratings for the network. Many newspapers and magazines called me the "breakout star" of the show. Trump liked what I was doing. We were winning our time slot every week! Winning *bigly*. On many phone calls with me, and in many media interviews, he attributed the winning to me.

Winning is a prerequisite for entering Trump's orbit, populated, almost exclusively, by people like him, entertainers who said things to get a reaction or garner attention. He cultivated these people and encouraged them to exaggerate the unique part of themselves and to live up to the hype. He saw the value in drama, aesthetics, conflict and theatrics, and in having a personal brand. The reason he often referred to himself in the third person was to reinforce the name of his brand. I started to do it as well.

The Apprentice was a branding opportunity for Trump, and nearly every task was self-promotional. Of course, the main location was in Trump Tower; this is where all the candidates were housed and the boardroom meetings on the show occurred. A giant sign for TRUMP ORGANIZATION was right behind a secretary's desk. And the winning team was promised an aerial tour of Manhattan on Trump's private helicopter, which is also featured in the opening scenes. We would gather at a location in New York to receive a task from Trump. He would say something like, "Today you're standing in front of my amazing Trump SoHo. It's the greatest Trump hotel in the world. You're going to sell condos in this building, the greatest building in the world," etcetera. Or we'd gather in front of a delivery truck and he'd lift the side panel to reveal cases of Trump Ice, his water brand, that we were to sell.

We all tried to make a positive impression on "task delivery" days, but it rarely happened. The only chance to have dialogue with Trump was in the boardroom. Everybody else was trying to stay *out* of the boardroom so they wouldn't get fired. I gambled the other way and tried to get *in* the boardroom. If I could talk to him directly often enough, he would get to see me in action, see my value and appreciate my strengths. The other women repeatedly nominated me for the boardroom, which helped me get more face time with Donald J. Trump. It was a big risk that paid off.

While in the boardroom, I continued my Trump studies. I observed his nonverbal cues. For example, whenever there was a disagreement or an argument, his eyes lit up. He loved conflict, chaos, and confusion; he loved seeing people argue or fight. He sat up even taller when people made a strong case when defending themselves. I adapted my boardroom strategy accordingly. Sometimes I gave backhanded compliments to my fellow contestants—and Trump would zero in on it. If I was openly critical of them, he'd smile.

I had an advantage over the other contestants because I wasn't easily intimidated by authority. Walking into the boardroom with Trump was a cakewalk compared to working with political powerhouses, law enforcement, cabinet secretaries, Congress members, and heads of state who came to the White House. I was conditioned to deal with the egos, the personalities, and the quirks of very strong, powerful people and not to be afraid of them. Powerful people like individuals who don't seem overwhelmed or nervous around them. Trump demanded respect and deference, but if you showed fear, he couldn't return that respect. My calmness helped me in the boardroom.

The boardroom tapings were brutal marathons. We spent hours in there with no bathroom or food breaks. It was like an interrogation. I specifically remember a contestant asking to use the bathroom once. She was told to "just hold it." We all learned to go to the bathroom before the boardroom and never to ask for a break in the middle of one.

Five hours is a long time. Everyone lagged, except for one person—Trump himself. His energy was high and his focus sharp. He engaged on an elevated level and had a full grasp of the rules and parameters of each task. He knew each of our names and performance histories, show by show. He spoke with a wide-ranging vocabulary, made eye contact, and sat still. He analyzed our performance and arguments on the fly. He kept all these balls in the air at the same time, without any sign of fatigue or stress. Trump seldom took food or bathroom breaks, either. He didn't ramble or get confused. He bragged, of course, but his stories were relevant to the discussion at hand. The conversations were productive, and the man couldn't have been more impressive. The Donald Trump of 2003 was as smart and shrewd as he claimed to be.

The task on episode four was to take over the dinner rush at Planet Hollywood. The woman on the team ran the bar and flirted with customers to entice them to order more drinks. The boardroom discussion focused on the profitability of women using their sexuality to sell. A sanitized version appeared on TV, but the outtakes and off-camera moments were not appropriate for a family show. Trump asked personal questions of the female contestants, like "What do you think she's like in bed?" and "Do you think she's sexy?" Then he turned to the male contestants and asked, "Who do you think would be better in bed between the two of them?" and "Rate how you think she'd be in bed."

At the time, I didn't think much of these exchanges. The conversation was about the marketability of sexuality, and he was asking about the potential of each candidate on that measure. I thought it was just part of TV production, Trump being provocative. Now I know better.

In episode six, the task was to enlist celebrities to do a charity auction at Sotheby's. I was selected to be the project manager and our team lost the task. I was eager to go into the boardroom to make my case to Trump and the advisers. As the losing team manager, I got to choose who to bring into the boardroom with me, and I tapped Heidi Bressler and Jessie Conners. Donald asked me, "How did Heidi do?"

"Heidi was fantastic," I said. "And I will tell you that I haven't always been a fan of Heidi. I haven't always thought she was professional, nor did she have much class or finesse."

"That's the worst compliment I've ever heard," said Donald. To Heidi, he asked, "Do you think Omarosa has class?"

"You know, in the beginning, I didn't think she had a lot of class," said Heidi.

"You like her now?"

"I do like her."

"You mean after that last statement, you like her?" Trump prodded. "If somebody said that about me, I wouldn't like her. I don't care what they do. And just now she—she knocks you and you're saying how much you like her. There's something wrong."

Then he moved on to Jessie and asked her whether she liked

me, despite the way I was talking to her. Like Heidi, Jessie said she "liked" me.

"How can you like her the way she's talking to you?" Turning back to Heidi, he said, "She destroyed you with a compliment." Back to Jessie: "She knocks you, and you say how much you like her . . . either you're not telling the truth, or you're not very bright."

He was shocked that they didn't defend themselves. Shrinking from conflict, in his eyes, was worse than a poor performance on the task. I'd insulted them, and Trump credited me with "a very sharp edge." He fired Jessie.

His praise meant a lot to me. I started to feel like my efforts to show him my value and toughness were working. He seemed to be singling me out with questions, and compliments, and I reveled in it.

WE FINISHED TAPING in the beginning of November 2003. NBC started running our promos during Thanksgiving while I was in Youngstown visiting my family. Everyone was in awe. It was the first time I'd seen them since the show ended. My tagline was something like, "Omarosa comes from the cutthroat world of politics." They were already packaging us and framing our characters to the American public. I was the tough political aide with a cutthroat attitude. Everybody I knew was fascinated by seeing me on television with billionaire Donald Trump. I got calls and notes from a lot of my old friends who said things like, "I knew you would be a star," or "I knew you were going to do big things." I'd always been ambitious, and all those years of hard work were paying off.

The show aired at the end of January 2004, and overnight, I went from anonymous to famous. *The Apprentice* was a mega hit, seen by more than twenty million viewers, and creative editing solidified my role as the supervillain, the person you loved to hate. I was a bit concerned about that. I was going for strong black woman, *not* angry black woman. There is a *big* difference. One of my former colleagues at CNN said not to worry about the portrayal. It would work out better being the villain. He told me, "I'm a big wrestling fan, and you have to remember that there is always a hero and a heel—and the heel is the most popular and sells the most merchandise. The heel also gets the biggest ratings and all the attention."

I went to Times Square to try to see the promos NBC had running on the Jumbotron screens. *The Apprentice* was everywhere you turned in the Big Apple: on the side of buses, billboards, on top of taxis, in the subway, and in print ads in newspapers and magazines. It was surreal. I'd craved the success and the spotlight all my life, and there was no brighter, bigger spotlight than being on the inaugural season of Donald Trump's reality show, produced by Burnett, the king of reality, on the number one network at the time, NBC.

On episode nine, teams gathered outside the Metropolitan Museum of Art to receive their task: choose "from a group of young emerging, brilliant artists" and sell the artist's work at one of the city's private galleries. The team that generates the most money wins; a difficult task given that art is subjective and there is no set market value. In the end, we only sold one piece for $869, while the other team sold eight pieces for thousands of dollars. Trump told me I had a big chip on my shoulder, was always making excuses, and had a "terrible attitude." I got fired at the end of that episode, but came back for the finale between Bill Rancic and Kwame Jackson. I supported Kwame in organizing a Jessica Simpson concert. Just as I'd predicted, Bill Rancic was hired as the first apprentice.

An estimated 27.6 million viewers tuned in to see Trump say to Rancic: "You're hired!" in the season finale. He may have been the winner, but I earned "the ultimate pop-culture salute," according to *Today*: I was spoofed on *Saturday Night Live*. My name became synonymous with the Trump brand and *The Apprentice* franchise. As soon as the final show aired, NBC offered me a talent development deal to create a talk show, to appear on soap operas and sitcoms.

Being the heel was working out quite well.

In interviews, Trump continued to give me a lot of the credit for the show's success. He was very generous in his praise, and I responded to it. I was grateful for everything he'd done for me. The feeling was compounded whenever he gave me credit for his show's success.

The first season of *The Apprentice* opened a whole new world for me, a career in entertainment. In 2004, I moved from DC to Los Angeles to pursue it full-time.

Trump and I stayed in touch through NBC. The network used me to campaign for *The Apprentice* to win an Emmy. I appeared on the cover of *Variety*, *TV Guide*, and *Hollywood Reporter*, my early adventures in surrogacy work, speaking in public on behalf of a person or entity.

For that *TV Guide* cover, Ereka Vetrini and I perched on the arms of the gilded chair with Trump sitting between us. We wore short skirts and Brioni ties with our shirts open. Trump was in a suit, as always. At that shoot, he paid particular attention to one of the magazine staffers. He was engaged to model Melania Knauss by then.

Trump told the *TV Guide* staffer how attractive she was and smiled at her in a way that could not be misinterpreted. It was the first time I'd seen this kind of behavior from him, but it wouldn't be the last. Still, I chose to ignore it. His personal life was not my business. The *TV Guide* woman acted like she was flattered.

As I continued to do dozens of promotions and events with Trump on behalf of the franchise, I noticed a pattern emerge. Trump made no secret of his appreciation for beautiful women. And the women seemed to be appreciative of his overtures.

The Apprentice was nominated for an Emmy, and I was invited to the show. I dazzled on the red carpet in an orange Fushá gown by Haitian designer Marie Claudinette Pierre Jean, the wife of musician Wyclef Jean. We were in the reality category, up against *The Amazing Race, American Idol, Survivor,* and *Last Comic Standing.* We lost to *The Amazing Race.* Trump was in the audience with Melania. I saw him briefly as he was walking up the aisle to leave the auditorium, and he was livid. "We were robbed! They cheated us!" he said. He called the system rigged. "I'm so pissed, Omarosa. They cheated us!" And then he was gone. That loss, and another two in 2005 and 2006, and then failing to earn a nomination again, infuriates him to this day.

I wasn't upset. I was a huge reality TV fan. I knew that *The Amazing Race* had won the year before. And, although it sounds insincere, it really was an honor just to be nominated and to be in that room.

I felt as if I had hit the jackpot with *The Apprentice.* Trump and I both did. Our connection to the show, and to each other, was sealed.

Chapter Three

The Ultimate Merger

I got to spend more time with Donald Trump than any other *Apprentice* alum, doing promotions and photo shoots, but we never socialized outside of work. Although I believe I was his favorite, our interactions remained professional.

When he and Melania got married in January 2005, none of the contestants were invited to the wedding but I read all the coverage of the event. I remember being happy for them and hoping that it would last. I'd had many opportunities to observe their relationship at events. She would gaze at him with adoration. She loved him. Of that, I was convinced. Before him, she'd been a model, and now she was a billionaire's third wife. As for his feelings, I wasn't so sure.

In March 2006, Melania gave birth to Barron, Donald's fifth

child. If she had any idea about his extracurricular activities, I didn't know, and again, it wasn't any of my business.

I'd seen him at events that Melania did not attend—his birthday parties, fund-raisers at Mar-a-Lago, golf tournaments—and he behaved like a dog off the leash. He never hid his appreciation for beautiful women. We all know about Stormy Daniels, whom he met in 2006 at a charity golf event in Lake Tahoe and allegedly had no affair with, and Playmate Karen McDougal. It would be safe to assume that there were many others.

Only Melania knows the bargain she made in her own mind to tolerate her husband's behavior. I will say that she is an incredible mother. She goes to all of Barron's activities and school events and meets with all his teachers. I've seen them at Mar-a-Lago together and remarked on her adoring attentiveness and affection. She watches him running around with his friends, wipes dirt from his forehead, pulls him into hugs, and gives him kisses. The world doesn't get to see this side of her, but I have, and I respect her deeply for it.

While the Trumps were newlyweds, my divorce became final and I was free to pursue my career full-on. The usual trajectory for a reality TV star in Hollywood is to burn hot and bright for about five minutes. But not for me.

I booked shows as often as I could, but I also had a balance. With my master's, I lectured at colleges and taught seminars. Opportunities to do public speaking flowed my way, and I gave speeches about leadership in business and in life. Throughout my entertainment career, I'd been focused on relationship building. I learned in Washington that careers in politics were driven by connections.

Why would entertainment be any different? When I did a show with a production company, I worked hard to build relationships, befriended the producers, the sound people, the camerapeople, the showrunners. So when they went to their next job and someone asked, "Who should we get for this show?" those same people would say, "Omarosa is amazing to work with. She gets it."

I had name recognition. I established a reputation as the consummate professional. The relationships I brokered with producers, network executives, cast, and crew made it possible for me to go from one show to the next. My fifteen minutes stretched into years. Some of Trump's successful branding secrets—referring to himself in the third person and by one name, Trump—rubbed off on me. I insisted that people call me only by my first name, too.

I was still closely associated with *The Apprentice* and was often called to do promotional events for seasons that I didn't have anything to do with. Hardly a casual observer, I kept an eye on how the show was performing in the ratings. Donald was *obsessed* with the ratings. I've heard that when the numbers declined, he became apoplectic. Then he'd do an interview and say that the show was still number one. Sound familiar?

Every year, the show dipped in popularity. Season one premiered in January 2004, and we had more than twenty million viewers. Season five premiered in February 2006, just two years later, and had fewer than ten million viewers. By season six, NBC had to scramble for a way to boost the ratings or face cancellation.

First, they tried moving the shooting location from New York to Los Angeles. The stunt failed. While the premiere attracted more than

9 million viewers, by the second episode, ratings plummeted to 7.3 million. During that season, one episode filmed at the Playboy Mansion in Holmby Hills, LA, the home of Trump's longtime pal Hugh Hefner. At that taping, Trump met Playmate Karen McDougal. A photo exists of Karen, Ivanka, Melania, and Donald posing together with some other Bunnies, the craziest family snapshot in history.

According to a written statement of McDougal's that was excerpted in *The New Yorker*, Trump complimented her, told her how beautiful she was—his MO—and got her number. They began speaking frequently on the phone, and soon after arranged to meet at the Beverly Hills Hotel in a private bungalow, where they began an affair that would last for about ten months, until April 2007, just after Barron turned one.

The Karen McDougal story eventually looped in another one of Trump's longtime cohorts, David Pecker, owner of the *National Enquirer*, a man I'd had dealings with, too.

But I don't want to get ahead of myself.

After the Los Angeles season tanked, NBC threatened to cancel *The Apprentice*. The Hail Mary idea was to change the name to *The Celebrity Apprentice* and have famous people compete for charity instead of a job in the Trump Organization. Trump called me to ask me to join the cast. "You made the show a hit before," he said. "You can do it again."

In January 2007, I went to a party for the first season of *The Celebrity Apprentice* at the Playboy Mansion along with some of the upcoming season's contestants, network suits, production people, members of the Trump family, and a lot of naked women.

The clothed people mixed and mingled, sipping their cocktails and snacking on hors d'oeuvres, as if it were completely normal for half the crowd to be practically or completely nude. I remember one Playmate was completely covered . . . in paint.

What kind of prime-time TV show would allow their launch party to take place at the Playboy Mansion? Who could get away with that? Only Donald Trump, because only he would think to do it or want to do it, and no one would dare say no to him.

Throughout the 2016 campaign and his presidency, many pundits have talked about the dangers of "normalizing" Trump's offensive, inappropriate, provocative comments and behavior. But for as long as I've known the man, being offensive, inappropriate, and off-color *is* normal for him. The longer you live in Trumpworld, the more normal things like a work party at the Playboy Mansion seem to you. *The Apprentice* events were always populated with celebrities and models and his family. It wasn't so far a leap to include nude models and porn stars. I made the rounds, skirting the grotto because God knows what went on in there, and talked to anyone who wasn't in a thong.

I always had a great connection with Melania and made a point of chatting with her whenever I saw her. A lot of people didn't approach her at events because they found her beauty to be intimidating. She also projected an aura that said, *Keep back two hundred feet!* But I had no problem approaching her and asked my usual questions. "How are you? How's the baby?" She lit up when she talked about Barron. He was our usual topic of conversation, and that day, the only topic. Melania always keeps things on the surface. We weren't going to talk about art, religion, or philosophy at the Playboy Mansion anyway.

Directly opposite us, in full view, Donald posed for pictures with lingerie-clad women. Melania stared at her husband and the Bunnies while we chatted about their almost-one-year-old son. She didn't flinch. She just stood there, stoically elegant. Her husband was in the middle of the action, while she watched and waited to go home to her son.

He had all the power, and she had none. That would change when she became First Lady. But when they were in the first years of their marriage, it was not what anyone would call an equal relationship. The fact that Melania had given him a child didn't turn him into a doting husband. Trump's first wife, Ivana, has said many times that he doesn't relate to children and barely interacted with Don Jr., Ivanka, and Eric until they were grown. He famously put young Ivanka on speakerphone when she called him during his business meetings. It's a good metaphor for his parenting style: he phoned it in.

Don Jr. was at that party as well, and he seemed as delighted to be among sexy naked women as his father, despite the fact that his wife, Vanessa—who was pregnant with their first child—was also there, appearing to wish she were invisible. Don Jr. told Adam Carolla, who was broadcasting his radio show live from the party, "Can you believe the hell I'm going through? I'm at the Playboy Mansion with a pregnant wife! It doesn't get worse than that, does it? Now, I love my wife, but that is rough. And I'm going to pay for these statements later on tonight. I'm gonna pay." I can only hope he did.

I don't remember seeing Eric Trump at this particular event. He might've been in Washington, DC, at Georgetown University.

Ivanka was definitely there. I remember, at one point, pausing to take in the Trump family dynamic. Over there, Donald was flirting with Bunnies. Hovering nearby, Don Jr. kept a wary eye on his father, both in awe and terrified of him. Across the room, Melania stared at her husband, mysteriously, intensely. And Ivanka laughed and charmed anyone nearby. Donald never looked over at his son or his wife. But he glanced often at Ivanka.

Don Jr. and Ivanka were going to appear on the upcoming season of *The Celebrity Apprentice* as advisers and sit on either side of their father in the boardroom to evaluate our work on projects. At the time, Ivanka was twenty-six years old. She'd had one job at Forest City Enterprises before taking her place in the Trump Organization in 2005. Don Jr. was just shy of thirty and had only worked for his father's company, apart from a stint as a bartender in Aspen.

To Trump, it didn't matter that his children were not seasoned professionals. He prized loyalty over experience; Don Jr. and Ivanka were nothing if not devoted to their father. His children would *never* challenge his judgment or overshadow him as the show's star.

THE CELEBRITY APPRENTICE started filming in late 2007. My TV persona was baked in by that point and I was an unscripted pro. I'd learned the secret formula to getting big ratings and making headline-grabbing, watercooler-worthy scenes. On the show every argument, every confrontation, every conflict I created was working to my benefit. I knew the producers were looking for dramatic tension from the cast. They needed it to save the show.

Some of that tension was sexual. One of the candidates was Tiffany Fallon, a Playmate, who was criticized and fired in the first episode—one that featured a cameo appearance by porn star Jenna Jameson—for not using sex enough to sell hot dogs on the street. In the boardroom, Donald said, "I've known a lot of Playmates of the year . . ." to which Tiffany Fallon responds, "I'm sure you have."

Candidate Gene Simmons of KISS, a close friend of Donald's, was the most disgusting misogynist I had ever met. On day one, he walked right up to another candidate, Carol Alt, a model and former *Playboy* cover girl, talked revoltingly about his famously elongated tongue, and then stuck it into her mouth. She gagged in front of me. When he started walking toward me with his tongue out, I ran. At one point, Simmons was taken off the men's team and put with the women's team, despite the fact that just about every one of the women on the show had complained to producers about his offensive behavior. As far as I could tell, they didn't care. The producers loved it. Trump loved it, too.

I hadn't been on the show for nearly three years, and during that time, the off-camera outtakes in the boardroom were still very revealing. During one long break, Gene and Donald engaged in language so profane, it would have raised eyebrows in prison. Donald asked Gene, "What do you think of Ivanka? How's she doing?" What followed was a vile exchange, right in front of Ivanka, with Gene Simmons talking about her in a room full of people. While leering openly at her breasts, he said, "She's a very, very sexy, desirable young woman who I'm looking forward to getting to know much better if you know what I mean, with all due respect." Her father egged him on. Ivanka groaned dismissively and tried to get them to change subjects. I have to assume she'd been dealing with this her whole life and was used to it. Everyone else in the room was shocked, not by Gene's language (we knew he was a disgusting pig), but by Donald's obvious delight in hearing it. He had complete control of the boardroom. He could have shut it down at any point. But he didn't.

Gene was a big star, and a star could say and do what he liked. Trump said so himself to Billy Bush on that infamous bus ride: that when you're a star you can do what you want, you can grab them by the you-know-what. Gene's decades of rock-star fame, and Trump's decades as America's gold-plated dealmaker, had normalized their sexist treatment to *all women*.

Including Trump's own daughter.

For as long as I'd known Trump, I'd observed the way he hugs, touches, and kisses Ivanka; the way she calls him Daddy. In my opinion, based on my observations, their relationship goes up to the line of appropriate father/daughter behavior and jumps right over it. I believe he covets his daughter. It's uncomfortable to watch them carry on, especially during that season of *Celebrity Apprentice* when she was so young. For her part, she knows she's Daddy's little girl, and I believe she exploits his fixation with her to get her way.

(Ivanka, by the way, has the worst potty mouth, which is such a contrast to her completely poised, sophisticated presentation.)

Don Jr. had to submit to his father's hazing as well. If Donald didn't like Don Jr.'s assessment in the boardroom, he'd berate him in front of everyone, using words like *wrong* and *stupid*. Don Jr. was clearly terrified of his father. People interpreted his fear as complete and total respect and deference. I did. But now, I see the verbal abuse as a method of control. He was rough on them, so they tried even harder to please him and avoid further abuse.

I remember during one boardroom outtake that season, it came out that Donald Trump and Carol Alt had once dated in the nineties. Donald said something like, "Yeah, those were the good old days." He turned to Don Jr. and said, "You've got to get ass like that. You got to get some ass like that." Carol just sat there, Ivanka-like, and took it. I remember being disgusted, thinking, *Donald, what are you talking about? Your son is married. His wife is pregnant.*

As we all know now, Don Jr. followed his father's advice and example. In 2011, he had an alleged affair with *Celebrity Apprentice* candidate Aubrey O'Day. Aubrey and I knew each other in LA, so when she did the show, she called me to ask for advice. I next heard from her when she started seeing Don Jr. She told me, "He's leaving his wife. They basically aren't together anymore. They're separated."

I didn't believe that. "Don Jr. is not leaving Vanessa," I said. Like father like son.

The next time I saw Aubrey at a diner in LA, she showed me very personal photos that Don Jr. had sent to her, and a long chain of dirty texts between them. If she hadn't shown me those photos and texts, I wouldn't have believed it. I filed their affair under "not my business," a list that was growing longer every day, but my heart went out to Vanessa. She was popping out children and holding down the fort in New York while Don Jr. was allegedly running around the world, cheating on her with somebody from work.

MY SEASON OF *The Celebrity Apprentice* taped during October and November 2007 and aired in January through March 2008.

As you might recall, something else was going on during that time frame: From our first day of shooting, the country was in the throes of presidential election politics.

Leading up to the Iowa caucus and the New Hampshire Democratic primaries in January 2008, Barack Obama and Hillary Clinton had been slugging it out and would continue to for months to come.

During boardroom outtakes, Donald talked about Obama often. He hated him. He never explained why, but now I believe it was because Obama was black. At one point during the shooting, Donald said, "I've got to wrap up this boardroom because I'm going to be making a major announcement at a press conference." He said that his investigators had discovered key information that would prove definitively that Barack Obama was not born in America.

As I mentioned, I'd first met Barack Obama in Chicago at a DNC fund-raiser in 2003 and knew he was a man to watch. I'd always kept my hand in Democratic politics, and I'd met Barack and Michelle Obama several times over the years and liked them both. So there I was, at my job and my boss was plotting to destroy a man I knew and respected deeply.

If your boss expressed political views that differed from yours, would you protest and quit your job? I reasoned that he had a right to his opinion, just as I had a right to mine. The difference was, he had unlimited cash and a big bullhorn, and if he could try to use them to keep Obama from getting the nomination of his party, he would.

I remember thinking to myself, *Does he really have proof?* By this time, Trump was known for these stunts so you could never be too sure. It was possible that he had unearthed some information that he thought the world needed to hear. But then, the press conference didn't happen and his birther rhetoric died down and didn't heat up again for another few years.

Let me be clear, we weren't equals. Donald Trump was the star of the network. He controlled the conversation. We never talked politics at work or otherwise, so I had no notion of his party affiliation changing from Democrat until he started talking about Obama's birth certificate.

Trump was accused of being racist toward Obama. His defenders said he was politically motivated, not racist. At that point, I had known Donald Trump for years and had never heard any accusations of racism against him prior to the birther issue.

In hindsight, I think it's possible he decided that because he was being called a racist in the press, it behooved him to cultivate a closer relationship with me. It was to his benefit when we created *The Ultimate Merger*, a TV show with a black woman lead and a black cast, which would wind up airing on TV One, a black-owned network. Perhaps he worried that, after a rocky season on *The Celebrity Apprentice*, he was losing my devotion and that he hoped our new partnership on *The Ultimate Merger* would keep me as an upstanding member of the Trumpworld cult. Not only would I star in the show, but also I'd coproduce it with Trump. When he offered this to me, I didn't take it lightly. Trump didn't do anything he didn't believe would be a success. He tapped me; it meant he believed in me, a sentiment that kept me as loyal to him as ever.

The Ultimate Merger was a dating show, an African American version of *The Bachelorette* with an *Apprentice* twist. Men would compete for my affections and I'd eliminate one each week. Included in the lineup of my twelve suitors were R & B singers Al B. Sure! and Ray Lavender, in addition to an attorney, a foreign currency trader, a former NFL player, and an author.

We were staying and shooting the show at the Trump International Hotel in Las Vegas. During the course of production, we filmed a scene by the hotel's swimming pool, and some furniture was damaged. It was not that big a deal, or so I thought. The next thing I know, I got a call from Trump in New York.

He said, "Omarosa, what the f**k is going on down there?" His tone was aggressive.

I said, "We're shooting the show."

"I heard from the manager that you're out of control! You can't just let those people do whatever the f**k they want! What's the matter with them? They have no respect for my property. It's my f**cking hotel! Show some f**king respect!"

I'd heard Trump use profanity many times, but never had he spoken like that to me. He was furious. I said, "I'm sorry, Mr. Trump. It won't happen again."

"It better not, Omarosa. Or I'm going to come down there and straighten this shit out myself. You do not want that to happen, believe me."

He hung up, and I remember the phone shaking in my hand. I hadn't even been at the pool while that scene was shot. He should have unleashed his anger to the production team or the network. Screaming about "those people" and showing him the proper respect might have come off badly to the black TV execs. Trump couldn't speak that way to people he didn't know, or they would think he was unhinged. This was a type of behavior I would see again in the White House, which I came to call his "going nuclear" on someone.

When the show was projected to be a hit, Donald changed the name from *The Ultimate Merger* to *Donald J. Trump Presents The Ultimate Merger*. Putting his name on it didn't seem like a great fit for an all-black TV network, but I didn't say a word. It debuted in June 2010 and was a modest success. We thought we'd produce another season, and I'd continue my search for love on the show. But by then, I'd met and fallen madly in love with a wonderful man. I didn't need to find love on a reality show. I had found it in real life.

Chapter Four

Shattered

Michael Clarke Duncan and I met at Whole Foods in Los Angeles in 2009. He came over to me and started talking. I recognized him immediately from his Oscar-nominated role in *The Green Mile*. He told me that he was an *Apprentice* fan and that he wanted to get to know me better. After I returned from a planned trip back east, we went on our first date.

After a few months of dating, we were madly in love and inseparable. In Michael, I found the love I'd been looking for my whole life with a man I respected and adored. But nothing in life is 100 percent perfect. Michael's moods were unpredictable, and he had a temper. He was a huge man, six foot seven and three hundred pounds. Seeing a man that big in a rage was terrifying to watch.

He insisted that I move into his home in Woodland Hills, California, and he asked me to accompany him to movie locations. I would help him select movie projects, read scripts, and write synopses for him. Eventually, I was traveling with him as often as possible, which he preferred.

I decided that *The Ultimate Merger* would be my last reality TV show. I had been booking shows back-to-back-to-back for six or seven years by then and was ready to take a break. I shifted to doing more teaching and started doing missionary work. I visited an orphanage in West Africa and had a life-changing experience. I received my calling during that trip. In that one experience, I decided to change my life. When I got back to the States, I put everything on hold and enrolled in the United Theological Seminary in Dayton, Ohio, to begin my degree in religious studies and to become an ordained minister. There was some pushback from people who didn't think a reality star should be a minister. But I proved my commitment to service, faith, and my studies, and the doubters were silenced. The program required that I travel to Ohio from Los Angeles for about one week a month, the only times Michael and I were apart.

During this period of my life, I wasn't in regular contact with Donald Trump. We did some press together to support *The Ultimate Merger* in 2010, when it finally premiered on TV One, but I wasn't emotionally invested in its success. I'd moved on. There was a second season of the show starring model Toccara Jones, but I was not involved in the production of it. Trump and I discussed my starring in season two, which he preferred, but my life had taken a turn, and I wasn't interested in reality TV anymore. I was focused on my studies, my faith, and my relationship.

Donald had also found a new passion in his life: the birther movement. The spark in his interest in Barack Obama's nationality I'd seen back in 2007 had grown into a fire of discontent. He said in interviews for outlets like *The View*, Fox News, the *Today* show, "Why doesn't he show his birth certificate?" "I'm starting to wonder myself whether or not he was born in this country." "If he wasn't born in this country, which is a real possibility, then he has pulled off one of the great cons in the history of politics."

In June 2008, Obama's campaign released a copy of his birth certificate, proving he'd been born at Kapiolani Maternity & Gynecological Hospital in Honolulu. In March 2011, while contemplating a run for president, Donald said that he had "doubts" about the birth certificate. More than anyone else, he continued to carry the birther torch.

Barack Obama's presidency incensed Donald Trump. In his mind, Obama wasn't just black, he was foreign, with a father from Kenya. He was suspicious of Obama's *otherness,* which is an actual term in the study of "whiteness." The otherness wasn't just being black; it was being African. Foreign. Exotic. Other. By Barack Obama becoming president, he made Donald Trump look like a fool. Trump took it personally, that the nation chose Obama over him, even though he wasn't running.

At one point, I asked him, "Why are you advancing this birther foolishness?"

He said, "It's just politics. This is politics." He claimed it was part of his opposition research, which everyone did. Since he was contemplating a serious run for the presidency in 2012—just like he'd said in 2004 and 2008—he considered it all fair game, just what you had to do to compete.

I remembered this conversation five years later when the news broke about Don Jr.'s meeting with that Russian lawyer in Trump Tower after he'd been promised in an email, "Official documents and information that would incriminate Hillary and her dealings with Russia and would be very useful to your father." Was that just more opposition research, too? Just another example of what you had to do to compete?

AT THE 2011 White House Correspondents' dinner at the Washington, DC, Hilton, Obama came out and immediately started roasting Trump about the birther business. Both Donald and I were in attendance. I was sitting probably seven or eight tables away from Donald at the dinner. Obama made jokes about Donald Trump's "credentials and breadth of experience." Obama continued, "In an episode of *Celebrity Apprentice*, at the steakhouse, the men's cooking team did not impress the judges from Omaha steaks. And there was a lot of blame to go around, but you, Mr. Trump, recognized that the real problem was a lack of leadership. And so ultimately you did not blame Lil Jon or Meat Loaf, you fired Gary Busey, and these are the kinds of decisions that would keep me up at night."

I saw the expression on Donald Trump's face.

He was livid.

Obama's delivery, the words, the power, were not just funny, they were impactful. His joke about *The Apprentice* made people at my table glance my way while laughing. Barack said from the podium: "Well handled, sir. Well handled," and addressed the crowd, "Say what you will about Mr. Trump, he certainly would bring some change to the White House. Let's see what we've got up there." Then, on the screen behind him, an image appeared of the White House with a Trump sign branded upon it, like Trump Tower.

It was in that moment, in that room, that Donald Trump made the decision, not only that he would run for president in 2016, but also that he would take his revenge on Obama's humiliating him in front of all those influential people. I was there to witness it. Not a lot of people can make that connection, but I know what I saw. When Seth Meyers took the mic and called the very idea of a Trump presidency "a joke," I could almost hear Trump's thoughts from a few tables away: *Laugh now, but soon enough, the joke is going to be on all of you.*

If Trump could, against every odd there was, become president, the only item on his to-do list would be to erase the legacy of Barack Obama by undoing his policies. And it sounds shallow, it sounds stupid, it sounds harmful, but that's just the reality from my perspective, and I had a very unique view as this unfolded.

Six months later, in October 2011, my brother Jack was murdered. He was home sleeping in his bed in Youngstown when his girlfriend's ex broke into the house and shot and killed him in cold blood.

My brother had his share of problems growing up, but he'd turned his life around, found a vocation, and was making us all proud. This tragedy devastated our family, as you can imagine. First, my father killed, and now my brother. The funeral was agony. I spoke at the service and honored his life.

We didn't know that the *National Enquirer* had sent a reporter, a black woman who pretended to be a mourner, to cover it. She took the words from my eulogy, turned them into an article with quotes, and claimed to have interviewed me while we stood over my brother's casket. The paper called it "an exclusive interview."

I hired the best lawyers and, within a month, put the tabloid on notice that I was preparing to sue, because I was so upset that my grief had been exploited with falsehoods. Their calling it an "exclusive interview" made my case unbeatable. It's unethical to use that language unless the subject agrees to be interviewed.

Then Donald Trump called me. We hadn't spoken since the White House Correspondents' dinner. We caught up briefly, and he said, "Omarosa, you've got to drop this lawsuit against the *Enquirer*. David Pecker is my close friend. I've spoken with him, and he's willing to work with you. What do you want?"

It came out that Pecker, owner of the *National Enquirer*, had called Donald Trump and said, "Isn't Omarosa one of your mentees? Can you tell her to drop this lawsuit?"

As a personal favor to Pecker, Donald agreed to call me and talk me out of the lawsuit, but I was so angry they'd portrayed me as someone who'd seek publicity over my dead brother's body that I was reluctant to drop it.

Donald went back to Pecker and negotiated a deal for me. In

exchange for a settlement with American Media, Inc., the parent company of the *National Enquirer*, they would give me the high-profile job and title of West Coast Editor.

This was the first time that, in exchange for dropping a lawsuit, Donald Trump brokered a senior position for me instead. The similarities between that deal and the one I was offered after my White House departure—in that case, my silence in exchange for a job—cannot be denied. The pattern had been established six years prior. No wonder they thought I'd bite the apple a second time.

I was still considering Donald's deal when David Pecker called to apologize to me personally. He said, "It was that dumb reporter's fault. She did this on her own. We're so sorry. You're great. We would love for you to join the team. It's about reality TV, and you're the queen of reality."

He said all the right things. The job included travel, an office, a staff of photographers and reporters. But what sealed the deal for me was that Donald personally asked me to accept it. He'd been very influential in my life, and I was loyal to him and ever grateful for what he'd done for me. If he asked me, as a favor, to drop my lawsuit against another of his friends, I had to do it.

The more I thought about it, the better I liked it. It was a great opportunity, plain and simple. AMI, the parent company of *Us Weekly, OK!,* and *Star* magazines, published the celebrity magazines. I had a degree in journalism that I hadn't yet put to good use. And I would get to see the inner workings of the machine. My logic was, *If you can't beat them, join them.*

I worked there for two years and got to learn the magazine business from the inside. I got to see all their dirty tricks. Of course, in hindsight, we all know the seedier side to the friendship between David Pecker and Donald Trump. There are two instances that we know of the *National Enquirer's* buying exclusive rights to stories about Donald—Karen McDougal and a doorman at Trump Tower who claimed to have proof that Trump had a love child with his former housekeeper. The tabloid then suppressed the stories by never publishing them, a practice called "catch and kill." In June 2018, David Pecker was subpoenaed by federal prosecutors for their records about the Karen McDougal payoff as part of their investigation into Michael Cohen. It's suspected that Cohen brokered that deal for Trump, too.

Now, when I look at things, I'm stunned that I was involved in this kind of shady dealing. But I'd been in the Trump cult for nearly a decade, and by then I was all in. This kind of backroom dealmaking had made Donald a huge success.

My relationship with Michael Clarke Duncan was strong and life seemed to be moving in the right direction.

ON FEBRUARY 18, 2012, I was officially ordained as a Baptist minister. I had to go in front of an ordination council for an examination, and I passed with flying colors. It was the greatest moment thus far in my ministry. Also that month, Trump announced he would not run as an Independent if Mitt Romney became the Republican nominee. Even after he dropped out of the race, and after President Barack Obama finally released his "long form" birth certificate in April, Trump would not stop sowing seeds of doubt about it. In May, he said on CNN, "A lot of people do not think it was an authentic certificate."

In hindsight, I think that Trump was experimenting and testing the gullibility of the voting public. If he kept saying and tweeting that the birth certificate was "a fraud," as he would continue to do for years to come, would people believe him? Would repetition of a lie turn it into the truth? If he said what a certain segment of the population wanted to hear, would they run toward him, as if summoned by a dog whistle?

His birther movement was, in effect, the earliest stages of a political campaign that began in November 2007 and did not end until November 2016.

While Donald was appearing on cable news shows questioning the legitimacy of the first black president, I was out of the country, in Scotland with Michael for his spot on *The Late Late Show* with Craig Ferguson. We took the opportunity to tour the Highlands. Michael and I visited a glorious Scottish castle, and he surprised me by proposing. I accepted. Upon our return to LA, I immediately started planning our wedding. What many people—even those in my family—didn't know was that I was two months pregnant at the time.

In July, two months after our engagement, I fell ill. For two days, I was in severe pain. I was rushed to the hospital and learned that I'd miscarried and that I needed immediate surgery to remove a large fibroid in my uterus. I had the surgery and returned home to recover. Because of the placement of the fibroid, laparoscopic surgery was not an option, and the incision wound extended from hip to hip. I walked around doubled over, in a great deal of pain, unable to lift anything heavier than a pound or two.

I was lying in bed with Michael the night of July 13, several days post-op, still in pain, still grieving for the lost pregnancy, when I noticed a change in his breathing. His soft snores became ragged, and then stopped altogether. I put my hand on his chest and realized he wasn't breathing. I called 911 in a panic and told the operator what was happening, that my fiancé wasn't breathing and might be having a heart attack. The operator gave me instructions to perform CPR, which I did, as I'd been trained to do in college, until the paramedics arrived and took Michael to the hospital.

He was still alive—the paramedics told me if it hadn't been for my efforts, he would have died—but the ER doctors told me he needed to be rushed to the more sophisticated cardiac trauma unit at Cedars-Sinai Medical Center, six miles away. I hired a private ambulance to take him there, riding with Michael in the back, my abdomen pain completely forgotten.

He lingered in the hospital for days, then weeks, regaining consciousness here and there, but never fully aware of where he was or what had happened. I sat at his side praying every day and couldn't help remembering sitting by my father's bedside when he held on for two weeks and then left this world.

I focused on what needed to be done in the now. What did the doctors say? Which friends were visiting? What paperwork needed to be executed? I didn't allow myself to even think about anything other than his making a complete recovery. My emotions stayed locked up, a coping mechanism I'd learned throughout my child-hood. But my supreme control was undone every time I came and went from our house.

Michael died on September 3, 2012. At the funeral a week later, I walked behind his casket, shattered, crying, and broken, com-pletely consumed by grief with an emotional intensity I had never experienced before. His memorial service was beautiful and unbear-ably sad for me. His family and friends, including Tom Hanks and Jay Leno, gave touching eulogies. I received a letter from Trump after the memorial service. In his note, he wrote, "I'm sorry about your loss. I heard Michael was a good guy."

After the memorial, I went home to find his fans had created a shrine outside our gate, lighting candles and leaving flowers. It was so large, it was hard to get through. I sat down on our couch, still in shock that his life and our future were gone, along with our baby, and my brother, and my father. I'd experienced so much loss in my life. If it weren't for my faith and my family, I don't know how I could have gotten through that time. Michael and I had two dogs, a shar-pei and a rottweiler, as well as a couple of cats and fish. We were the parents of our happy menagerie, and the dogs and cats just stared at me crying on the couch, not knowing what was going on, but obviously feeling the loss. It filled every inch of our home and every being living inside it.

A month later, a dear friend of mine came to visit, and she said, "At some point you're going to have to take the memorial down." I agreed with her, but I couldn't just throw it away. His fans loved him, and so did I. Removing their cards and candles would be agonizing for me. It all felt like too much to bear. I told myself, just get through today. I wound up taking the dogs to our weekend vacation spot on the beach for two days. When I got home, the shrine was completely gone. My friends took care of it for me, even scraping the wax off the cement. I will be forever grateful to them for that.

My family and friends helped, but living in such a massive house alone and sleeping in the bed where he'd had his heart attack was agonizing for me. Additionally, I had to deal with all of Michael's long-lost family members and associates who came out of the woodwork making demands for money and inheritance. His lawyers and executor of his vast estate handled the claims one by one until they were resolved. Under the stress, I felt that my very existence was spinning. I was in a deep state of grief and dealing with depression and needed to turn things around before they spun out of control.

The election in November went by in a blur. Obama beat Romney, and Donald went on a classic Twitter rant about the "rigged election." I'd supported Obama and was glad he won, but I was so deep in my grief that I barely noticed.

I'd taken a leave of absence from my magazine job and now regretted that decision. Work had always been all-consuming. I needed to work through the pain.

That fall, Donald called me personally and said, "How are you doing, Omarosa?"

"Not too well, Mr. Trump." Every day, my depression darkened. It seemed bottomless.

"I'm sorry to hear that. Listen, I need your help with something. I'm doing another season of the show. I really need you to come back one more time."

Again? I didn't know if I could. "I'm flattered . . ."

"I can't do it without you. I need you as an all-star."

I was in no condition to do a TV show. But he persisted. "Look, it will be good for you to get out of the house, and you can raise money for charity. What was Michael's charity? You can do it for him, as a way to honor him."

One part of me knew that Donald only did things that served his own agenda. He wanted me on his show, and he would exploit my grief to do it. On the other hand, he was right about my needing to get out of the house and think about anything besides fighting to stay out of the ever-widening, ever-deepening hole of grief.

"It would be great to do something for Michael's charity," I said. It was the Sue Duncan Children's Center. Ms. Duncan (no relation) was the mother of Michael's childhood friend Education Secretary Arne Duncan, and ran a center for children from the South Side of Chicago. He bequeathed a large sum to the center in his will, and I could add to that amount on the show. Just the thought of that lightened my grief.

"Great! I'll have the producers call you."

He was self-serving, yes. But his being self-serving, this time, helped me.

• • •

IN CLASSIC CONFLICT-BAITING style, the candidates were separated into two teams, one predominantly white (Trace Adkins, Gary Busey, Dee Snider, Penn Jillette, Marilu Henner, Lisa Rinna, Stephen Baldwin) and the other team, predominantly black and liberal (myself, Lil Jon, La Toya Jackson, Dennis Rodman, and others). There was a joke made about our being the black team and that the other team was like the Republican National Convention.

The racial tension in our nation was being played up for ratings on the show. Mark Burnett was the mastermind of creating conflict. Burnett had been in the British military, where he'd learned tactics like creating conflict to divide the enemy and conquer them. I'd been involved in the franchise from the very beginning, and I saw how he divided teams by gender, by class, by race. He honed this type of conflict-baiting on the social experiment of *Survivor*, and he naturally brought those tactics to *The Apprentice*.

Gary Busey was annoying but entertaining. He had terrible body odor and horrible breath, and no concept of personal space. In his original season on the show, he'd established a crazy-person persona that had been marketable, packaged, and presented to the audience, who ate it up. Judging by his antics, he'd decided to double down on his persona this time around.

La Toya Jackson's energy was very dark. Anytime someone mentioned my Michael's death, she brought up her brother's death in 2009, and how her brother's ghost visited her at night.

Dennis Rodman had issues with sobriety. His apartment in Trump International was just a couple of doors down from me, so I could literally look out my peephole and see him getting off the elevator with what looked like transients, dealers, and hookers. Throughout the taping, he seemed inebriated at least half the time.

I noticed a contradiction in Donald Trump's patience and tolerance of Rodman, the future ad hoc diplomat to North Korea, and his addiction. Trump didn't have the same compassion for Khloé Kardashian. He fired her on season eight in 2009 because she'd been arrested for a DUI in the past.* The DUI hadn't happened during the course of taping, but years before. Dennis Rodman's drinking was forgiven, but Khloé was taken to task on national television about her arrest and fired. I believe sexism played a part, but I also think Donald was a little jealous of the Kardashians' fame. Their reality TV franchise was on a meteoric rise, while *The Apprentice* was barely hanging on.

It's easy to see his pettiness now so clearly. I see the little man behind the curtain. But for all those years, I forgave him his insecurities. It made me feel a sense of compassion for him, which only increased the ferocity of my loyalty.

While in the midst of shooting season thirteen, *Inside Edition* announced that they were going to release a recording of my 911 call on the night of Michael's heart attack. Anyone who cared to click

---

* There were reports in 2016 that claimed he'd actually fired her because of her weight. According to anonymous *Apprentice* staffer sources, he'd called her a "fat piglet" and bemoaned that they didn't book "the hot one," referring to Khloe's sister Kim Kardashian.

would hear the desperation in my voice to keep him alive, everything I did, everything the operator instructed me to do. Nothing could be more personal than what transpired on that tape. The idea of it being leaked felt like a physical violation. It was certainly an emotional one. And it would happen while I was shooting the show, all playing out on TV. I had to leave the competition for a couple of days to try to stop the release.

When I was fired on the fifth episode, I was relieved. I was able to win $40,000 for the Sue Duncan Children's Center, which was the bright point. Another positive was during a boardroom session when Donald said to me, "Can I be honest? I almost consider you a friend." When I responded that we brought this show to number one, he replied, "We did. Do I like Omarosa? I love Omarosa, okay?"

When the show aired in early 2013, I just knew the series had run its course. There was one more season with Trump, but then it was over. I looked back at my three seasons on *The Apprentice* as life-changing and, for the most part, positive. As for my friendship with Donald—a unique kind of work friendship, now ten years along—I felt a deep respect for him, too.

When people try to understand the dynamic between Donald and me, it begins with shared triumph. Donald likes winners. He likes people who make him money and get him attention and head-lines. I did all that for him and for the show. *The Apprentice* storm that first season was so massive, so defining for both our careers, that we are forever connected because of it.

Donald and I had a symbiotic relationship, as I've said. I gave him ratings, and he gave me, a woman of color, opportunities, again and again, which, in turn, gave him someone to point to and say, "I'm not a racist misogynist! Look at all I've done for Omarosa!"

At no point during our mutually profitable, loyal connection did I stop to think, "Is he using me?" We'd both gained tremendously by being in each other's lives, personally and professionally, for a long time.

I couldn't imagine that ever changing.

Part Two

The Campaign

Chapter Five

The Woman Problem

In early 2013, the Democratic Party's presumptive front-runner was Hillary Clinton. She'd waited for Obama's two terms to wind down, and now it was her turn. The idea of Hillary shattering the glass ceiling to become the first woman president was almost as thrilling as Barack Obama's becoming the first black president. Although I'd been disappointed by her handling of her husband's infidelities in the nineties, I knew her to be a strong, smart woman of conviction, and an inspirational figure.

Then First Lady Hillary Clinton actually gave the commencement address when I graduated with my master's degree from Howard in 1998, and parts of her speech had stayed with me all these years. The speech spoke to me more than ever in 2013, given the surprising turns my life had taken. "I think you can be a good citizen by defying conventional wisdom," she'd said in that address. "And helping to track down the stereotypes that keep us locked in our little worlds. I'm sure that all of you have had moments when your expectations of who someone was—because of what they looked like, or where they were from—were shattered—because you took the time to sit down and talk, or grab a meal together, or share a book. You've had the opportunity to spend the last four years in one of the most diverse settings imaginable—yet I would bet it still takes courage to take that first step, and to put yourself beyond a place of comfort."

I'd certainly bumped up against people's expectations of who I was because of where I came from, my gender, the color of my skin, what I chose to do for a living, and have always known that those prejudices would shatter if someone sat down with me and just had a conversation. I'd been fighting the stigma of extreme poverty and coming from a single-parent household nearly every day for the last ten years. Now I was going to step outside my comfort zone again, by jumping back into politics, in support of a woman I deeply admired.

My fellow Howard grad Quentin James—political influencer, community organizer, and then NAACP board member—was heading up the African American finance committee for the Ready for Hillary PAC, and I was excited to work alongside him and his team. Our clear understanding was that the members of the African American finance team would become an arm of her official campaign when the time came, but until she announced her candidacy, she couldn't have anything to do with her PAC. It is standard procedure for the candidate to keep a PAC at arm's length, although it seemed obvious to everyone that Ready for Hillary would be the rudimentary structure upon which her official campaign would be built.

During this time I reached out to longtime Clinton adviser and political consultant Minyon Moore to see what the overall strategy was for her presidential campaign. She assured me the best vehicle to help HRC was the Ready for Hillary PAC. So I doubled down on my efforts to raise money and awareness for Hillary. As a celebrity, my networks were vast, and I drew big crowds to the events I organized for Ready for Hillary.

I was the special guest speaker at a fund-raiser organized by Quentin at a Los Angeles nightclub on November 7, 2013. Part of my speech was quoted in the *Los Angeles Times* the next day: "All of us have to stick together and get behind this sister because I'm going to tell you, when I was at the White House, she cared about each and every one of us and she made sure we stayed connected to the issues that were important." I meant every word. I believed that Hillary truly cared about the African American community.

Minyon assured us that the powers that be were very pleased with our committee's contributions. "You will have a role," she said. It only made sense. We'd all worked together to create the infrastructure. It was logical that the people who had laid the foundation would build the house.

When Hillary announced her candidacy on April 12, 2015, the Ready for Hillary PAC closed down, and all the resources shifted to the official presidential Ready PAC. We were all excited to make that transition and join what would surely be a historic campaign. I remember feeling a sense of belonging to something meaningful.

But we didn't hear from them.

We waited. And waited some more.

On May 29, Quentin forwarded an email to our committee saying he would not be joining the Hillary for America campaign as African American Outreach Director after all, and that someone else would be serving in the role instead.

I read this email in shock and called Quentin immediately. He was as angry and upset as I was. We felt duped and insulted. The woman they'd replaced him with had not been involved with Ready for Hillary, and I later heard that her appointment had been a quid pro quo deal to secure a key endorsement from that person's mentor, a representative in a swing state, a.k.a. swamp politics.

I'd given Ready for Hillary two years of my life. So had Quentin. After this unceremonious rejection, my support for her was now tepid.

Moving forward, the Hillary campaign would rely heavily on data collection and analysis (Democrats do love their data), and not on face-to-face outreach and human connection. This approach would prove to be their downfall in the end.

THE ENTIRE TIME I'd known Donald Trump, he'd been talking about running for president. In 2003, he talked about 2004. In 2007, he talked about 2008. In 2011, he talked about 2012. There had been many efforts to recruit him to run, but none of those runs ever materialized. Each election cycle reporters would ask me if Donald Trump was ever going to run. I would respond with a Donald-like "Never say never."

On June 16, 2015, just two weeks after I'd been misled by the Clinton campaign, he proved many naysayers wrong. Trump and Melania descended that famous gold escalator in Trump Tower and he declared his candidacy for president.

I watched the announcement from my home in Los Angeles, and, when I heard his comments about Mexican immigrants— "When Mexico sends its people, they're not sending their best. . . . They're sending people that have lots of problems, and they're bringing those problems with us. They're bringing drugs. They're bringing crime. They're rapists. And some, I assume, are good people"—I thought, *This is over before it's even gotten started*. A traditional political announcement does not include such provocative statements. But Trump wasn't a traditional candidate, and he knew that bringing up this particular issue would appeal to a subset of the American population, the so-called forgotten man.

His comments were strategically controversial, and sure enough, he had the media riveted. Once again, he was topic A across the country. I remember receiving an avalanche of texts and calls from various people who all asked me the same question, "What do you think?"

I wasn't sure.

I was bemused, like many Americans, by the spectacle of a

Trump candidacy. Part of me thought he was dead in the water. Part of me knew never to bet against Donald Trump. I thought, *We'll have to wait and see.*

Until the day he entered the race, I'd never heard anybody say, "Donald Trump is a racist." He was a pop cultural superstar, referenced by dozens of rappers in their rhymes. He was close friends with P. Diddy, Russell Simmons, and Don King. Donald Trump does not discriminate in his workplace against people of color. I'd visited a dozen Trump properties and spent time in his organization, and his staffs are diverse at every level.

As I thought at the time, he is *racial*, though, in that he uses race and racial relations to manipulate people. I believed the birther movement stuff was opposition research, as he claimed, but it also had the purpose of riling up the Republican base of white voters. Trump's racialization of illegal immigrants and his rhetoric about "building a wall" served the same goal. I believed then that Donald Trump was intentionally pitting races against each other for political gain, just as he'd pitted races against each other on *The Apprentice* for ratings.

In hindsight, I see the flaws in my thinking. And it probably should have bothered me more than it did. But, as I've mentioned, I had a blind spot where Trump was concerned. Because of my proximity to him, I couldn't see him from a certain angle that everyone else did. When I met him, he was the famous billionaire, and I was a hopeful, aspiring businesswoman trying to impress him. The *Apprentice* experience changed my life from anonymous to famous, from weary to wealthy. As a girl who'd lived in extreme poverty, I equated wealth with security. As I'd come to learn, money does not protect you from pain. I associated the Trump way of life with security and freedom. When people accused him of intolerance, I simply couldn't see it.

One of the earliest showcase events of the Republican primary season was the Fox News–hosted debate on August 6, 2015. I watched along with 24 million other viewers, the highest rated primary debate in history. I was not part of the campaign at this point; I was an outside observer with personal knowledge of Trump.

Ten candidates crowded the stage, but all eyes and most of the questions were directed at the most controversial candidate, Donald Trump.

Megyn Kelly, the debate moderator, asked him directly, "You've called women you don't like 'fat pigs,' 'dogs,' 'slobs,' and 'disgusting animals—' "

He replied, "Only Rosie O'Donnell." The crowd cheered.

He was not happy with how she put him on the spot. The next day, he complained about Megyn Kelly's treatment to CNN's Don Lemon and said, "You could see there was blood coming out of her eyes. Blood coming out of her wherever."

At the time, I believed that the "war on women" Kelly was describing was really only a war on Rosie O'Donnell, too. I didn't believe he was at war with all women, rather, he had personality clashes with specific women, just as he'd had personality clashes with specific men. I see the holes in that thought process now. I can look back and see a pattern of sexist treatment and derogatory comments toward women going back to my first season on *The Apprentice*. But, again, I had that blind spot. I couldn't see what I should have. I felt protective of this man who'd never said an inappropriate thing to me—or, to my knowledge, about me.

There had been rumblings about him in the past, though. In *Lost Tycoon: The Many Lives of Donald J. Trump* by Harry Hurt III, the author quoted from Ivana Trump's sealed 1990 divorce deposition, accusing her ex-husband of a violent sexual assault, a violation that she referred to "as a rape." In July 2015, Ivana Trump released a statement that said, "The story [of the violation] is totally without merit," saying it was an overstatement made in the heat of a divorce battle. Allegations of sexual harassment emerged from women ranging from an up-and-coming model to a former receptionist. Jill Harth, a Florida woman who, with her boyfriend, was seeking a business partnership with Trump, detailed numerous incidents over a six-year period—Trump allegedly groped her between her legs and pinned her against a wall at Mar-a-Lago—in her 1997 sexual harassment suit. The couple had also filed a breach-of-contract lawsuit, which was settled on the condition that Harth withdraw the harassment suit. She did.

Like his alleged racism, his sexism could be explained away or somehow justified, if you were inclined to do so—as I was back then.

Trump's woman problem of 2015 seemed reminiscent of what Bill Clinton had faced back in the late nineties and was mostly limited to spats with Megyn Kelly and Rosie O'Donnell. It would be another fourteen months before his woman problem of 2016, with the *Access Hollywood* tape and the accusations from more than a dozen women of sexual harassment. And, of course, his woman problem of 2017 would bring porn stars and Playmate payoffs.

Who knows what the rest of 2018 will bring?

I'd been through the Clinton White House, so I'd become desensitized to politicians being accused of behaving badly—with and without cause. In a political environment, it was all too common for a man to be accused of misbehavior.

Along with Katrina Campins, my *Apprentice* season one roommate and current Trump International Realty employee, I appeared on CNN's *Reliable Sources* with Brian Stelter on August 9 to talk about Trump's bad attitude about women.

I said, "Donald Trump does not have a woman problem. I think this is equivalent to going through somebody's trash and cherry-picking the things you think will bring down his campaign. Going through comments that Donald Trump has made in the last thirty years is just the lowest form of journalism. . . . Just because he doesn't like Rosie O'Donnell doesn't mean he hates all women. . . . He does not have a woman problem. . . . It's so clear to me that Megyn Kelly has a bone to pick with Donald Trump. Everybody saw it. . . . I call it very, very personal. Donald Trump is really good about reading people's intentions, and her intention was not to give him a fair chance of showing where he stands on women's issues."

My next media hit was on CNN on August 10, an interview with Don Lemon, who also asked me about Trump's woman problem. I said, "We've squandered a whole weekend speculating whether or not he's talking about hormones or not instead of trying to figure out about the gender wage gap, talking about reproductive health for women, talking about funding or defunding Planned Parenthood. Shame on the press, shame on the media, shame on people wasting women's time. We need to know where the candidates are on these serious issues."

Trump and his bare-bones campaign must have liked what they heard. A few days later, on August 15, I received a phone call from Michael Cohen, vice president of the Trump Organization and special counsel. He was on the case to fix the woman problem.

Michael Cohen is a "what you see is what you get" kind of guy. He comes off profane and blunt, with bravado, and that's exactly who he is. He's also very funny and very street-smart. He'd have to be: he graduated from an average law school and managed to hustle up clients and a career.

From the bottom of the food chain, he rose to become the personal lawyer to the president of the United States. That took a lot of imagination, maneuvering, common sense, and creative problem solving—not to mention a flexible ethical code—that most people don't have.

I liked Michael. He came into Trumpworld a few years after I did, and we sized each other up as straight shooters. He thought of me as a rebel, as someone who woudn't be taken aback by his colorful use of language or intimidated by the threats that flowed from his lips toward anyone who put down or disrespected Trump. Because he liked me, he was courteous, comfortable, and friendly. Around anyone he didn't trust—which was nearly all of humanity—he was aggressive, in-your-face, curt, and unapologetically brazen.

For his part, Trump was not always respectful to Michael, often mocking him and belittling him. Trump had sussed out that Michael would work ten times harder to earn praise if it were rarely given.

Michael began the call by telling me how ridiculous it was for anyone to accuse Trump of sexism and talked about the Trump Organization's roster being full of female executives. He proceeded, very excitedly, to talk about how I could continue doing, in an official capacity, what I'd been doing as a surrogate to help change the public perception about Trump's attitudes toward women and African Americans. "And that kid who shot up the black church doesn't help us, either," he said, referring to Dylann Roof, the twenty-one-year-old white supremacist who had recently opened fire during a church service, killing nine, in Charleston, South Carolina. Hillary Clinton had said on Nevada PBS the day after the shooting, "We have to speak out against [hate and prejudice]. Like, for example, a recent entry into the Republican presidential campaign said some very inflammatory things about Mexicans. Everybody should stand up and say that's not acceptable."

The campaign must have seen me as a two-pronged solution. I was black and a woman. I said I'd be happy to discuss it, and he rushed me off the phone with promises to call back with Corey Lewandowski, the campaign director, very shortly. "Give me one hour!" he said.

The Clinton campaign had squandered my support, but it seemed like I was about to be offered a position on Team Trump. His politics at that point—with the exception of immigration and trade—were still very murky, and I'd known him to be socially liberal. I was curious what they'd offer, but I hadn't made up my mind about whether I'd sign on.

Corey and Michael called back. "Any help you can provide would be greatly appreciated," said Corey. His team was small, only twenty-five people at that point.

I still wanted to hear their offer, and I discussed what plan they envisioned to reach members of the African American community who were disgruntled with the DNC (I knew they were out there, having just dialogued with them while on Ready for Hillary). I suggested that I could engage with black religious leaders and in the black business community.

"I'd love that!" said Corey. "You're intimately involved in black social and professional networks. How can we harness all that?"

Michael chimed in. "It's a misconception that Democrats own the African American vote. You could be the greatest surrogate for talking about how Trump is really the person they should want and need to make this country great again. He's inspirational and a job creator. He can deliver greatness. Everyone is looking for a leader. I've watched you on TV and in the boardroom. You could be the messenger for him. You can deliver his message better than anyone."

Michael tended to speak in these kinds of paragraphs with cult-like rhapsody about the wonders of Donald Trump. Corey and I would just pause and wait for him to finish.

"The Congressional Black Caucus is meeting right after the next debate," I said. "Trump should go and meet a lot of people."

Corey and I came up with a game plan for me to generate media discussion as a surrogate, and to create my own events with my networks. The campaign was very small, with zero infrastructure, no housing, and operating out of an office in Trump Tower.

On September 9, when the newest edition of *Rolling Stone* came out, Trump exacerbated his "woman problem" by criticizing candidate (and former Hewlett-Packard CEO) Carly Fiorina to a reporter, saying, "*Look* at that face! Would anyone *vote* for that? Can you image that, the face of our next *president*? I mean, she's a woman. And I'm not s'posedta say bad things, but really, folks, come on. Are we *serious*?"

When I read that, I leaned away from boarding the Trump train.

But then, as if sensing my hesitation across time and space, I got a phone call from the candidate himself on September 13, 2015. We hadn't spoken in some time.

Donald Trump said, "Hi, honey. I remember my pals. How do you like Arnold [Schwarzenegger] doing *The Apprentice*? I own it, so I had to approve it. I like the idea." *

I said, "I haven't had a chance to watch it."

"How are you doing?"

---

* The optimism was short lived. At the National Prayer Breakfast on February 2, 2017, Trump said, "They hired a big, big movie star, Arnold Schwarzenegger, to take my place and we know how that turned out. The ratings went down the tubes, it's been a total disaster. . . . And I want to just pray for Arnold, if we can, for those ratings, OK?" Arnold tweeted a video of him saying, "Hey, Donald, I have a great idea. Why don't we switch jobs? You take over TV because you're such an expert at ratings, and I take over your job and people can finally sleep comfortably again?"

"All is well, Mr. Trump."

"Did you meet a new boyfriend? You probably have them eating out of your hand."

"I'm still single," I said, not flinching at his asking about my sex life. It was normal for him, and therefore normal for our conversation. "Mr. Trump, I'm getting an overwhelming response of people wanting to help you. It'd be great to do more outreach."

"You know what happened, twenty-five percent of the African American people are supporting me. No one's had more than nine percent.* I'm not surprised. Twenty-five percent support for a Republican is unheard of. It's the biggest in the history of politics. I love you getting involved."

"I've been speaking with Michael and Corey."

He said, "You said on one show that you hadn't made up your mind. You said you were a Democrat or some shit. Melania loves you. That killed a great interview. Hopefully you can make a decision. It hurts me that you're not voting for me."

Well, I couldn't vote for a Republican in a primary election. "I'm a registered Democrat," I said, "I'd have to register as a Republican to vote for you."

"Okay, I love you. Take care."

Donald often signed off with an "I love you."

The next thing I know, Michael Glassner, Trump's political director, called me and encouraged me to come to New York and

---

* Actually, since 1980, Republican candidates have gotten up to 12 percent of the black vote.

support Trump. He said he got a call from Trump and he needed to firm up my coming on board.

After much thought and prayer, I decided to proceed. No one— *no one*—thought he had a remote chance of winning the primaries. The field was full of veteran politicians like Jeb Bush, Ted Cruz, and Marco Rubio. I thought it might be an interesting experience to work on a campaign at a high level. I'd been planning on doing just that, albeit for another candidate across the aisle. And, since Trump had little chance of winning, it would be "no harm, no foul" for me to have worked with the campaign for however long it lasted.

The day after I signed on, a Dallas rally outside the American Airlines Center drew a crowd of fifteen thousand people inside, and one thousand protesters outside. In his speech, he said, "If I'm elected president, you are going to be so proud of your country again. . . . You're going to remember this evening . . . and you're going to say we were part of a movement to take back our country. And we will make America great again."

From my unique perspective, having gotten to know his marketing tactics for appealing to mass audiences on a TV show, I recognized this performance for what it was: a branding opportunity. The previous month, in an article titled "What Omarosa Gets Right about Trump and Why That's Horrifying," the *Washington Post* printed parts of my interview from MSNBC's *Up with Steve Kornacki*. I said, "Reality television has now taken over television. People want to see real moments and see life unfold in front of them. Not scripted, but real moments. When you have a big reality TV star as the front-runner for the Republican nomination, there is no way to separate it. This is the new reality. Donald Trump is the front-runner, and you have to deal with everything that comes with it . . . He's going to have to give his position on serious issues, and he may also call people pigs, but that's part of the Trump thing that comes with the package."

Trump appeared as himself on *Saturday Night Live* on November 7, 2015, almost one year to the day from Election Night. The cold open was about the utopia of a Trump presidency: great economy, the obliteration of ISIS, a trade war victory with China, and according to Secretary of State Omarosa (played by Sasheer Zamata), a Russian retreat from Ukraine. When Ivanka came out for a brief cameo, no one applauded for her. Presidential candidates did appear on *SNL*, but I thought it was bizarre for him to do so when he was trying to legitimize his candidacy to a doubting public. But, then again, the nation as a whole seemed desperate for something different—and entertaining—in a presidential candidate and campaign. I was disenchanted with the Democrats after being duped by the Clinton people, but it went back further than that, all the way to the Bill Clinton White House and my time with the DNC. I could see clearly that Trump was in a unique position to get Americans who'd never engaged in politics before to vote, not only rural whites, but young African Americans and Latinos, anyone who would respond to his star power. He could appeal to Independent black voters and Reagan Democrats. I made it my goal to reach those people—Trump Democrats—with outreach to women, Independents, and minority voters.

Once I committed, I was all in, and I hoped he'd win a few primaries at least. I knew we had to move fast. Candidate and surgeon Ben Carson was making inevitable inroads with conservatives and minorities. But because of Trump's past history as a Democrat and an Independent, he could compete for that support. In my time with him, he'd been more liberal than conservative. I convinced myself that my historical knowledge of his views would match his current positions on broader issues. Even on immigration, he wasn't so far off from Hillary's. In 2006, as a senator for New York, she'd voted in favor of the Secure Fence Act's seven-hundred-mile fence between the United States and Mexico.

All of this might have been how I rationalized joining him. But I didn't have to push myself too hard to do it. Trump, my mentor and friend, had asked me to support him. His staff had given me the full-court press. I'd been ready for Hillary, but when push came to shove, she hadn't been ready for me. Team Trump *was* ready, willing, and eager for my help.

Not only that, Donald Trump gave me everything I asked for. In April, with Michael Cohen, Pastor Darrell Scott, and Georgia businessman Bruce LeVell, the National Diversity Coalition for Trump (NDC) was born. There was no office of engagement or diversity outreach for the campaign, so we established the NDC to handle diversity matters. Our mission was to represent the voices of our communities and to recruit, mobilize, and educate citizens to help us support Trump.

Pastor Darrell Scott wanted to organize black ministers to come to New York on November 30, 2015, to announce the coalition and meet with Mr. Trump at Trump Tower. My efforts on the coalition, later as the director of African American outreach for the campaign and as the director of communications for the Office of Public Liaison in the White House, was to get minorities, particularly African Americans, to sit down at the table with the leadership and discuss issues that were important to them. We got one hundred church leaders into a closed-door conference with Trump.

The meeting lasted two and a half hours, and, afterward, Trump told the media—up to one hundred outlets covered the event—about wanting to help the African American community in any way he could. Inside the room, there was a lively discussion, and the candidate expressed his desire to raise employment rates for African Americans and provide better education and safety in predominantly black neighborhoods.

It was the first sign of the disconnect between things Trump said privately to people face-to-face, and what he'd say from the podium at rallies.

There was some controversy about what was otherwise a very positive, successful event. Hope Hicks, the campaign spokesperson, had originally described the ministers' participation as a prelude to their endorsement of the candidate, which was not true. So instead of headlines about Trump opening a dialogue with black church leaders, there were headlines like *Esquire*'s "No, 100 Black Pastors Are Not Endorsing Donald Trump Today." This would be the first of many, many communication issues that would undermine or sabotage my African American outreach during the campaign and throughout my year in the White House.

I always found Hope to be very nice, capable, sensitive, and out of her depth. She handled PR for Ivanka's fashion line, and then she became a press secretary in a presidential campaign. She lacked the understanding of politics for the job she was given. She didn't even know the basic terminology. I remember once talking to her about GOTV for one of the primaries.

She said, "What's GOTV?"

"Get out the vote," I said, surprised. It was politics 101, basic political jargon, and she didn't know that. She was always Googling terms while we were in meetings, always playing catch-up, always sensitive about what she didn't know.

She was so painfully aware of her inadequacies, she refused to speak publicly about the campaign or as a surrogate to express the candidate's views. For every other press secretary on any politician's campaign, the number one job is to talk to the press. She *never* did on camera. Hope was terrified to give statements or even entertain the idea of it. She lacked confidence because she knew she wasn't qualified to talk about policy or the political process. She had no insight into or understanding of what was going on and could not speak on behalf of the candidate, or later, the president.

So why was she there at all?

Trump has an affinity for pretty women. He'd rather have a pretty woman with no experience around than a qualified, less-attractive woman.

Through our work on the NDC, I spent a lot of time with Michael Cohen and came to understand that there was some tension between him and Corey. They were both jockeying for their attention from DJT and wanted to firm up their positions in Trumpworld, but they clashed big-time. Corey didn't see the importance of having diversity outreach, but Michael, my fellow rebel, did. Because of his long-standing position with Trump, Michael won out. Donald encouraged us to launch the National Diversity Coalition officially as an organization, which we did a few months later.

Michael was one of the most fervent Trump worshippers/cult followers, among many, with whom Trump surrounded himself. Trumpworld is a cult of personality focused solely on Donald J. Trump. And Donald, like a cult leader, can spot susceptibility in people in an instant. They were fascinated by fame, power, Trump's charisma, and would do anything to be close to Trump and win his favor. Michael Cohen would pay off porn stars and make questionable deals, which would ultimately be his undoing. Corey's loyalty continues to be strong to this day. And mine? I'd like to think I wasn't as susceptible, but I allowed myself to be swept up, as a member of Trumpworld. Until I wasn't.

Chapter Six

Winning Votes and Defeating Opponents

The candidate-Trump brand was controversy and ratings, just like during *The Apprentice* years. Conflict sells. You could liken the entire GOP primary season, from February to June 2016, to a season of *The Political Apprentice*, with Trump "firing" his sixteen opponents one by one.

Many of them dropped out well before the Iowa caucus on February 1, including Rick Perry, Bobby Jindal, George Pataki, and Lindsey Graham.

The results of the first contest in Iowa were humbling for Trump. Ted Cruz defeated him by over six thousand votes. Publicly, Trump accused Cruz of stealing his victory. Apparently, Cruz's camp had posted a false report on Twitter that said Ben Carson was dropping out of the race (at that point, he wasn't), and many of Carson's supporters caucused for Cruz. Trump was livid! He blasted Cruz at every chance he got from then on.

One by one they started to drop.

Arkansas governor Mike Huckabee withdrew from the race that night after the results were in. Kentucky senator Rand Paul dropped out on February 3, two days after his dismal performance in Iowa, and eventually endorsed Donald Trump, whom he had called "a delusional narcissist and an orange-faced windbag" during the campaign.

Former Pennsylvania senator Rick Santorum also dropped out on February 3, and endorsed Marco Rubio.

Trump's bluster came roaring right back on February 9 with a landslide win in New Hampshire. They loved him in New Hampshire. He beat the number two, John Kasich, by over nineteen percentage points (Trump won 35.3 percent of the vote; Kasich 15.8 percent).

New Jersey governor Chris Christie dropped out on February 10, and endorsed Donald Trump two weeks later.

Carly Fiorina dropped out on February 10. After Trump's "Look at her face!" comment back in September, Fiorina, the only woman in the field, had risen to number two in the polls. But her ascent didn't last. After she dropped out, she endorsed Ted Cruz and in late April, became his running mate. Trump dismissed it by saying, "Cruz can't win, what's he doing picking vice presidents?" Less than a week later, Cruz dropped out. In September, Fiorina endorsed Donald Trump, only to rescind it three weeks later when the *Access Hollywood* tape came out and she called for him to drop out of the race.

Former governor of Florida Jeb Bush dropped out on February 20, winning none of the contests and ranking very low in the polls. Trump said that his describing Bush as "low energy" was a "one day kill."

Dr. Ben Carson announced on March 4 that he was skipping the upcoming GOP debate in his hometown of Detroit the next night, preceding his dropping out the day after the debate. By the end of the week, he'd endorsed Trump.

The field was down to four—Ted Cruz, John Kasich, Marco Rubio, and Trump. On March 3, the eleventh GOP debate was held in Detroit and, for the third time, hosted by Fox News, moderated by Bret Baier, Chris Wallace—and Megyn Kelly. Donald Trump and Megyn Kelly had not come face-to-face since the "bleeding from her wherever" dust-up back in August 2015. (Trump had not participated in the second Fox debate in January, in protest over how he'd been treated by Kelly previously.)

To attend the debate, I flew to Cleveland with the intention of driving to Detroit with a friend. There was a snowstorm, and the roads were so icy that I didn't think we could attempt it. But we did, and after that scary drive, we arrived at the Fox Theatre to find hundreds of protesters outside, despite the weather and the cold. We parked in a reserved area and had passes to use the VIP entrance, but we still had to walk through the pack of very rowdy, seething, angry, vocal protesters.

Once we got inside, I ran into Richard Grenell, now the US ambassador to Germany, in the lobby. Ric was one of my LA friends, a Republican correspondent who appeared on multiple news outlets. He asked me if I'd be in the spin room later and offered to help get me booked to do TV interviews after the debate.

Viewers were anticipating round two between Trump and Kelly, but the two were cordial to each other from the start. He said, "Nice to be with you, Megyn. You're looking well."

She said, "As are you."

From my seat to the far right of the stage, I exhaled deeply. I'd hoped Trump's performance would be disciplined and substantive. The nomination was within his grasp, and a solid showing tonight could be enough to clinch it.

Throughout the two-hour debate, Kelly's questions to Trump were tough but fair. The only glimmer of tension between the two was over the Better Business Bureau's ranking of Trump University; he said it'd been awarded an A rating, and she corrected him and said that it had actually received a D–.

Next to me in my row was Pastor Darrell Scott and his wife, my friend from Cleveland, and several other VIP Trump supporters. In front and behind, to the left and the right, we were surrounded by supporters of Rubio, Cruz, and, for the most part, Kasich. They'd driven across the border from Ohio to Michigan in droves.

Rubio supporters had high hopes coming into this debate because their candidate had taken some low blows at Trump. I suppose their new strategy was "let Rubio be Trump." A few days earlier, on February 28, in retaliation to Trump's calling him "Little Marco," Rubio said at a rally in Salem, Virginia, "He doesn't sweat because his pores are clogged from the spray tan that he uses. Donald is not going to make America great, he's going to make America orange! I'll admit the guy, he's taller than me. He's like six two, which is why I don't understand why his hands are the size of someone who is five two. Have you seen his hands? And you know what they say about guys with small hands . . . You can't trust them! . . ." Had he hired a joke writer from *Saturday Night Live*?

Rubio couldn't pull off the crassness like Donald. The media pounced on it, though, almost begging for a debate confrontation.

I was afraid Donald would not be able to resist taking the bait and was pleasantly surprised that he didn't attack Rubio unduly. He didn't need to. He was so close to winning it all. He didn't have to do more than show up. But he did very well. It was his most disciplined and prepared debate yet.

Until.

Toward the end of the debate, Marco Rubio said, "Trump has basically mocked everybody with personal attacks. He's done so to people that are sitting on the stage today. He's done so about people that are disabled. He's done it about every other candidate in this race. So if there's anyone who's ever deserved to be attacked that way, it has been Donald Trump, for the way he's treated people in the campaign. Now that said, I would much prefer to have a policy debate. Let's have a policy debate. . . . Talk about Donald Trump's strategy and my strategy . . . and on healthcare and on the important issues facing this country."

Trump responded, "I have to say this. He hit my hands. Nobody has ever hit my hands. I've never heard of this. Look at those hands.

Are they small hands? . . . And he referred to my hands, if they are small, something else must be small. I guarantee you there is no problem. I guarantee it."

I was flabbergasted. Had Donald just referenced his penis onstage during a political debate? My hopes of a sober performance from Donald came crashing down. Of course, in the days to come, the pundits were outraged by the vulgarity. Everyone in the Trump section was extremely uncomfortable with the exchange, and we'd all been so pleased with his performance until that moment. Knowing him as well as I did, a part of me knew he couldn't resist going there. His ego would not allow him to ignore an insult to his manhood.

As one of the few female surrogates for the campaign, it was my responsibility to respond to this latest Trump outrage in the spin room that night and media hits for days to come. The last thing I wanted to do was answer questions about the size of Trump's hands or any other body part. I went on MSNBC and a couple of other networks that night. I couldn't reach anyone from the campaign for talking points, so I had to wing it.

ON MARCH 8, right after a Florida rally, just days after Handsize-gate, Corey Lewandowski grabbed the wrist of Michelle Fields, a Breitbart reporter. When she was trying to ask Trump a question, Corey yanked her back so forcefully, he left bruises on her wrist. Now Corey was part of Trump's ongoing "woman problem," not to mention the growing "violence problem."

The MAGA rallies were getting hostile. Reporters and photographers were being roughed up by supporters and security. Angry confrontations were sprouting up. We had a big rally scheduled for March 11 at the University of Illinois Chicago Pavilion, and we all worried about an escalation of the by-now established pattern. In the week leading up to this particular event, in Barack Obama's hometown, organizations such as MoveOn.org, Black Lives Matter, and College Students for Bernie had been mobilizing their members to lobby UIC to shut down the event, and, when that failed, they showed up with bullhorns, signs, and sore attitudes. Thousands of protesters arrived the night before the event and held a vigil.

I was never intimidated by aggressive protesters, because I'd made a practice of being nonconfrontational. When I walked through a group of them, I was respectful and friendly and did not engage. I firmly believed that they had every right to be there. Protesting is one of the most fundamental rights and freedoms that we enjoy in this country. Our great democracy was created to ensure freedom of speech, freedom of protest, and freedom to assemble. I am *not* opposed to anti-Trump protests, but I am opposed to violent attempts to shut down free speech.

I was among the surrogates scheduled to attend this rally. I'd been in Columbus, Ohio, doing another event, and was at the airport to fly to Chicago. Moments before I boarded the plane, I texted Trump's bodyguard Keith Schiller and he said that the event wasn't going forward, that Donald would not be attending. Immediately,

I found a TV in a sports bar to see what was going on at the UIC Pavilion.

It was the first time that I thought being part of this campaign could be dangerous for me.

Outside the venue, thousands of protesters were screaming at the supporters. People held up signs denouncing Trump as a racist and sexist, and pictures of Trump as a Nazi. I was taken aback by the sheer size of the crowd, and the massive force of three hundred armed police in riot gear surrounding the venue to control the crowds, scores of them on horseback. Many blocks surrounding the venue were shut down to vehicles. The images from inside the venue were even more alarming. Security forces escorted protesters out, but there were too many to control. More than nine thousand supporters had waited for hours to see their candidate—Trump liked to start his rallies at 9:00 p.m. or later—and only moments before he was supposed to speak, it was announced that, due to security concerns, he would not take the stage. The protesters inside whooped with victory. The supporters were furious and frustrated. Instantly, like a lit match igniting a dry forest, throngs of warring groups and individuals started shoving and yelling. Heightened tensions were close to or beyond the breaking point. People started chanting, "Bernie! Bernie! Bernie!" Other people chanted, "Hillary! Hillary! Hillary!" And, of course, since it was a Trump event, there were chants of his name: "Trump! Trump! Trump!"

The crowds inside didn't want to leave, but they were forced to exit by the police. The organizers were criticized for pushing thousands of disappointed Trump supporters onto the streets, exactly where the protesters were assembled. Inevitably, mayhem followed. Multiple arrests. Skirmishes on the street. Protesters blocking traffic. Citizens and police bloodied.

I did not condone the violent behavior by any Trump supporters or the protesters, nor did I agree with threatening violence against anyone. But we had reason to believe that at least some of the hostile participants were not doing it out of the passion of their convictions.

Based on internal reports not made public at the time, we suspected that the protesters had been organized by the opposition. And in fact, later that year, an explosive investigation would be released by Project Veritas Action that showed secretly videotaped conversations of Scott Foval, the field director for the Americans United for Change, and Bob Creamer of Democracy Partners, two consultant groups working with organizations supporting Clinton. In the videos it appeared that Foval and Creamer were basically bragging about having their people wear Planned Parenthood T-shirts and wave Nazi Trump signs to get Trump diehards to "pop off" and to "draw them to punch you" at Trump/Pence events. The Project Veritas Action investigation provided evidence that both the Clinton campaign and the DNC were supporting disruptive activities. Their objective was to cause anarchy at Trump events, and to make his supporters look subhuman and deranged in front of the media.

Did you ever hear about Trump supporters crashing Clinton or Sanders rallies? No. We didn't resort to planting agitators at their events. But according to Project Veritas's investigation, the Clinton campaign not only knew about the plants, they requested them. In the WikiLeaks dump of Clinton emails, there were allegedly references to "birddogging," or the practice of having people sit in the front row at Trump events to stir things up, in full view of the cameras.

We believed that the Clinton camp was doing what the Clintons had always done—playing dirty. Having worked in the Clinton White House and in the early parts of the Ready for Hillary campaign, I felt that was their modus operandi.

When Trump said from the podium in Alabama in 2015 about a rowdy protester, "Get him the hell out of here, will you, please? Get him out of here. Throw him out!" and on Fox News the next day, "Maybe he should have been roughed up," he suspected this person to be a planted agitator.

There were a few other statements of this nature, too. In Cedar Rapids, Iowa, in February, "If you see somebody getting ready to throw a tomato, knock the crap out of them, would you? Seriously. I promise you, I will pay for the legal fees."

Same month, in Las Vegas: "Oh, I love the old days, you know? You know what I hate? There's a guy, totally disruptive, throwing punches. We're not allowed to punch back anymore. I love the old days; you know what they used to do to guys like that when they were in a place like this? They'd be carried out in a stretcher, folks. Oh, it's true," Trump said. "The guards are very gentle with him. He's walking out with big high fives, smiling, laughing. I'd like to punch him in the face, I'll tell you."

With his rhetoric, Trump encouraged his people and gave them license to behave in exactly the way the Clinton plants hoped they would. It wasn't hard to agitate the darker elements of society, susceptible idol-worshippers who looked up to the candidate/cult leader on the stage and had a physical, if not violent, orientation. Members of the Trumpworld cult would do anything he said or asked, directly or indirectly.

People texted and called me to ask how I could support a man who threatened protesters with violence. I wasn't at liberty to explain that we suspected a good number of them to be plants. I did think that Trump's rhetoric went too far. Behind the scenes, everyone on the campaign advised him to tone it down and said that it was dangerous. I remember speaking with Michael Cohen about my concerns, and he said, "This whole situation is out of control. It's time to f**k people up. If they are bringing people in, we should bring people in." I'd get no help in deescalating the tone at rallies from him.

But no matter what Trump said or did, no one could control everyone who came to events and supported him. The thinking was "the show must go on." As long as supporters weren't harming anyone, everybody was welcome.

There was a lot of blame to go around for the failure of the Chicago event. We blamed the protesters. We blamed law enforcement for not properly managing the situation. We blamed Chicago and its mayor, Obama acolyte Rahm Emanuel, for not supplying adequate security resources. We blamed everything and everyone, except for Donald Trump. No one talked about what we could do to change him or his message. The divide in our nation was simply too big to bridge, even if the candidate wanted to (he didn't). He relished the conflict.

I was concerned, but trusted that he knew best how to handle the matter. The way things were talked about, you were either on his side or working to undermine him. When I look back and try to pinpoint the moment when, in my own heart, I adopted an "us" versus "them" mind-set, it was that night in Chicago in March 2016. We all had a bunker mentality. We were hunkered down, ready to battle for our candidate. I had picked my team, and I wanted my team to win. The longer I stayed involved, the deeper my loyalty was to Donald Trump and the bigger my blind spot became. As I've said, he chooses people who are very loyal, who subscribe to the fame and charisma that is Donald Trump's magnetism. And I was one of those people.

I never stopped to ask myself what all this conflict meant for the future of the country. If I acknowledged my role in what was happening, I would have had to come to terms with nearly thirteen years of suppressed doubts and concerns about Donald Trump, and I was simply incapable of doing that at that point. I'd wake up the next day and put out a new fire, or do damage control about a new tweet or one of his crazy claims. There was always an emergency to manage. I focused my mind and energies on short-term Trump problems, which allowed me to avoid thinking about my own long-term Trump problem of having given him the benefit of the doubt for more than a decade, despite having many reasons not to.

When you work on a campaign day in, day out, you're only thinking about the next rally, the next primary, the next debate. It was all about winning, winning, winning. Winning votes and defeating opponents. When things came up, we would say, "It's the opposition creating problems. They're crooked and corrupt," and then we'd pivot back to the issue at hand or putting out the next fire. We had an answer for everything.

And the response, nine times out of ten, was always "What about Hillary Clinton's emails? What about her use of a private server? What about her emailing classified documents that put our national security at risk?"

I called our number one campaign strategy "whataboutism."

In all of our talking-point memos and emails, we were instructed to bring up her emails. No matter what a reporter asked us, we pivoted to that. It was the only thing we had. At that point, we lacked a platform, plans, big ideas about foreign or domestic policy. All we had was Trump's bluster, the MAGA slogan, and Hillary's emails.

The night of the Chicago rally left a deep scar on my consciousness, and I'd never even reached the city.

From my place in the figurative bunker, I came out aggressively to support candidate Trump and believed the argument that the protesters were at fault. I spoke to MSNBC host Chris Matthews later that night, and said, "This is a country that you have the right to assemble, you have the right to free speech. But you have no right to go into a closed, private event, and, if you do, you get what's coming to you. I do not condone violence, but if you go into an environment where you're interrupting thirteen, fourteen times, do you expect a hug or kumbaya? Come on, Chris. These protesters know exactly what they're getting at this point. . . . He's from New York. He's not going to be pushed around."

I got a lot of flak for that interview. The media used the clip to insist that we condoned the violent attacks on protesters. They generally portrayed the protest as organically occurring, and rarely explored whether they might be staged. I could not share the details we had internally with Matthews or anyone, but I stand by my convictions that these were tactics and that they came straight out of the Clinton playbook.

Shortly after that dark spot, a bright light came into my life. In late March 2016, I was invited to the board meeting for the charity Golf. My Future. My Game, a nonprofit organization whose mission is to teach African American kids how to play the sport, founded by Craig Kirby, a Democratic political strategist, a fellow Ohioan, and a colleague of mine from the Clinton White House. The plan was for me to fly in from LA and meet Craig at DCA with the board chairman, a man named John Allen Newman, a pastor, who was flying up from Jacksonville, Florida. The flight was delayed, and John waited with Craig to pick me up. He greeted me in a dark suit, looking very handsome.

We spent the day running around, doing things for the charity. Our chemistry was instant. On our first date, we went to see DC's cherry blossom festival and walked under the trees around the Washington Mall water basin as pink petals drifted down. It was pure romance. I'd been dating on and off in Los Angeles but hadn't been in anything serious since Michael died. This felt different, though. John was a Democrat, as I'd been for most of my life. He didn't judge me for my allegiance to Trump, although he was concerned about his rhetoric. We didn't discuss politics that much, and chose to discover what we shared. Our connection was undeniable.

John and I started a long-distance relationship. He was in Jacksonville, and I was all over the map. Once, when I was in LA, I got a text from him, and he asked me to dinner. Turned out, he was already on a plane, flying across the country just to have a meal with me. I was flattered and charmed, but I wasn't ready to give up my dating life yet. I made it clear that until I had a firm commitment, I was going to continue seeing other people. He didn't like the sound of that.

I was so busy with the campaign, I took a wait-and-see attitude about John. If we were going to get serious, I'd know soon enough.

SENATOR MARCO RUBIO lost to Trump in his home state of Florida. He dropped out on March 15, and on July 20, he endorsed Donald Trump.

Only three contestants—I mean *candidates*—remained in the reality show that was the GOP primary race. It was down to Trump, Cruz, and Kasich.

Things had already gotten personal, but the acrimony intensified when the battle between candidates turned into a beauty contest between their wives. An anti-Trump super PAC, which we thought was working in secret collaboration with Cruz's camp, released a raunchy photo of Melania from her modeling days. The aim was to disparage her and, through her, her husband. As always when he felt insulted, Trump reacted aggressively and tweeted that he could "spill the beans" about Ted Cruz's wife, Heidi, who'd struggled with depression. A Trump supporter created a meme with an unflattering photo of Mrs. Cruz on one side, and a modeling headshot of Melania on the other, and the caption, "No need to 'spill the beans.' The images are worth a thousand words." Trump retweeted the meme.

Cue media firestorm and the Cruz camp accusing Trump of being a "coward" and "classless," who'd launched another cruel attack on a woman.

On March 25, while two husbands vociferously defended their wives, I appeared on Don Lemon's show on CNN along with the political strategist and head of Ted Cruz's super PAC, a woman named Kellyanne Conway, who was not a Trump fan to say the least.

It started badly. Lemon asked me for my personal opinion about Trump's retweet, and I pivoted to talking about anti-Trump super PACs. Lemon said, "I'm not going to let you do that! Omarosa, stop!"

When I tried to explain myself, he said, "Okay, let's stop, everybody, cut the mic, everybody. We're not doing that. I want everyone on this panel to answer the questions directly."

He cut me off. He silenced me. I was shocked. Why have me on the show if he wasn't going to allow me to make my case? I was incensed.

After a commercial break, I made the point that it was honorable of Trump to defend his wife.

And Conway, ready with "Trump's woman problem" talking points, interrupted, "If you want to defend your wife, and let's be very clear, it was not a pro-Cruz super-PAC or the Cruz quote team that put that picture out there, it was an anti-Trump PAC. Number two, and most importantly, if you defend your wife, why do you have to attack someone else's wife? I mean that's really the core question here . . . Seventy percent of all women say that they have an unfavorable opinion of him. And, look, there are those who say if you attack someone else's wife, it is petty, it is rude, it is undignified. . . . Women out there are telling pollsters they don't appreciate a leader who is—has to get the last word all the time or uses certain words. . . . Do you think he wants to talk about health care, education, taxes, destroying ISIS, or you want talk about wives? So let's be honest who created this mess."

I was used to talking circles around my opponents, but Conway could slither her way out of any debate.

On March 29, it was announced that GOP political operative Paul Manafort was coming on as the campaign convention manager and Rick Gates, a veteran political consultant, would be his deputy. I got a bad feeling about Manafort. He was the opposite of what we'd been campaigning for. We'd been rallying against special interests and Washington insiders; Manafort had worked for everyone in the establishment including Ronald Reagan, George H.W. Bush, and Bob Dole. New York billionaire Tom Barrack recommended Manafort to Trump, though. Jared supported it. The argument was that we needed someone who'd done all this before.

I was worried about what direction he'd take us in. But then again, the GOP establishment hated Trump. Jared saw him as a bridge to unite the party before the convention. Corey could only see him as a threat.

The same day, Trump defended Corey against the battery charges that had recently been filed by Michelle Fields. At a Wisconsin rally, he mocked her complaint and insinuated that she'd changed her story many times: "I did not witness any encounter. In addition to our staff, which had no knowledge of said situation, not a single camera or reporter of more than 100 in attendance captured the alleged incident." People in the crowd chimed in that her claim was "bullshit." and that she was a "liar." Trump also said he was a loyal guy, and he would be loyal to Corey.

I was booked with Wolf Blitzer on CNN's *The Situation Room* to talk about Corey's evolving role in the campaign. I declined to comment on the legal aspect of the case, but said, "I mean, Donald Trump was leading by a great margin up until these recent events. I will tell you that, if he loses Wisconsin, I can guarantee that you don't have to worry about Corey any longer, because he will become a liability and Donald Trump will get rid of him. . . . Whether he's right or wrong, whether he did or didn't, that's not what's important. The optics of this does not look good, and it does not reflect well on Donald Trump's campaign."

On April 15, four days before the crucial New York primary, we were blindsided when six former *Apprentice* contestants—season four winner Dr. Randal Pinkett, Kevin Allen, Tara Dowdell, Marshawn Evans Daniels, James Sun, and my old teammate Kwame Jackson; all of them black, except for James, who is Asian—rented a ballroom in New York and held a press conference to speak out against Donald Trump's racism. The timing was intentional, to tank Trump's chances in the New York primary. The blaring headlines—in CNN, NBC and *Vanity Fair*—were all versions of *"Apprentice* Stars Denounce Trump."

I was at the campaign office in Trump Tower when the drama

started. Trump heard about it, and I was called into his office to watch it with him.

Kwame Jackson started with, "Let us choose Kennedy over Kardashianism each and every time as a leading nation." I thought, *Here we go*.

"Trump has created a toxic ecosystem in our political discourse," he continued. "Trump has appealed to the lowest common denominator of fear, racism, and divisiveness in our populace. . . . You don't have to lynch someone, you don't have to burn a cross in someone's yard these days to be a racist. There are very nuanced forms of being racist in 2016."

My heart dropped as I watched this press conference. I knew that his words would strike a chord as he talked about Trump's violence-inciting rhetoric, which we had been struggling to justify. Here were six former constants who, like me, were people of color, and they were calling him a racist. As the only *Apprentice* alum on the campaign, I knew that it would be up to me to figure out how to combat these accusations.

At my side, Trump said, "You f**king believe these people? F**king Kwame! I made these people, and this is how they repay me. No loyalty! Randal worked at Trump and now he hates me? No loyalty! *None!*"

I flashed back to taping season one of *The Apprentice* and rumors I'd heard ever since of Trump describing Kwame throughout the taping as "uppity." Kwame got his MBA from Harvard. The University of Pennsylvania Wharton School of Business was also in the

Ivy League, but compared to Harvard, I suspected that Trump felt that UPenn was a lesser Ivy. I always thought that Kwame's Harvard credentials—like Obama's—rubbed Trump the wrong way.

He asked me if I'd help to fix this. I said, "I'm on it!"

I booked several interviews on cable news, including a face-off with Randal Pinkett on MSNBC. My strategy was to say how much Trump had supported me in my career and to present myself as a counterpoint to their argument, a.k.a., "He can't be a racist if he's been so good to me."

Meanwhile, Hope Hicks wrote a statement for Trump describing the former contestants as "six failing wannabes out of hundreds of contestants. How quickly they forget. Nobody would know who they are if it weren't for me. They just want to get back into the limelight like they had when they were with Trump. Total dishonesty and disloyalty. They should be careful, or I'll play hours of footage of them individually praising me." In hindsight, it's unlikely Trump would have pulled out any old footage. The world didn't know about things he'd said in outtakes yet, but *he* did.

A few days later, we were all charged up. Finally, it was the New York primary. Trump really wanted to win in his home state. That night, Fox was broadcasting live in the middle of Times Square, and I was booked for an exclusive sit-down with Greta Van Susteren.

While I was doing that, the rest of the campaign staff was back at the Trump Tower party, watching me on the big TV screens. Immediately after the Fox interview, I was booked to do another hit with Katie Couric for Yahoo! Also on that panel was Kellyanne Conway, who seemed distraught that Trump was about to win the New York primary. When I saw Donald later that night, he said, "Great job on Greta! We all watched you live." In the end, Trump won over 59 percent of the vote, and we watched as the Empire State Building lights turned crimson red, to indicate a Trump victory (if Cruz had won, it would have turned coral).

Hillary won, too, and the Empire State turned dark blue, not light blue for Sanders.

Everyone knew it'd be Trump versus Clinton in the general election now, but before we could shift to that contest, we still had to clinch the nomination.

SENATOR TED CRUZ dropped out on May 3, having put in a decent run, winning eleven contests, including the first, the Iowa caucus, and his home state of Texas.

Governor John Kasich ended his run on May 4. His one victory was my home state of Ohio.

In the end, Trump won an astounding forty-one contests. It was never even close. The Trump train was on track and unstoppable, despite concerted efforts from the opposition to do so.

On May 19, Paul Manafort was promoted to campaign chairman and chief strategist. Corey would stay on, Hope Hicks said in her statement, to manage day-to-day operations while Manafort would work on big-picture political strategy for the general election.

On June 20, Corey Lewandowski was fired. His exit was instigated by the Trump children and put the reins of the campaign solely in Paul Manafort's hands. I had an uneasy feeling about this.

Yes, Manafort had experience and a good relationship with the establishment. But couldn't we have found someone who wasn't an establishment denizen and better represented the campaign and the candidate?

Trump didn't seem to like him, either. From the beginning, Manafort said, "I'm the one who can rein him in. I can make him more presidential."

As soon as anyone tried to control Donald, he rebelled against them. Whatever Manafort asked for—that he use a Teleprompter, for example—Trump dug in his heels and refused.

On July 1, two months after Cruz dropped out, Trump hired Kellyanne Conway in a senior advisery position. Considering her previous vocal support for Ted Cruz and her earlier denunciations of Donald Trump, you can imagine my surprise when that happened. I thought it was a bit odd. One day, I was facing off with her on CNN, her saying rough things about Trump. The next, she was standing in front of me as part of the team.

We had made it. Trump was moving into July with the electorate united behind him. The Republican National Convention (RNC) on my home turf of Cleveland, Ohio, was just around the corner. I was ready for things to solidify for us.

Chapter Seven

Unconventional Standards

As we started our descent into Cleveland, it all hit me. This was my home state, and I was returning in triumph for the Republican National Convention, with my mentor about to be nominated as the party's choice for president. As I deplaned, and walked through the airport, I saw Trump fever had broken out. Everywhere you looked, Trump posters, MAGA hats, buttons, and bobbleheads. The excitement was palpable, and I was there to see and experience it all.

It reminded me of flying into Los Angeles the year we were nominated for the Emmy for *The Apprentice*, hoping we were going to win against the odds. That time, we didn't. But this time, we did. Throughout the primaries, the campaign and the man himself had been called a joke, and no one in the media thought he'd win. We arrived in

Cleveland having defeated sixteen other contenders, winning forty-one contests, and now Donald Trump was about to accept his party's nomination. After all the pain and anguish and challenges that we'd gone through to get there, I was just so excited, in part, because I thought, *Now people will finally respect us and take us seriously.*

As soon as I arrived at the Quicken Loans Arena, I started doing a series of media hits. MSNBC's Craig Melvin broke the news that I'd just been appointed the campaign's director of African American outreach. Even though I'd been one of the top media surrogates for nearly a year, the announcement made plenty of headlines. The Trump team, unlike HRC, was true to its word and had officially brought me on board as a senior adviser and director. Regardless of whether Mr. Trump was being taken seriously, I was.

Shep Smith at Fox News, asked, "Is the diversity thing going well?" By the end of the convention's four days, I would speak to dozens of anchors for dozens of shows and on every news channel, a myriad of reporters from publications across the country. Along with my surrogacy work at the convention, I also hosted and spoke at diversity events around Cleveland, a panel, a lunch here, a meeting with various state delegations there, all with the goal of communicating to the world about the importance of diversity and the issues around minority communities.

I knew my work was cut out for me, but I was on top of the world that first day in Cleveland. Every media eruption I'd dealt with since his announcement, every time I went on TV to defend a controversial tweet or remark, every rally I'd attended, every constituent group I'd met with, had all led up to this crowning moment.

All of us felt a bit like we'd survived a shipwreck and had washed ashore at a luxurious resort. Inside the arena, it was bright, colorful, and exciting, nothing but positive feedback flowing my way.

I met many familiar faces for the first time there, like Ben Carson. As the director of African American outreach, it was my job to cultivate any prominent black support, and Carson was high on the list. In politics, your foe becomes your friend in the blink of an eye.

Outside the arena, hundreds of angry protesters raged on the streets of Cleveland, disgusted and upset that Donald Trump was about to accept his party's nomination. The number of police and security guards and their intense, grim expressions reminded me of Chicago. We'd put up fencing around the venue, and people said we'd "built a wall" around Cleveland.

The largest and most vocal were the Black Lives Matter (BLM) groups. Many different chapters had descended on Cleveland, and it was my job to listen to them and respond to their issues. I'd been trying to sit down with leaders from the movement for a while, but since Black Lives Matter is decentralized—many small groups but no one leadership body—I'd reached out to Melina Abdullah, a professor of Pan-African studies at California State University in Los Angeles, and one of the coorganizers of BLM in LA. I'd been trying to sit down with her since October 2015. I thought it could be an opportunity for us to talk about the issues and hear what BLM wanted from the Trump campaign, or in the unlikely event, his presidency.

In Cleveland, I reached out again, contacting several chapters' leadership to arrange a meeting with me. They all flat-out refused.

It wasn't about meeting and talking. They were there to protest, and that was what they were going to do. My job was outreach, and I made a concerted effort, but whether someone agrees to meet with me is not up to me. I had hoped to take their concerns and requests to the leadership so we could resolve the issues, but we didn't get a single step toward that.

I worked hard to meet with BLM because I believe the movement is needed. Too many African American men are being killed by police officers. Gun violence had taken my brother. I was most certainly aware and concerned about police violence, gun control, and systematic racism! I had protested the killing of Trayvon Martin, and in Ferguson, Missouri, about the shooting of Michael Brown. BLM is important and vital to African Americans.

I was disappointed that I didn't have an opportunity to talk with the group during the campaign. I still think about the good it might have done, not only for BLM but also for DJT. Martin Luther King Jr. had met with Lyndon Johnson, and, against all expectations, the two joined forces to fight poverty in African American communities and to push for (and pass) the Civil Rights Act in their respective areas of influence.

Two days before the RNC, the NAACP kicked off its 107th annual convention, also in Ohio, in Cincinnati. I had reached out to the NAACP in early 2016 to set up a meeting, but it never happened. Then, as luck would have it, they were having their convention at the same time, in the same state as the RNC. The NAACP thought it'd be a great idea for Trump to hop on Trump Force One, fly to Cincinnati, and meet with leadership. I agreed to try to set it up. Unfortunately they invited him to come on the same night of Melania's speech. He was not going to leave his convention and miss his wife's big moment. We offered to send surrogates, like Ben Carson, Mike Pence, me, but they said no. The headline, of course, was "Donald Trump declines invitation to speak at the NAACP convention," per the *Los Angeles Times* and dozens of other outlets.

Like I said, uphill battle.

INSIDE THE BUBBLE, support and excitement.

Outside the bubble, hate and tension.

On social media, hate flowed like a river of lava at me. I would post a photo from the RNC floor, and the comments were full of racial slurs, insults, and death threats.

"House n****r."

"Sellout."

"Trump whore."

"Token."

"Her black card should be taken away."

"Die, bitch."

The ratio was about ten vile comments and death threats for every positive one. I reported the death threats to Secret Service, Trump's bodyguard Keith Schiller, and local police. So while I was fighting to be a voice and advocate for the African American community, external forces were trying to attack me. I was living in the dichotomy of joy and pain.

On July 19, Spike Lee posted on Instagram a photo of me with a clown nose and turned sideways with the caption: "Ms. Theresa 'Omarosa' Manigault 'Pic Is Like This Cuz I'm Looking At Her SIDEWAYS," he began in the caption. "Trump Has Named Her As His 'Director Of African-American Outreach. You Might Know Her From Trump's RealityTV Show The Apprentice. #Who's Next? Step N' Fetchit? Aunt Jemina? Uncle Ben? Sleep N' Eat? Rastus? Lil' N----r Jim? Omarosa Gonna Give Out Free Popeye's Chicken With Sides To Deliver Da Black Vote To Trump? YA-DIG? SHO-NUFF. #blacklivesmatter."

He used my mother's name, Theresa. I can only assume that was to shame me to my mother? Why bring her into this at all?

I replied in a Tweet that has since been deleted: "You attack me, I can deal with! You attack my mom, NOT cool!! How does this help our community? You attack my mom?? Wow! #newLow!" My mother, Theresa, is a Democrat and had nothing to do with this. I was livid that he or anyone would sit in judgment of me when all I was doing was advocating for the African American community.

Throughout the primaries, we fought a tirelessly aggressive race. We were told we could never win, that he should never win, but he did win, despite the best efforts of his sixteen opponents and the majority of the media. I should have felt only pride and happiness. And yet, I was conflicted. Yes, I'd been part of an extraordinary phenomenon. I'd accomplished something incredible that precious few people who grew up where I did ever would. But so many members in my community resented my being a part of the team.

I ran into Donna Brazile coming out of the CNN booth at the

RNC. She congratulated me on my appointment. She'd always been supportive and real with me. She reminded me that we need people in both camps. In the past months, she'd sent me gentle warnings about my affiliation with Trump and his fringe supporters like white supremacist and former Grand Wizard of the Ku Klux Klan David Duke, but always with concern, never accusation—and would continue to do so in the coming months. In a text about my switching parties, she said, "We need you there. We are comforted that you'll be in the room and at the table, as long as you are there we're going to be okay." I will always be grateful for her counsel at the time.

As a senior adviser and director on the campaign, I was on both the RNC and campaign mailing lists, and my email boxes started filling up with daily talking points (TPs; an apt acronym), updates, schedules, media-hits lists, headlines, Trump travel logistics information, etcetera. I was sending and receiving up to five hundred emails per day. The campaign memos I received were cc'ed to Hope Hicks, Rick Gates, and veteran Republican political operative Kevin Kellems (a Dick Cheney guy who lasted only two weeks). It was expanded to include ex–Ted Cruz comms director Jason Miller and speechwriter Stephen Miller, a Jeff Sessions's protégé. The daily memo had the Trump/Pence logo on top, followed by a subject like, "How to Talk about Brexit" or "Fifty Facts about Hillary Clinton from Trump's 'Stakes of the Election' Address."

We had an entire daily memo devoted to "Trump Tweets Alerts," just to handle talkers on his favorite platform of all. FDR used the radio to reach the public. JFK used television. DJT uses Twitter. He's addicted to it because he's a narcissist, and he revels in his many million followers. The likes and retweets feed his ego. It's the ultimate power tool for him because he controls his content. It's not censored or even spellchecked. No one can tell him what to write or say. He can tweet about anything in the world, and does, with a rawness that is decidedly not presidential. He loved the idea that any tweet could set off a firestorm and that they allowed him to get his message directly to his base.

Our job was to turn his tweets into targeted messaging. The Trump Tweet Alert memo came with specific TPs to respond to whatever he posted in the wee hours. The writer of the TPs depended on the subject matter of Trump's tweet. If Trump posted about domestic policy, the expert in that field would write them. If he posted about international foreign policy, the national security advisers would write them. Every adviser to the campaign was enlisted to contribute to these daily alerts to explain to the rest of the team how to deal with his 140-character policy statements and missives.

We had daily communications from the Republican National Committee, which isn't so surprising. A little more strangely, a select Trump campaign mailing list received daily emails directly from a producer at Fox News that summarized the news of the day, broke down talking points and spin suggestions, and offered resources. For example, a typical @foxnews.com email would have a complete transcript of a recent Hillary Clinton speech, a second-by-second breakdown and analysis, with specific suggestions for how to respond to her, line by line.

People suspected that there was a relationship between Fox News and the Trump campaign, and that there were people at Fox work-ing tirelessly to get him elected. To all those people, I can confirm that you have no idea just how right you were. The back-and-forth of daily communications between individuals at Fox and the Trump White House continues to this day. People joke that Trump gets his talking points by watching Fox News, and that is certainly true. But individuals at Fox News are also speaking directly to his team of advisers every single day. The channel's channels are wide-open.

The first marquee event of the convention, on opening night, was the speech by Melania Trump. Her profile on the campaign had been extremely low. I could count on both hands how many appear-ances she'd made for him for the campaign. On the rare occasions she came to an event, we talked backstage in the green room or the hold room or when she and Donald came out of the motor-cade. I would give her an update on how things were going, and she was always polite and friendly. It reminded me of the first time we'd met, during my first season on *The Apprentice* while filming the very first episode. Melania gave us, the winning team, a tour of the famous Trump Tower triplex. She came down the gilded staircase and greeted us warmly, the stunning lady of the manor.

As I watched her speech that night, I was so incredibly proud. The crowd received her well. My favorite line was, "The only limit to your achievements is the strength of your dreams and your willing-ness to work for them." Amen, sister.

I thought to myself, *We could have utilized her more during the primaries.* I understood and respected her choice to stay in New York with Barron and not join the campaign trail full-time. We had plenty of Trump family members already involved, Don Jr. and Eric, and Lara Trump. The best way to combat the woman problem was to showcase Trump's beautiful, intelligent wife. I made a mental note to talk to her team about that in the morning once the rave reviews came in.

Unfortunately, the next morning, there was breaking news. A freelance TV reporter named Jarrett Hill noticed similarities between Melania's speech and another convention speech from eight years ago, Michelle Obama's at the Democratic Convention in Denver.

From Michelle's speech: "And Barack and I were raised with so many of the same values: that you work hard for what you want in life; that your word is your bond, and you do what you say you're going to do; that you treat people with dignity and respect, even if you don't know them, and even if you don't agree with them. And Barack and I set out to build lives guided by these values, and to pass them on to the next generation. Because we want our children—and all children in this nation—to know that *the only limit to the height of your achievements is the reach of your dreams and your willingness to work for them.*"

From Melania's speech: "From a young age, my parents impressed on me the values that you work hard for what you want in life, that your word is your bond and you do what you say and keep your promise, that you treat people with respect. They taught and showed me values and morals in their daily lives. That is a lesson that I continue to pass along to our son. And we need to pass those lessons on to the many generations to follow. *Because we want our children in this nation to know that the only limit to your achievements is the strength of your dreams and your willingness to work for them.*"

Internally, the texts between the spokespeople and comms teams were nonstop. The TP emails were coming one after another. The decision was made to place the blame for the plagiarism on Meredith McIver, who was an in-house staff writer from the Trump Organization and coauthor of two of Trump's books. It was painful to watch her take the blame, because she was one of the higher-ranked persons of color in the Trump Organization. She was asked to fall on the sword, and she did. In her July 20, 2016, statement to the press, she explained that snippets of Michelle's speech did wind up in Melania's in the process of creating it.

"This was my mistake, and I feel terrible for the chaos I have caused Melania and the Trumps, as well as to Mrs. Obama. No harm was meant," she said. "Yesterday, I offered my resignation to Mr. Trump and the Trump family, but they rejected it. Mr. Trump told me that people make innocent mistakes and that we learn and grow from these experiences. I apologize for the confusion and hysteria my mistake has caused. Today, more than ever, I am honored to work with such a great family. I personally admire the way Mr. Trump has handled this situation and I am grateful for his understanding."

They chose McIver as the sacrificial lamb, but they needed to keep her under control, so she was not fired. If they had fired her, she would have been free to tell the world any number of Trumpworld secrets. The ending about "honor" and "gratitude" toward Trump is classic loyalty-oath behavior. Many canny people have figured out that praising him is the only way to get his attention and approval.

The negative exposure destroyed any hope of Melania joining the campaign efforts. She appeared reluctantly onstage when Trump accepted his nomination a few days later, but behind the scenes, she was humiliated and furious at Donald for forcing her into a position of scrutiny and vulnerability. My heart went out to her during this horrible time of being mocked. It had to be devastating to be in that position. It was a blow to her, and a loss to the campaign. She practically disappeared for the rest of it.

I WENT ABOUT my business, and spoke at an evening reception for black GOPers, participated in town halls, attended events, in and out of the arena, picking my way through angry protesters and city police. I was able to leave the convention and attend a family reunion for a few hours. My cousin Darian Rushton was there. A Democrat, Darian is one of my favorite cousins. He served in the army and works at the VA in Ohio. I brought him back to the convention with me and took him to a few events.

In the Trump family spectator box, there was a constant stream of GOP players like Karl Rove and former primary foes like Chris Christie and Ben Carson. The future Women for Trump team was always around: Lynne Patton, and Lynnette Hardaway and Rochelle Richardson, a.k.a. Diamond and Silk, YouTube stars and Trump diehards.

Tiffany Trump, the only child of Donald's second wife, Marla Maples, gave a warm-up speech on the second night. I watched her from the family box, sitting with the three children of Donald's first wife, Ivana. It was America's first chance to get to hear and see Tiff, and I thought it was an important moment for her. She'd always been treated like a California castoff, but that night, she was given a platform, and she did a great job.

Don Jr. spoke sometime that night after Tiffany. I remember feeling anxious for Don Jr., because of how hard his father was on him. If Don Jr. flubbed his address, Donald would surely make cracks about how "disappointed" he was, as he often did with his firstborn. He hit his regular-guy "pouring concrete and hanging sheetrock," "doctorates in common sense," and "dignity of hard work" talking points about his father. An avid hunter, he spoke passionately about Second Amendment rights. I wished I could have seen Donald Trump react to his son's fiery address, but he wasn't in the arena that night. Much to my relief, Don Jr. did very well. But no matter how good a job Don Jr. did, I was sure his father would find some fault with it. Don Jr. was desperate to please his father, and that same desperation caused him to trip up.

My heart went out to Don whenever I saw them interact. Having lost my father very young, I understood Don Jr.'s longing for his father's approval, which was not forthcoming. Ivana Trump, Don Jr.'s mother, wrote in her recent memoir *Raising Trump* that when she and her husband were deciding what to name their firstborn, she suggested Donald Jr. Trump was against it. She asked why, and he said, "What if he's a loser?" His father was afraid that his son was going to be an embarrassment. Don Jr. has been struggling against the negative expectation of his namesake since the moment he was born.

The family box was the best place to watch the speeches and take photos. I must have snapped several hundreds of them. While flipping through them, I came across many of Vanessa Trump, Don Jr.'s wife, sitting next to him. They never held hands or touched. They never even looked at each other. She had a dour expression on her face the entire time. I believe that as far back as July 2016, if not even farther, their marriage was hanging by a thread. But she showed up at the convention and the debates anyway, taking her seat in the row of Trump wives out of respect for her father-in-law.

The third night of the convention, June 20, there was a technical snafu in the middle of Eric Trump's speech. The electrical system shorted out, and all the video monitors went down—but not the teleprompter, thank God. Eric stood onstage when the forty-foot LED screens behind him started to flash and then go dark. Eric didn't miss a beat. He continued with his speech and hit every line. He earned big points with his father that night. He'd carried on triumphantly, regardless of glitches or obstacles, and that was the Trump way. Donald was sitting in the family box that night, between Don Jr. and Ivanka Trump. He beamed with pride at his second son. Traditionally, the candidate doesn't sit in the family box to watch the speeches. When Donald sat there to watch Eric, I felt sorry for Don Jr.

The monitors were repaired by the time Mike Pence took the stage. I'd only just met him in the family box that day. He came right over to me and said, "Omarosa! I know all about you and how helpful you've been to Mr. Trump, and I'm so looking forward to working together." He waved over three men who looked like his clones. "I'd like you to meet my brother, and my other brother, and my other brother." I liked the Pence clan. "We always knew this would happen to Mike. He's always wanted to be president . . . I mean *vice* president!" one of his brothers said with a wink. It was a real joking-not-joking look, and I filed it under "keep an eye on that situation."

On the final night of the convention, Ivanka Trump walked out to the Beatles' "Here Comes the Sun," and gave her MAGA-power speech. Like all of his children, she was articulate, poised, and well prepared. Unfortunately, her polished address was overshadowed by controversy the next day. Ivanka tweeted a photo of herself that showed her blush pink dress to great advantage, with the caption, "Shop Ivanka's look from her #RNC speech" with a link to Macy's retail page. The $138 Ivanka Trump Collection dress quickly sold out, but the media was in an uproar about her using her convention address as a branding opportunity. She'd be similarly criticized for plugging a gold bracelet on *60 Minutes*. I am sure Donald loved Ivanka's selling of her dress, seizing each and every opportunity to advance the Trump brand.

It was a hard habit to break. In February 2017, when Nordstrom stopped carrying Ivanka's brands due to either poor sales or political pressure, depending on whom you spoke to, her father tweeted that the retail chain treated his daughter unfairly and that "She is a great person—always pushing me to do the right thing! Terrible!" Soon after, Kellyanne Conway appeared on *Fox & Friends* and said, "Go buy Ivanka's stuff! I own some of it. . . . I'm going to give a free commercial here. Go buy it today, everybody. You can find it online." That set off yet another firestorm about the ethics of using public office for private gain. Some said that a veteran surrogate like Conway should have known better. I believe she *did* know better.

-125-

She was playing to an audience of one, the candidate. Part of her role was to say whatever Trump wanted or would have liked to hear, and she did exactly that, every time, with a huge smile on her face.

When Ivanka finished her speech, she presented "my father and our next president, Donald J. Trump!" The nominee walked onstage from the wings, went over to his daughter, placed his hands on her bare upper arms and kissed her. Then he placed his hands low on her hips while appraising her, and then patted her on her hip. The placement of his hands made *everyone* uncomfortable. But I was used to the sickening feeling I had whenever they touched or kissed or he openly admired her form. Usually, it was in private, like the time not too long before the convention, during the campaign, when Trump and I and a few other people were in a meeting. Ivanka came into the room wearing a fitted skirt. The entire meeting had to stop so he could gush about her body. "You look great! I like the way that skirt fits. Doesn't Ivanka look great?" He insisted that we all agree that his daughter's tight skirt was very flattering. I thought, *Why don't the two of you cut it out?* It appeared to me that Ivanka had gotten so used to his touching her in ways that made others cringe and either didn't notice it anymore or purposefully allowed it to happen—as I've said, Ivanka uses his obsession with her to her advantage.

Donald proceeded to deliver his Stephen Miller–penned speech. The speech was referred to by liberals as "Midnight in America," a dark twist on Ronald Reagan's famous "Morning in America" speech. The speech focused on the dangerous state of our nation. Murders on the rise. People killed by the thousands on our streets. Nearly 180,000 illegal immigrants with criminal records, roaming free across the country. The millions of blacks and Latinos living in poverty, and the escalating crime rates. Police officers gunned down. Islamic radicals streaming across the borders. Terror everywhere.

Trump was the law-and-order candidate. He was going to go to war against terrorism, street crime, and illegal immigration. When I'd read this speech on paper, it didn't sound as dark and menacing as it did when he delivered it. He was speaking to his cult—not the country.

Although Trump said he wanted to improve the lives of all Americans, he blamed our country's problems completely and specifically on certain subsets of the population: black and brown people. It was hard to miss the racial undertones of his speech. When he railed against criminals, terrorists, and gangs, many figured he was not talking about white people. He said, "I am your voice." And by "your," he meant steel workers and coal miners in the Rust Belt. It was classic dog-whistle racism.

When I read the headlines, I knew I had to talk to him, to get him to understand that words matter. Thirteen months later, when white supremacists rallied in Charlottesville, I would realize that Trump's acceptance speech at the convention had set the standard for his racial agenda. But that night, I tried to qualm the uneasiness that I felt. I checked myself and my thoughts. I was in the moment, feeding off the excitement in the convention hall. As the balloons dropped, I said a prayer for Donald and for the country.

After Trump formally accepted the nomination in his speech, there was a private reception for him in the penthouse of the hotel. Many high-level donors were there. Donald spent much of the night watching cable news reactions to his speech. I was mingling, eating, and enjoying myself. At one point, Trump motioned me over and I said, "Congratulations, you did it."

He said, "No, Omarosa, we did it."

I HAD A couple of days off after Cleveland, and went to Jacksonville to see John. At the end of a church service, in front of the entire congregation, John proposed. I said yes! It was one of the happiest moments of my life. He is a man of God, brilliant, charming, and down-to-earth.

I asked him when he knew he wanted to marry me, and he said it was when he watched me preach at his church for their Youth Recognition Day. He told me later, "Watching you ministering at my church, I knew you had to be my wife."

My candidate won. I was in love and engaged to the love of my life.

Four years before, I was in a deep, dark depression after Michael Clarke Duncan's death, and couldn't imagine ever being happy again. Life has a way of challenging your faith. But in John, God had sent me a new beginning.

Chapter Eight

Trump vs. Clinton

As a senior adviser and the director of African American outreach, my mandate was to engage the community on behalf of the candidate and to increase black voter turnout for Trump.

In 2012, Mitt Romney garnered just 6 percent of the African American vote against President Obama. I felt optimistic that we could reach or exceed that number. The headlines said otherwise. One headline read, "No Matter What Omarosa Says, Trump Is Not Getting the Black Vote." It seemed I had been brought in to do an impossible task.

At the convention in July, reporters kept asking me about recent polls that claimed Trump had *0 percent* of the African American vote. Few people believed that I'd be able to get any support from the black community, given the extraordinary opposition I faced.

But I was determined to make it happen. I asked National Coalitions Director Alan Cobb to approve a budget for African American outreach. He stated that there was little to no money allocated for actual engagement events, only diversity media buys. I pushed back and was told that expenses would be approved on a case-by-case basis. I forged ahead, determined to make something out of nothing. But at each turn, there was a hurdle.

It would be impossible to go through every single hurdle of that summer and fall before the general election, so I'll do a lightning round of some of the high and lows of those days.

JULY 27

The O'Jays sent a cease-and-desist letter to Congressman John Mica (R-FL) and copied Paul Manafort via their attorney, demanding that the campaign stop using their 1972 hit "Love Train" (which we'd changed to "Trump Train") or 1973's "For the Love of Money," which had been *The Apprentice* theme song for fourteen seasons, at any Trump or Republican rally or event. The O'Jays's Walter Williams and Eddie Levert said in a press statement, "We don't appreciate having our music associated with a campaign that is hurtful to so many with whom we have common ground. . . . Our music, and most especially 'Love Train,' is about bringing people together, not building walls." I was devastated—not only were the O'Jays one of my favorite groups, they were friends from Ohio, and I participated every year in their charity events. That one hit close to home.

AUGUST 4

The first Women for Trump event was held in Charlotte, North Carolina, at the Trump National Golf Clubhouse. The concept for the event was the brainchild of Lara Trump. Lara, Lynne, Katrina, and I went down south to meet and greet Republican women and persuade them to vote for Trump. The event was so well planned and attended, Lara ran with the template, which quickly evolved into a women's empowerment tour, which at times had all of us on a tricked-out tour bus—with a huge wrapped image of Donald Trump's face on the side—driving from place to place. Often, I'd attend a women's event in the morning and piggyback it with an African American event in the evening. The Women for Trump tour was well funded, unlike my outreach agenda, which received nothing for events.

That event also set a precedent for future appearances as Women for Trump. Whether we did a fancy reception, like in Charlotte, or an arena rally in the Rust Belt, Lara insisted that we wear dresses and heels. Many of us would have preferred campaign T-shirts and jeans. But Lara always reinforced that "Trump men" required "Trump women" to look and dress a certain way, and because we were on the Women for Trump tour, we weren't allowed to wear standard campaign T-shirts. Later on, the unofficial dress code of the Trump White House of "women dress like women" set off some controversy. Hope Hicks pushed her fashion choices as far as possible, wearing miniskirts with thigh-high boots or diaphanous summer dresses in the dead of winter, the opposite of traditional Washington conservative style.

We pushed back, and eventually designed pink Women for

Trump jackets and T-shirts as a kind of uniform for the rallies, and Lara reluctantly approved them in the last two weeks of the campaign, but only if we wore short skirts and heels with the jacket or skinny jeans or slacks. If you look at photos of those appearances, we look like we're about to go to a cocktail party, not a campaign rally.

AUGUST 14

Manafort had proven to be a liability ever since the convention. Reporters started asking questions about his foreign clients and why the official RNC platform had suddenly softened its stance on arms dealing among the US, Russia, and Ukraine.

The New York Times revealed that Manafort's name appeared in a "black ledger" of the Ukrainian president. Manafort had apparently received payments of $12.7 million over five years. The link between the pro-Russian Ukrainian language in the RNC platform and this new information was too much for anyone to stand. Combined with Donald's fascination with Vladimir Putin, Manafort's connections threw a new, dirty light on the campaign. He had to go.

AUGUST 17

Steve Bannon was hired as campaign chief. I found this new addition to the team alarming. Steve Bannon, the chairman of the Breitbart News website, was widely considered to be a sexist and racist. This was not going to help me with women and minorities.

AUGUST 19

Manafort was fired—and I was relieved—amid sliding poll numbers and rumors about his shady business connections to pro-Russian political leaders in Ukraine. Manafort is currently in jail while he awaits trial.

What disturbed me the most about the Manafort situation was the lack of vetting. This was a major party presidential campaign, and it seemed like no one was being sufficiently legally checked out before being put in leadership roles. This would come back to bite us again and again.

Kellyanne was promoted to campaign manager. She was my third campaign manager—first Corey, then Manafort, now Kellyanne—in less than a year. I'd managed to weather every storm so far and hoped that the turnover rate would slow down.

At a rally in Dimondale, Michigan, Trump asked black voters, "What do you have to lose?" in voting for him. I put out a statement that said, "The Democrats continue to take the African American community for granted. It is disconcerting that they would rather pander than formulate substantive policy plans that would actually improve conditions as opposed to continue down the current path of the last eight years."

SEPTEMBER 3

In conjunction with NDC and Pastor Darrell Scott, we organized an event at the Great Faith Ministries Church in Detroit where Donald would address the congregation. Ben Carson came along with us.

Right off the bat, there was some trouble with Pastor Wayne T. Jackson. Because of the vocal protesters outside, he was waffling about letting Trump speak from his pulpit. Donald snapped at me, "Why did I come here if I'm not going to speak. You have to fix this."

The pastor and I had a heated exchange. Donald walked up and watched me handle it. It was a bit odd to be arguing about him, with him just looming there. The pastor agreed that he could speak, and then I escorted him into the sanctuary. I had a lot of organizational things to do, so I got up to take care of them. He grabbed my wrist and said, "You can't leave me with these people." The look in his eyes was like a lost child.

I stayed with him, sitting to his left for the whole service. The praise dancers came out before the sermon, and Donald said, "Wow, there's entertainment before church? I had no idea."

We'd only gotten through the devotional part of what would be a two-hour service when he leaned toward me and said, "This is the longest I've been in church in my life." A bit later: "When is this going to end?" And again: "God, how much longer do I have to sit here?" When he finally got to address the congregation, I hoped he'd speak from the heart, but he pulled out a piece of paper and read some bland, stump-speech remarks. I'd pushed Pastor Jackson so he could just say, "I want to help you build and rebuild Detroit. I fully understand that the African American community has suffered from discrimination and there are many wrongs that should be made right." This community didn't need reminding that their lives were hard.

The singing and dancing at the end might've been a relief, but he was still at odds. "What do I do?" he asked.

I said, "Just go with the flow."

He started swaying creepily, and I wanted to tell him, "Okay, stop going with it."

As we were leaving, the pastor loaded up Donald with a Bible and some accessories. He placed a prayer shawl around his shoulders. Donald thanked him, but as soon as we got away, he said, "Take this thing off me!" Ever the germaphobe, he was horrified to wear a shawl that might have been on anyone else's shoulders.

He picked up an African American baby, and the baby started screaming. I wanted to scream, too. Outside the church, protesters chanted, "What do we have to lose? Everything!"

For all the tension with the pastor, he did well for himself in the end. In exchange for letting Donald speak that day, Trump let Pastor Jackson give a prayer at the inauguration. Everything with Trump was transactional.

SEPTEMBER 7

Matt Lauer moderated a forum with Donald Trump and Hillary Clinton at the Intrepid Sea, Air & Space Museum in New York, and

Donald praised Vladimir Putin as a strong leader, "far more than our president has been." We cautioned him against pro-Putin rhetoric, saying, "He's not somebody that you want to align yourself with." He didn't understand why.

It became immediately apparent that Trump lacked basic comprehension about the very complicated relationship between the United States, the former Soviet Union, and modern Russia. History didn't seem to matter to him. Donald was not a student of history. He wasn't a student of anything but what he was doing and has done. He'd never been a big reader, either, and I'd be shocked if he'd ever read a book about the Cold War. I just don't think that he had the attention span to even watch a documentary about Russia. He was fixated on Vladimir Putin as a feared, respected, and admired leader. I believe he was envious of the control that Putin exerts over his people. Trump went with his gut, and his gut told him, "I like Putin, and I want him to be my friend." Nothing else mattered.

SEPTEMBER 11

The Women of Trump Tour was in Cleveland, and I'd been to a service at Darrell Scott's church that morning. After Lara was invited to give remarks, our group was heading to the cars, and Lara said, "Guys, look at this." All our phones had multiple messages. We stopped on the landing in a back stairwell to watch the video of Hillary Clinton fainting as she walked to her SUV after a memorial service at Ground Zero in New York. I said, "Oh my God, is she okay?"

Lara and the others said things like, "She's sick! She's not going to make it to election night! She's sick!" They were gleeful that Clinton appeared to be gravely ill. Many people in Trumpworld believed that she was concealing a serious neurological medical condition—Parkinson's was mentioned often. They thought that her untreated pneumonia might have been the cause of her collapse, but if you truly had pneumonia, why would you go visit your infant grand-daughter? Many suspected there was an underlying condition as well.

SEPTEMBER 15

At the 46th annual Congressional Black Caucus Legislative Conference in DC, I had a brief run-in with Hillary Clinton. My friend Darren Peters from my White House days was advancing her. When she approached, he grabbed my phone and snapped a picture. She gave me a lukewarm smile and said, "Donald? Really?"

SEPTEMBER 16

Trump held a press conference at DC's Trump International, his new hotel, to make a major announcement about veterans. He spent a while showing off the hotel and bringing out decorated veterans, then said, "Hillary Clinton and her campaign of 2008 started the birther controversy. I finished it. You know what I mean. President Barack Obama was born in the United States—period. Now we all want to get back to making America strong and great again." Along with promoting his hotel, he needed to preempt anything Clinton might say about his birther blather at the upcoming debate. He wanted to "put it to bed," a phrase he often used to mean "take care of it; make it go away."

SEPTEMBER 19

Don Jr. likened Syrian refugees to a bowl of Skittles, reigniting the outcry that the entire family was racist, hated Muslims, and equated immigrants and asylum seekers with terrorists. Trump just shook his head and said, "Look at what he did now. He screwed up again. What a f**kup."

SEPTEMBER 22

I filmed an episode of *Say Yes to the Dress*, a TLC network reality show. I took some flak for doing that, too, but it was only a two-hour shoot and it was one of my favorite shows. It was also the first time I was getting to see my bridesmaids in months because of the campaign, and one of the few wedding items I had attended to. The dress, one of the most important elements for the bride, was key. The show was shot at Kleinfeld, which is heaven on earth for brides. I was thrilled to go and be the blushing bride for a couple hours before returning to Trumpworld across town. It was a wonderful reprieve and, among the many perks, production gifted me the full cost of my dress and veil.

SEPTEMBER 26

Lester Holt moderated the first presidential debate at Hofstra University in Hempstead, New York. In their preparations with Donald, the campaign staff tried to convince Trump to be more "presidential," and coached him to shift his tone away from that of the primaries—the interruptions and use of monikers for his opponents. But Trump had his own ideas about being spontaneous and Trump-like.

Right out of the gate, he seemed agitated. Hillary was expertly prepared, and he seemed nervous. She hit him hard by saying, "I think Donald just criticized me for preparing for this debate. Yes, I did. And you know what else I prepared for? I prepared to be the president. And I think that's a good thing."

During a segment on jobs that should have been a home run, he kept sniffing loudly and weirdly. He reverted to interrupting and saying, "Wrong!"—the very things he had been urged not to do. For me, it was unusual to see him succumb to the pressure. I was not used to seeing Donald fumble. He was not himself. Something was off.

He was unprepared with basic information on the issues. He

showed his age by mocking her campaign website. He didn't seem to understand what a website was used for.

After the debate, members of the Trump team, including Sarah Huckabee Sanders, communications adviser Ashley Bell, Bruce LeVell, Republican correspondent Scottie Nell Hughes, and I huddled in the war room with Jason Miller, the comms director, and his deputy, Bryan Lanza, for a rapid-response briefing about what we were going to say in the spin room and for the upcoming news cycle.

First order of business, the weird sniffing. It was decided that the debate room's high-impact air conditioning had caused postnasal drip. We had no idea why he'd been doing that.

Second order of business, race. Hillary brought up Trump's long record of engaging in racist behavior, including a 1973 Department of Justice lawsuit accusing him of not renting apartments to black people in a building he owned. His defense included praising himself highly for letting black people into his Palm Beach country club "in probably the wealthiest community there is in the world." I cringed. Trump continued: "And I'm so glad I did it. And I have been credited for what I did. And I'm very, very proud of it." He also extolled the success of "stop and frisk" policing in New York, which Hillary knew was untrue. It was difficult to watch.

It was my job to prepare him to respond to the media on his racially insensitive remarks. I pushed the campaign to prepare Trump with counterpunches about Clinton-era racist policies and rhetoric. She had called young black men "superpredators" in 1996.

The Clinton crime bill in 1994 had resulted in the mass incarceration of low-level offenders, the vast majority of them young black men. I had the facts and figures. The person I spoke to on the debate team said, "He can't retain that much information. We have to simplify it. Put it in basic terms."

I said, "Well, I can make simple talking points for him, but we've got to counterpunch. She's kicking his butt on race issues." He never bothered to get up to speed on any of it.

One more thing about that first debate: the woman problem came up again, and Hillary mocked Trump's love of "hanging around" beauty contests and how he'd called Miss Universe 1996 Alicia Machado "Miss Housekeeping" because she's Latina, and "Miss Piggy" because he thought she was fat. While she was delivering this takedown, Trump interrupted her, which only reinforced her point that Trump was disrespectful and dismissive of women.

When Donald began attacking Machado on Twitter, calling her "disgusting" and "my worst Miss U" in addition to saying she had a "sex tape" and questioning her citizenship, I groaned. His woman problem might not have a solution—no matter how many stops we made on the Women for Trump bus.

OCTOBER 7

Donald Trump told CNN, "[The Central Park 5] admitted they were guilty. The police doing the original investigation say they were guilty. The fact that that case was settled with so much evidence against them is outrageous. And the woman, so badly injured, will never be the same." The young men—four black and one of Hispanic descent—who were arrested and convicted for the vicious 1989 crime spent between six and thirteen years in prison. Years later, when another man confessed to the crime, DNA evidence proved their innocence. They were exonerated in 2014 and were paid a $41 million settlement from New York for their wrongful conviction.

Hope Hicks and I emailed about talking points. I wrote, "Even though it's old news, this story, his response, has legs. I'm concerned it will be brought up in the debate and in any press that he does, in attack ads in battleground states." This was going to hurt us badly with African American voters. It was just like his birther claims that stretched out over years.

I spoke with him about it myself. I prepared a briefing about the case. I asked him to look at the available information and to come to terms with the fact that they were indeed innocent. He rambled, rehashing his misinformation and refusing to look at anything new about the psychology of innocent people confessing under duress. For him, it was black and white (no pun intended). They confessed, so they were guilty. His mind was like a brick wall. He refused to take back his words or admit he was wrong.

I told him that his stubbornness and ignorant position were irrational and hurting us, but he refused to budge, which put me on the front lines on the issue. I was constantly in fight mode, fighting to correct him on these crucial issues.

This is the big one, I thought. *This is as bad as it's going to get.* Boy, was I wrong.

4:00 p.m.

The *Washington Post* put up a video on its website that has become known the world over as the *Access Hollywood* tape.

I was at an airport, on my way home to LA, when the news broke. The text chain with the Women for Trump group was full of swear words, anguish, and disbelief. Watching that footage was the most shocking moment of my life with Donald Trump. I can only describe it as a punch in the stomach. I knew all those people on the bus: Billy Bush, Jim Dowd, Keith Schiller. I'd heard Trump speak crassly before, on *The Apprentice*. I'd heard him talk about women as objects of beauty before. But I'd never heard anything like *that*. It struck me the same way it struck everyone else: the man is bragging about a sexual assault. But because of my blind spot, or my history with him, or just because I couldn't emotionally allow myself to believe it, I tried to rationalize it, thinking, *It's offensive, but he says offensive things. It's normal for him. He wouldn't assault a woman. He loves women! He's just trying to impress the guys on the bus.*

5:30 p.m.

Hillary's campaign tweeted, "This is horrific. We cannot allow this man to become president." She was roundly mocked on social media. One person commented, "Your husband got a blowjob from an intern and used a cigar as a dildo. And *this* is horrific?"

Throughout the afternoon, I was receiving texts from the campaign. Lara was giving us updates on the back-and-forth behind the scenes. Apparently, RNC chairman Reince Priebus wanted Trump to bow out of the race, but Steve Bannon would not hear of it. Lara was fielding panicked texts from all of us, but she said, "I know this is bad, but we have a plan."

11:00 p.m.

When in crisis, the unofficial Trump family strategy was to go dark for twenty-four hours. But this time, Trump released a video statement after only seven hours, the famous "locker-room talk" sorry-not-sorry apology. The strategy was conceived by Bannon, Jared, and Kellyanne.

This was the big plan? People wanted him to express shame, but he refused to do that. He simply couldn't admit that he'd done anything wrong and he had no empathy for anyone he'd offended, because he had no empathy for anyone, period. Donald Trump's single greatest character flaw as a leader and human being is his complete and total lack of empathy.

Not too long after the video was released, Melania told Anderson Cooper, in what was, for me, an excruciating video to watch, that she accepted her husband's apology. I could not help but think about Hillary Clinton when all this was happening. Melania, like Hillary, had an unfaithful husband exposed in a very public space. Melania carried it differently, though, like a woman who was fully aware of who her husband was and what she'd gotten into by marrying him. Remember, Donald met her at a club while he was with another woman and not yet divorced from Marla Maples. I don't think that Melania ever had an expectation that Donald was going to be faithful. Not that I thought she condoned the *Access Hollywood* content.

OCTOBER 8

In the morning, I went to the church of my friend, the head of the Saint Louis NAACP, because I needed Jesus. We all did at that point.

At 2:44, Bill Pruitt, a producer from the early *Apprentice* seasons, tweeted, "As a producer on seasons 1 & 2 of #theapprentice I assure you: when it comes to the #trumptapes there are far worse. #justthebegininng" [*sic*]

The comms team called me to see if I knew anything about what Bill was talking about.

Over the day, people speculated what could be on these #trumptapes, and the N-word was mentioned often.

7:00 p.m.
Trump had a press conference with Juanita Broaddrick, Kathleen Willey, Kathy Shelton, and Paula Jones, all of Bill Clinton's accusers, less than two hours before the second presidential debate in Saint Louis. It was classic Trump tactics, to discredit and distract. I have no idea if it worked, but it did send the message that he would keep swinging.

Clinton's accusers sat in the family box, along with all the women who had forgiven and stayed loyal to Trump: Melania, Ivanka, Lara, and Vanessa. Me. I hoped Melania was okay. In her Anderson Cooper interview, she'd looked shell-shocked.

Don't ask me to parse the debate. I barely heard a word of it.

In the spin room afterward, I was surrounded by a throng of reporters who wanted to get my reaction to the *Access Hollywood* tape and the debate antics of the campaign. In the middle of this very hectic scene, a young woman started yelling at me, "I was sexually assaulted! I was raped!" *Who is she?* I wondered. *Is she a journalist? How did she get in here?* I was in the middle of answering reporters' questions about Trump's debate performance, but she kept yelling at me.

I said, "I'm sorry about what happened to you, but I didn't do that to you." I urged her to seek help and got back to work.

The next thing I knew, there's a viral video shot by a reporter of this woman in the bathroom crying, saying that she had hoped to speak to a Trump surrogate about rape culture and Trump's permissive attitude about sexual assault, as a survivor, and that the woman she tried to engage, "an African American," had been insensitive and insulting to her. She also said she did not know my name, despite my name appearing on a giant red sign right over my head.

I am convinced it was a staged stunt, that she was a plant. Why was she in the spin room, screaming, "I was raped"? And why, if she was so upset, did she then run into the bathroom and tell a reporter that I was mean to her? And why wasn't that reporter in the spin room, getting a real story? Trump was about to come out. Didn't she want to ask him about this issue? Did this smell right to anyone?

The "student" posted on Twitter about the incident, an account that appeared to have been created for this purpose and never used again. She had only two followers. I unleashed on Twitter about what I thought was an obvious setup. I'd been on edge, as you can imagine, and this put me over the top. I must have written half a dozen tweets about how staged I believed this was, which only made the story bigger.

OCTOBER 9

All day, I was getting texts and emails from people I knew asking why I hadn't already packed my bags and gotten the hell out of there. Lester McCorn, my classmate from seminary, texted, "Now would be a good time to resign and condemn Trump's behavior. This isn't about your public reputation. This is about a man and the spirit of hostility towards African Americans."

On social media, people had ideas whom the slur on the *Apprentice* tapes was referring to. A sample tweet: "Trump probably was calling Omarosa a n***er in those #apprenticetapes, I would not be surprised."

My mother checked in on me often. "I'm worried about you. I want to make sure you're okay," she said. She knew that I would do what I wanted and needed to do, regardless of anyone else's opinion. I'd heard them all out, but I'd make up my own mind. She was concerned, but she knew she had raised a daring child.

The MAGA messaging email of the day covered a lot of ground, avoiding an apology and relying on tried-and-true tactics. The points made, and selected quotes from the memo are as follows:

Despite his comments about women, we were to say, "Mr. Trump has the utmost respect for all of the women in his life—his wife, daughters, the women he has promoted throughout his businesses, and the millions of women who support him as the agent of change this country needs." It pushed our mentioning that if Melania accepted her husband's apology, so should everyone else.

Whenever someone mentioned *Access Hollywood*, we were to say, "Mr. Trump's words pale in comparison to the words and, vitally, tragic actions of Hillary Clinton. She has called tens of millions of Americans desperate, deplorable, irredeemable people who live in their parents' basement." No matter what, pivot to key words and phrases including, but not limited to: "Benghazi," "emails," "private server," "Hillary Clinton bullied and smeared Bill Clinton's accusers," "Hillary dreams of open borders," "Hillary Clinton has swanky fund-raisers with her Wall Street buddies."

Regarding the debate, we were to say that Hillary Clinton was "robotic," "scripted," "out of touch," and evasive about emails. On the contrary, we were to praise Trump's "wild success as a businessman, problem solver, and change agent." The catchphrase would be, "Mr. Trump will once again show himself to be the strong, focused, energetic leader we need" to Make America Great Again.

OCTOBER 11

On a conference call with Katrina, Lynne, and myself, we discussed all the information we'd gathered about the tape that Bill Pruitt had referred to. Lynne was familiar with Bill from *The Apprentice* days, too. Katrina had heard from her sources that the tape was of Trump using the N-word. Someone she knew, who knew political strategist Frank Luntz, told her that Luntz had heard it.

Lynne reported that she asked Trump about it on the plane, specifically whether it was possible that such a tape might exist, and he said "no." Then, she asked him what he wanted her to do, and he said, "Put it to bed."

Katrina cursed and said, "He said it."

In survival mode, I could only ask, "Oh, no! What do we do?" I was hoping it could not be true, but it probably was. I didn't know what to believe. If he'd said it during that time, he might have said it about me. The thought was too awful to contemplate. I pushed it aside. I was very good at doing that by this point.

Jason Miller was conferenced into the call, and we all discussed next steps. What struck me was that no one seemed shocked. No one said, "He'd never say that." He was such a loose cannon and there was no way of knowing what he had or hadn't said thirteen years ago.

OCTOBER 14

We were back in North Carolina, where the Women for Trump tour had started, with Lara, Katrina, Lynne, Diamond, and Silk, in a bus with Trump's face plastered on the side. We made a stop to give out bottles of water and boxes of food and diapers for hurricane relief. I was there in body, and put on a good show, but my spirit was lagging.

I stayed with Trump out of loyalty. I had been brought on to the campaign to deal with the ever-growing woman problem, and I could not abandon him now. The *Access Hollywood* tape had been spun internally as a dirty trick by the Clinton campaign, a strategic move. Why release the tape now? Why not back in July after the convention? It wasn't just to win the election, it was to humiliate and destroy a family, to steal an election.

The other part of it was that, after a brief dip, Trump's poll numbers were unchanged. His voters—men and women—didn't care what he said on that bus. We still had a chance to win, despite every major newspaper forecasting a huge Clinton victory.

OCTOBER 15

Saturday Night Live spoofed Beyoncé's "Lemonade" with the parody video "Melaniade," starring Emily Blunt as Ivanka, Cecily Strong as Melania, Vanessa Bayer as Tiffany, Kate McKinnon as Kellyanne, and Sasheer Zamata as yours truly, Trump's "one black friend." It showed a scene where my character walks in and tenders her resignation by slamming down a paper that reads, "I quit," signed Omarosa.

It was frankly hilarious.

As a huge Beyoncé fan, I laughed and danced while watching the episode live on TV. It was a much needed and appreciated dose of humor.

OCTOBER 19

The campaign traveled to Las Vegas for the third debate, moderated by Fox anchor Chris Wallace. The format allowed the candidate to move around the stage, and Trump's prep team instructed him to take advantage of the space, to use his large physical presence to dominate it.

As you recall, he took it a little too far by looming directly behind Hillary while she was speaking. He hadn't been instructed to be stalkerish, but his efforts to be physically intimidating had that effect. But the point is, every last detail of that debate was discussed and decided upon in the war room. I'd come around to seeing the *Access Hollywood* tape, and the possible *Apprentice* tape, as weapons used against us by the opposition. They weren't evidence of Trump's vulgarity and boorishness. As Melania and Ivanka had said in their response to the tape, what they heard did not match the man I knew.

Our internal data, tracked by our numbers guru Brad Parscale, showed that Trump was holding steady in battleground states. He had an office at headquarters, and a staff. One young woman I always said hello to was named Laura Hilger. She was the head of research for a firm called Cambridge Analytica. Yup, *that* Cambridge Analytica: the UK firm that harvested Facebook data to influence the election.

In a few days, I caught the *Washington Post* headline: "Donald Trump's Chances of Winning Are Approaching Zero." I felt sick.

OCTOBER 27

Surprise! FBI director James Comey announced that they were reopening the investigation into Hillary's emails. As he wrote in his famous letter, "In connection with an unrelated case, the FBI has learned of the existence of emails that appear to be pertinent. . . . I agree that the FBI should take appropriate investigative steps designed to allow investigators to review these emails to determine whether they contain classified information, as well as to assess their importance to our investigation."

Basically, he was just saying they were looking at some emails, but didn't know if they had anything. Later, it was revealed that the potentially questionable communications were between Clinton aide Huma Abedin and her soon-to-be-ex-husband, Anthony Weiner.

Trumpworld was thrilled with the move, naturally. If the *Access Hollywood* tape was NBC's attempt to kill us, Comey's letter was like a death blow to Hillary's campaign.

Without that letter, she might have won.

Internally, we were delighted and relieved. We weren't popping the champagne, but it felt like a cause for celebration. For how to handle it publicly, we huddled and came up with the strategy of resolve. We were told not to gloat. The talker guidelines were to hammer it home, to pivot toward Comey and the emails. No matter what we were talking about—say, education or the economy—always shift to the reopened investigation. Little did we know, the FBI was investigating our campaign at that point, too. If that news had gotten out during the campaign, it might've neutralized the Clinton situation. But it didn't.

OCTOBER 31

I didn't vote at the polls. I voted on Trump Force One. I filled out my absentee ballot on the plane while we were flying to a campaign rally. I showed Trump that I'd voted for him. He took the ballot and looked at it for a long time, turning it over and studying it for a while. He saw me looking at him looking at the ballot. He regained his composure. He said, "But it's California, so it won't matter."

I sent in my ballot anyway. I really wanted to win. Yes, my candidate was deeply flawed. So was Hillary. It had been a long battle, and I'd taken a thousand blows along the way. The only thing that would make it all worthwhile would be to get that victory on Election Day.

With one week to go, we pulled out all the stops. Literally, we made up to eight campaign stops per day. It was a crazy rush to the finish. Although *every* poll predicted a Hillary win, there was one—a *Los Angeles Times* USC poll—that had Trump slightly ahead. We clung to that poll. It was at the top of our MAGA messaging daily emails. As long as we had one reason to hope, we could keep going on a relentless path to uncertain victory.

Chapter Nine

Election Day

"HuffPost Forecasts Hillary Clinton Will Win with 323 Electoral Votes," *The Huffington Post*, November 7, 2016

"Optimism from Hillary Clinton and Darkness from Donald Trump at Campaign's End," *The New York Times*, November 7, 2016

On November 8, Election Day, we were back in New York. I returned to my suite at Trump International Hotel at Fifty-Ninth Street and Central Park West. That morning, I took a car through Central Park to Trump Tower at Fifty-Seventh Street and Fifth Avenue, up to the campaign headquarters, and into the comms shop to get my media-hits list. Most of my hits were on African American and other minority radio stations. I did back-to-back interviews until 2:00 p.m. I also did a hit on TMZ, which was a fun reprieve from the other more serious interviews. We had a satellite broadcasting station in Trump Tower, so all I had to do was sit in front of the camera and answer questions live.

TMZ founder and on-air TV host Harvey Levin asked about Trump's demeanor, and I replied, "He's real chill today. I thought he'd be tense, but he's relaxed. We're all very relaxed. There's a light mood here today. His grandchildren were here eating chocolate chip cookies. We're all just enjoying the fact that we did it. There's a ton of gifts and food here, but we've also got stacks and stacks of briefings. We are prepared to lead this country."

In the early afternoon, I popped upstairs to have a brief talk with Trump. When I arrived in his office, he was on two phones, his cell and a landline. I asked, "You good?"

He said, "I'm good, come back after I finish this."

I went back downstairs to the war room, intending to go back up in an hour, but Donald and Melania eventually came to us. When they walked into the room, everyone there applauded. They were both ebullient. They had their coats on, and I believe they had just come back from voting. Donald and Melania made their way through the room, shaking hands and chatting briefly. When Donald got over to me, he grabbed me by both shoulders and kissed my cheek. He asked, "How's it going?"

"Very well," I assured him.

Melania was right behind him, and I remember thinking, "She's *smiling!*" Melania rarely smiles. Reports that Melania spent Election Day sobbing in a corner are inaccurate. Melania was as upbeat as I'd ever seen her in thirteen years of our acquaintance, and very engaged by what was going on. She, like everyone, wanted to win, desperately. I suppose she had some concerns about how her life would change tomorrow, but on that night, she was hoping for a victory.

I have many videos and photos of that day, including a striking one in the data shop office at 3:00 p.m., of me standing over Brad Parscale, with Eric Trump, Pastor Darrell Scott, and Bruce LeVell all standing by Brad's desk, with Rick Gates and Avi Berkowitz, Jared Kushner's assistant, looking on.

Brad sat in front of his computers and could zoom in on any county in any state to see the incoming data. Even that early in the afternoon, our numbers showed Trump winning in key battle-ground states. I was focused on African American turnout, keeping in mind how Romney performed in 2012, how Trump did in the primary, and what was happening there in real time. Despite the erroneous reports of pessimism the Trump campaign was *reported* to have by the *New York Times* and other outlets, we were looking at · very encouraging numbers.

Our figures were different from the ones you might have seen on CNN, based on exit polls. We were basing our numbers on reports from our state directors, who were being informed by county heads. We coupled the anecdotal information we were getting from our folks with analytical data from our operation, which included the Cambridge Analytica research. The company was instrumental early on in helping us pinpoint where to dispatch resources at the beginning stages.

Of course, I am completely opposed to any voter suppression or anyone interfering with a person's fundamental right to cast a vote. I had previously been on the board of an organization called Transformative Justice Coalition (TJC) until I took my appointment in the Trump White House. The TJC had an apparatus in place to monitor any voter suppression incidents. So while I was watching Brad's data flow in, I was simultaneously checking TJC's feed and information from other civil rights organizations like the NAACP, the National Urban League, and the Lawyers' Committee for Civil Rights Under Law. They had volunteers stationed at poll places in the event that African Americans or minorities in general reported that they had been turned away. I was concerned about the disenfranchisement of black voters from either side, whether Democrat or Republican.

After the election, Donald Trump made some controversial statements that were very troubling to me, saying that black voters came through for him "big league," and that the ones who stayed home had been almost as good for him. I sent a warning email to Sean Spicer, Jason Miller, Bryan Lanza, and Ashley Bell that said, "We must be careful that this statement is not interpreted as encouraging voter suppression."

The RNC, under the direction of Reince Priebus, is accused of engaging in some tactics that would be considered voter suppression. For example, in North Carolina, state Republicans took advantage of obscure rulings to target predominantly African American districts and ban early voting, enforced strict voter ID laws that most impacted people of color, severely restricted the number of early-voting sites, making it impossible for working people to cast their ballots, canceled voter registrations by the thousands if the voter had one piece of returned mail. Early reporting found that those efforts had been successful.

What Brad and his data team were most concerned about were the key factors in his algorithm for a Trump victory, our pathway to 270 electoral votes. For example, according to the stats, Hillary needed African American turnout to be high, at Barack Obama 2012 levels. From the information I'd gathered leading up to November 8, African American turnout was expected to be 20 percent *lower* than the previous elections in traditional Democratic strongholds. If she were looking at the same data, Hillary Clinton had to be on pins and needles. She needed that 20 percent, particularly in states like Florida and Michigan, to win. If those projections held up, then we knew Michigan would go our way.

But since I'd worked for the Clintons, I knew they had a big, deep bag of tricks and they could get the turnout they needed. Bill Clinton had already won *two* presidential elections. They had a tremendous amount of experience, an extensive network, huge resources, momentum, and a message they thought would win. Their major setback had been the Comey letter. No one knew how that would impact the election turnout.

And yet, I was cautiously optimistic that Donald Trump was going to win. On my media hits, I said that we felt that he was going to pull it off, no problem, as we'd all been instructed to do. But I also knew how powerful the Clintons were.

Donald Trump had talked about the possibility of a loss. He said at a Nevada rally, "If I don't win, this will be the greatest waste of time, money, and energy in my lifetime, by a factor of one hundred." There was also some hedging on his behalf. In a tweet, he wrote, "If they win, it's because they cheated." He made no secret of the fact that he thought the entire system was rigged. He'd said it when Obama beat Romney four years ago and had been saying it throughout the election. His saying "rigged" over and over, and then his winning the election, exacerbated the Russian discussion.

It was widely speculated that, if he lost, Trump could move on to his next venture, Trump TV, a Fox News–like news channel that would provide twenty-four-hour news coverage. He experimented with a streaming Facebook live broadcast; I called it the "Live from Trump Tower Hour." I did a few spots on it, and the number of people who watched and engaged was very high. So if Trump TV was his backup plan, I was sure it'd be a *huuuge* success.

I didn't have a backup plan. I was getting married in April 2017 to the love of my life, John, a pastor, and I was going to move to Florida to help him with the work of the church and we'd live happily ever after. My plan B was returning to my life of service to God and community—a beautiful life. I'd heard that others on the campaign (like Sean Spicer) had started looking for other jobs before Election Day. Most of the loyal soldiers, like Michael Cohen, would never say die. I spent some time with Michael in Trump Tower that day, and he was prepared for a battle, ready to do whatever was needed to challenge the election results if Hillary won and take it all the way to the Supreme Court! He was in "they're going to steal it" battle mode.

Everyone else said, "We've got this. We're going to win" on repeat, with the glazed conviction of Trumpword's most dedicated followers. This optimism wasn't just part of the loyalty requirement of being in Trump's orbit. We already had a precedent of beating the odds and defying predictions, going back to the New Hampshire primary. We'd had months of headlines saying he'd never win the nomination, but one "more qualified" candidate after another fell to Trump in the primaries anyway. We were preconditioned to ignore media predictions. They'd proven to be wrong, over and over again. When people said things like "I never saw that coming" or "I was shocked by the results on election night," I had to wonder why.

In fact, I lay some of the blame for Hillary's low turnout on those assurances from the media that her victory was a sure thing. Voter behavior indicates that if voters believe their candidate has it in the bag, they will not, for example, take off work to go vote and lose a day's wages, believing their vote isn't needed. The press actually demotivated her base. If they'd reported the truth, that the race was very close, there is no doubt in my mind that they would have turned out for her.

At around 4:00 or 5:00 p.m. on Election Day, I had left Trump Tower and headed back to Trump International to get changed and touch up my makeup. The press team had compiled all the media requests that came through for Election Day. When they handed me the full list, I pushed back. I just could not do them all. I was given a revised media schedule, which included ten live standup hits from the party at the New York Hilton, and I needed to get camera ready. The crush of people around Trump Tower was so thick, the driver couldn't get to me. I ended up walking from Fifth Avenue back to Central Park West.

I was wearing a hat, so no one recognized me. I did stop to take a picture with several police officers. I talked to them for a minute, just to get a read on what was happening on the streets. A few of them whispered to me, "I voted for Trump." I wasn't too surprised, since he was the law-and-order candidate.

While I walked, I listened to the chatter around me. Every single person was talking about the election. Most of the people who I passed were Hillary supporters. Again, not surprising. New York City voted overwhelmingly for her; her campaign headquarters was in Brooklyn; she'd been a New York senator. A group of college kids came up alongside me, and they talked about going to the Javits Center that night, where Hillary was having her big party. The Javits Center is made of glass; she would be shattering the glass ceiling, etcetera. These young women couldn't have been more excited to celebrate Hillary's certain victory. Hearing them gave me knots in my stomach. Even with the data we had coming in, we could still be wrong. It could go either way, and it was possible that I'd wake up tomorrow morning to a Clinton presidency.

After I changed and freshened up, I had to go to the New York Hilton on Fifty-Fourth Street and Sixth Avenue. The traffic was even more congested now because there were even more sand trucks and police, and protesters. Roads were shut down. Mobility around New York City was extremely limited. I wanted to show our supporters what it was like out there, and posted a Facebook Live report of my commute between Trump International and the Hilton. It was about six or seven blocks, but it was slow going.

I arrived at the Hilton around 6:00 p.m. On the main floor level, there was the large area for staffers, supporters, and all the camera crews from every TV network, and press from every major newspaper and outlet. I would do my media hits on the floor level, and then in between I would go up to the invitation-only party to visit the VIP and the VVIP rooms, which were already packed with luminaries including billionaire David Koch, New Jersey governor Chris Christie, and actor Stephen Baldwin. Off to the side, there was a hold room with food, music, and a little side seating area where I could just take a break and think.

In the end, we achieved our goal. The exit polling showed that we received 8 percent of the black vote, beating Romney's 6 percent by two points. Thirteen percent of African American men voted for Trump, and I think that goes back to his aspirational image, the rappers and the actors he was friendly with. I was praised by the campaign, by the leadership, for that turnout. I didn't have a whole team like the Clinton campaign, which had twenty-five full-time staffers working on African American outreach. I didn't have the Democratic grassroots infrastructure. I was grateful to Bruce, Darrell, and Michael for the National Diversity Coalition efforts.

We had our eyes peeled on key battleground states—in particular, Florida and my home state of Ohio. Traditionally, if you win Ohio and Florida, you win the presidency, so when those states went for us, there were cheers, mayhem, total elation in the room. We were still waiting for Pennsylvania and Missouri, though. I didn't want to get overconfident.

But states just kept falling our way. The enthusiasm in the room was palpable. You could feel how excited and optimistic people were, and the momentum just kept building. Interestingly enough, the media still did not call the election. They seemed to drag it out, as if things were going to turn around. Their reluctance turned to despair once it was clear that Donald Trump was getting closer and closer to 270. Every time he won another key state, we thought they'd declare it, but they seemed to be drawing it out. For ratings? Because it was painful to accept the truth? Probably both.

Around 2:00 a.m. back at the war room, Kellyanne got the call we had all been waiting for from Clinton.

Hillary's concession didn't trickle down to the rest of the world for a while. Her campaign staff didn't tell the thousands who'd come to the Javits Center to go home until 2:00 a.m. I thought about those girls I'd seen on the street earlier. I didn't understand why they'd kept those kids standing there all that time. It seemed cruel, prolonging their hopes when the contest was already over.

We got word shortly after that that the senior staff and the Trump family were heading over to the Hilton. We had to navigate from the VIP room, through security, to the freight elevator they would be coming up in. Interestingly enough, in our little entourage of Lynne, Katrina, and myself, we picked up a stray. Sarah Palin found out we were going to meet the Trumps, and she joined us as we walked to the freight elevator. She wanted to be there when the group arrived so she'd be swept up along with the rest of us as we walked to the stage in the main room.

At two thirty, they started the walk. The room was at capacity; hundreds of screaming supporters went crazy when Donald came onto the stage.

And I was right there with him. It was just unbelievable, a thrilling moment for me. It was a rush, a surge of adrenaline. And it was emotional, the culmination of everything that we'd done. All the hard work, travel, rallies, interviews, death threats. They were all worth it for that moment.

Donald gave his victory speech, framed by Mike Pence and Barron Trump. I was on the stage along with the family members, Kellyanne, Steve Bannon, Stephen Miller, Lynne, everyone who'd played a major part in this win. After he finished, Donald made his way down the stage, shaking hands and embracing everyone up there. When he got to me, he gave me a hug and a cheek kiss. The moment was caught on camera and broadcast to the world.

That moment was one of the highlights of my life. I marked it down as proof of how wonderful and great this country had been to me. At that moment, I was living the American dream. I'd had many low points in my life: being on public assistance, going to the mission to get food from the food bank, the murders of my father and brother. And now I was standing on that stage with the president-elect of the United States, soon to be the most powerful man in the country, if not the world. That anyone could overcome such tremendous odds, so many hurdles and barriers, to wind up there, seemed incredible and humbling. I'd had to navigate the media, the meanness, the name-calling from petty people online and from members of the press, who mocked me with a clown nose on the cover of a newspaper. I'd faced it all down, stood strong in my sense of purpose and loyalty—just like Donald had—and now, against all odds, the two of us were on that stage together.

I walked with him and his family to the motorcade at 3:20 a.m. I congratulated him and said good night as he headed back to Trump

Tower. It was a good night, a crazy night. TMZ cameras caught me returning to Trump International in the small hours of the morning, still celebrating our victory. The headline on the video was "Omarosa Parties After Trump Win."

"It was amazing. I can't believe my mentor, my friend is now president of the United States!" I told them. I looked exhausted. I did not care. I was overjoyed.

After several hours' rest, I got up the next day, showered, dressed, and headed back to Trump Tower for a 10:00 a.m. meeting with senior staff. I was also planning on stopping in to congratulate the president-elect. As I entered the lobby of that building on 725 Fifth Avenue, where it all began for me, I realized I'd come full circle. Thirteen years ago, I'd walked into the same building for the first time with my suitcase, a game plan, and the determination to win. Now I was walking in again, taking the same elevator to the same floor to wait in the same lobby area before going in to see now–President Elect Trump.

No one could make this story up.

Believe it or not, we worked all day on November 9. By the time I headed back to my hotel, protesters had swarmed Midtown and surrounded Trump Tower. Katrina and I were sharing a car from the Fox studios, and when we reached the spot where they'd have to go out of their way to take me to the hotel entrance, I said that I'd just get out and walk. I love to walk, and I was still full of energy. A nice little stroll for six blocks to Trump International along Central Park South seemed ideal.

"Are you sure?" she said. "You need to be careful, it's dangerous out there."

"I'll be fine," I said.

Traffic was at a standstill. Now I saw why: protesters had shut down Columbus Circle. As I was getting closer, I got a sense of how many there were. There had to be at least a few thousand.

I wasn't concerned—I put on a pretty good disguise when I walk and move around. But when I was crushed by the crowd and had to slow down, I started to get very nervous someone would take a close look at me. I kept thinking, *Okay, just focus on getting to the side door.* The front door was completely blocked by an angry mob.

All the doormen and hotel staff knew me because I'd stayed there for months. They would let me in the loading-dock entrance. As I was walking down a side street, I realized that the protesters had also figured out that there was an alternate entrance to block and had shifted their attention.

I just kept walking, and made it within a few feet of the door.

A man yelled out, "There's Omarosa! That sellout! Let's get her!"

They started rushing toward me. A Trump security guard was standing there, and, with perfect timing, he opened the door, grabbed me, threw me inside, and shut the door behind me, locking it.

It was just like that time my mother grabbed my sister and me away from that drug dealer and shooting cop back in the playground at Westlake Terrace.

Shaking, I went up to my room and turned on the TV, and was shocked by what I was seeing. The aerial footage showed blocks and blocks of people. News reports estimated ten thousand protesters, with filmmaker and activist Michael Moore leading the charge.

It was terrifying. So quickly, the feeling of victory descended into despair because of the images I was seeing. I was not thinking, *Wow, so many people are unhappy with the election results.* Sorry. I was thinking, *I don't want to die over an election!*

The next day, Trump Tower was under siege. It was impossible to enter the building. When I called in about my final meeting with DJT, I was dissuaded because it was deemed not safe. As always, I was not deterred by danger, and headed to Trump Tower anyway. I wanted that final talk with him before I flew home. The protests were escalating, a rolling anger that increased with every turn. A snowball effect of unrest.

My fiancé, John, had said on the phone the night before, "You need to leave New York. It's just not safe."

I was highly recognizable, associated with Trump, images of me with the president-elect seared in people's minds. I knew that the vast majority of the protesters were there to make a point. But some of them were violent. They had rushed at me last night, and said, "Let's get her!" (I assumed they weren't looking for a selfie or my autograph.)

That's it, I thought. *I'm leaving New York.*

That morning, November 10, the hotel people helped pack up my suite and helped me into a waiting SUV. I drove to Trump Tower, where they had security get me into that building. I made it to my meeting with Trump. He said, "You're coming to the White House with me, right? I have a beautiful new hotel there. The Trump International."

I knew all about it. I said, "It'll be interesting to go back to the White House."

"It's going to be so much better than your last time. My White House is going to be great, the best. Hey, Omarosa, I want to give you something." He pulled out a box of Trump ties. "Give these to your fiancé. He'll love them."

I thanked him for his gift.

Before I went to the airport to meet my fiancé, John, I sat down for an interview with *20/20*. I was emotionally exhausted. I didn't hold back.

"I was called every single racial slur in the book that you could direct towards an African American by African Americans. I got death threats," I said. "There are people who stopped talking to me," I said. "It has been a long, lonely time. . . . I will never forget the people who turned their backs on me when all I was trying to do was help the black community. It's been so incredibly hard."

Most people get a chance to process their intense emotions in private, with a friend or family member or a therapist. I didn't have a chance. I'd been running on pure adrenaline for months. I feared for my safety. When I started talking on that interview, my emotions and vulnerability just came out.

I took pride in showing only a pulled-together, grace-under-pressure persona on TV. That all went out the window.

I didn't have much time to process that once the interview concluded, either. I had to rush to the airport to catch the last flight out of LaGuardia to Jacksonville, where John was waiting.

The day the *20/20* segment aired, I got a hundred calls and texts from people who said, "I'm so sorry. I hope you don't think I abandoned you. I didn't know you were so lonely; I didn't know you were suffering. You are always so strong."

If I get hurt, if somebody cuts me, I bleed. I'm human, like everyone else. I'd been so isolated since I joined the campaign. It was the silence that hurt the most. Lifelong friends stopped talking to me and stopped inviting me to things. It had just gotten so bad, and then it all came pouring out live on national TV.

Donald was in DC meeting with Barack Obama. Even though he was very busy, of course, he was consuming the news. He saw *20/20* and had Lara call to check on me. "Hey. We're just calling to see if you're okay!" she said.

I was back with John by then, and everything was much, much better. I thanked her for asking, and assured her that I was fine. I didn't want Trump to think that the stress of what we'd been through had gotten to me. Donald hates weakness. The election was over, and now it was time to assemble a team and lead the nation. I was excited to play a big part in that.

Part Three

The White House

Chapter Ten

The Transition

"Firings and Discord Put Trump Transition Team in a State of Disarray," *The New York Times*, November 15, 2016

Donald Trump's first order of business as president-elect was to travel to Washington, DC, and meet with President Obama at the White House to discuss the successful transfer of power. According to the official line on the ninety-minute meeting, it went well. Trump said afterward, "I have great respect [for Obama]. We discussed a lot of different situations, some wonderful, and some difficulties. I very much look forward to dealing with the president in the future, including counsel." It was theorized in the press that, since Trump had never worked in government before, he'd rely on Obama for guidance during the transition and beyond.

It was the last time the two men ever discussed anything of substance.

This comes as no surprise to me. Donald has told me that he

thinks Obama is a fraud. He questioned his nationality, his citizenship, his scholarship. He's demanded to see Obama's birth certificate, his passport, and his Harvard transcripts. In 2011, Trump told the Associated Press, "I heard he was a terrible student, terrible. How does a bad student go to Columbia and then to Harvard? I'm thinking about it, I'm certainly looking into it. Let him show his records."

When I would challenge Trump on his erroneous assessment of President Obama, he would say, "Omarosa, you only support him because he's black! And he hasn't done anything for the black community, look at his Chicago—it's a mess, his people are dying and he does nothing!" In Trump's mind, Obama made up his credentials as a community organizer, and this became a common rant starting in 2007 and continuing to this day. "He's a fraud. A phoney! Organizer? What is that? They hyped him up and made him out to be some big shot, and he's not," he's said many, many times, over and over, for years. I believe Donald Trump was incapable of believing a black man could be all that Barack Obama is, and he was determined to expose him.

The irony is, Trump himself has greatly inflated his own wealth. He has said that he graduated in the top of his class, which has been proven to be untrue. Trump is the one who has the sketchy bio, and he overcompensates for it by attacking Obama to feed his base.

After the election, the Trump team was fully aware that the election had been contentious, to say the least, and that half the electorate was still reeling from the results. A smooth transition from the Obama administration to Trump's could go a long way to calming down the jittery public. Between Election Day on November 8 and the inauguration on January 20, there were only seventy-three days to form an entire government. The clock was ticking, and unfortunately for everyone on the Trump train, we were moving at a crawl.

The presidential transition, mandated by law, is a critical time for any incoming administration. It sets the tone for the years to come, in style and in staffing. When Obama took over from George W. Bush, his transition was praised for being seamless, upholding his "no drama Obama" reputation.

Trump's transition was chaotic from day one. Governor Chris Christie, tapped to lead the transition during the course of the campaign, was fired on November 11, and most of Christie's loyalists were purged. The driving force behind Christie's ousting was Jared. He hadn't forgotten that Christie, as New Jersey's US attorney, prosecuted Jared's father, Charles, for tax evasion in 2004. VP-elect Mike Pence took over the transition chairmanship with an enormous job to do and precious little time. Not only did the incoming administration have four thousand jobs to fill, from high-level cabinet and cabinet-equivalent posts to the rank-and-file posts known as Schedule C, they had to review existing agencies, set policy agendas, ensure that day-to-day operations continued to function, and divest from businesses that would be a conflict of interest—no small matter for Trump.

One of the first orders of business was for President-elect Trump to appoint a chief of staff. On November 13, Reince Priebus, chairman of the RNC, was tapped for the role. Paul Ryan and some other GOP players behind the scenes had pressured Trump to appoint Reince, arguing that he'd help bring the Republican establishment into line. Trump would have preferred one of his own people—

Jared Kushner, deputy campaign manager David Bossie, or Corey Lewandowski—but Ryan pushed back on the loyal followers' inexperience. From the beginning, the GOP was putting up safety guardrails so that Donald wouldn't drive the US government over a cliff.

I liked Reince, but he and Donald were a very bad fit. Trump demands loyalty. He can't work closely with people who have shown any sign of weakness or doubt. Unfortunately, that was all Donald knew of Reince. When the *Access Hollywood* story had broken, reportedly Reince and senior advisers met privately with Trump and said, "You have two choices: either you lose by the biggest landslide in presidential election history, or you drop out right now." People in the room at the time said that Donald was defiant, looked Reince in the face, and said, "I'm not dropping out. I'm going to win." He never let Reince—or anyone for that matter, ever—forget that Reince wanted him to drop out. He would demean Reince and mock that moment of weakness. Reince was starting with two strikes against him. So why did Donald give in to the GOP and Speaker Ryan? He really did want to be a good president and keep his campaign promise. If putting in Reincey (as he nicknamed him) would make peace with the Never Trumpers and the GOP, then it was worth it.

Around this time, immediately after the election, my longtime agent John Seitzer from Agency for the Performing Arts (APA) in Beverly Hills started calling me with offers from several Hollywood producers. The offers ranged from producing my own television projects to opportunities in scripted and unscripted shows, to entertainment and news, to having my own talk show and/or serving as a political correspondent. I also got a call from Robert Walker, my longtime agent at the American Program Bureau, my speakers' bureau in Boston, saying he wanted to schedule a nationwide speaking tour for me to talk about the election and the Trump presidency. He was optimistic that I could command top fees. Last, my close friend and Hollywood talent manager Tracy Christian called with myriad international offers that she said I should seriously consider. Before joining the executive committee, I'd flown to Los Angeles and took a series of meetings, sat there and listened to their pitches, and told the team I would consider each offer carefully. But upon my return to the hustle and bustle of the transition, nothing that was presented felt as fulfilling as hunkering down with my battle buddies and shaping policy and the direction of the country in the new administration. I could have returned to Hollywood—my comfort zone—to my home, my church, service to the chaplain corps of the California State Military Reserve (CSMR), and to all my friends and family. But Trumpworld needed me and I didn't want to let them, or the nation, down.

Pence went about assembling transition vice chairmen, loyal Trump people including General Michael Flynn, Jeff Sessions, Newt Gingrich, and Rudy Giuliani—all white men, all controversial figures, and all reviled by Democrats.

He also appointed an executive committee that included venture capitalist Peter Thiel; VIP donor Rebekah Mercer; Reince Priebus; Anthony Scaramucci; Steve Mnuchin; Don Jr., Ivanka, and Eric Trump; Jared Kushner—and me. As usual in Trumpworld, there was little to no diversity; I was the only African American woman on the executive committee. I was honored by the appointment to serve among this group of trusted, revered people in Trumpworld, placed on the same level as his children and future cabinet members—but I was worried that the lack of diverse voices might get us started on the wrong track.

If I didn't go back to DC and be part of Trump's White House, what other black woman in Trump's orbit would? I was the only one in the unique position to keep Trump accountable for his "What do you have to lose?" campaign promises to people of color. As soon as I officially joined the transition team, I wrote down every promise and commitment Trump had made to black and brown people during the campaign—from Chicago, to Flint, to young black men, to Haiti, to the black church—to fight poverty, to improve public education, to end gang warfare on the streets. I considered it my personal priorities list moving forward.

More controversies came up daily, taking precious time away from the impossible mission of assembling a team to start after inauguration day. Trump requested top security clearance for Jared Kushner, setting off cries of nepotism. (By the way, Donald wasn't always such a fan of Jared. When he and Ivanka first started dating, I asked Donald what he thought of Jared. "He seems a little sweet to me," he said, using his phrasing for "gay.") Trump gave the press the slip in New York in order to go out for a steak dinner, causing outrage about his lack of seriousness. While he was taking meetings at Trump Tower with Henry Kissinger and the prime minister of Japan, everyone on the executive committee, through weekly conference calls, was strategizing how to get things done. Simply put, we were scrambling. We were woefully unprepared and overwhelmed, and the clock was ticking. Mike Pence didn't seem to know how to get the job done. There was simply too much to do, not enough time, and not much experience among the staff we were selecting, most of whom had never worked in Washington before.

As for Trump, he was riding high. We were in the Presidential Transition Committee (PTC) office and he was in Trump Tower. Whenever he was given reports, they were upbeat only. As far as he knew, everything was fine and we were chugging along. The top advisers would give him a list of tasks—meet with someone or choose a cabinet pick—but he wasn't involved or aware of just how much there was to do, and how much wasn't getting done.

If Hillary Clinton had won, she would have brought in her eight-hundred-member campaign staff, along with people who'd worked in her husband's administration, and coasted right through the transition. We had only 130. She'd been through a transition before and knew exactly what it entailed. To put it bluntly, we hadn't and didn't. In fact, the transition office was decorated in a way that assumed that Hillary, not Trump, would win. The spouse suite was done up in masculine colors and the presidential offices were feminine colors. Melania took one look at that office space and relocated to working out of the Presidential Suite at the Trump hotel in DC. We also noticed that there were more than nine hundred work spaces—more than enough room to accommodate the voluminous Clinton campaign team.

For a while, we spun our wheels, and then, on November 18, Congress left for Thanksgiving break, and we were stalled again. I was commuting between Trump Tower in New York for meetings, the transition offices in DC, and Jacksonville, Florida, where I was also planning my upcoming nuptials. I was exhausted from travel and the uphill battle of filling some of those four thousand empty seats with diverse, qualified people—a nearly impossible task. I frequented the fifth floor, where the presidential personnel offices were located, asking daily for an update on printouts of diverse applicants from our database. The applications trickled in, but many were fraudulent submissions and profiles or had an insulting message in the body of the résumé.

At a November 29 transition staff meeting, I said to the room, "Donald Trump wants an administration that looks like America," which he'd expressed to me personally and I believed to be true. Falling just short of saying, "Please don't hire a whole bunch of white boys." Advisers Rick Dearborn; Sebastian Gorka; Bob Paduchik, Ohio state director for the campaign; and Ashley Bell, nodded in agreement. I reinforced this message publicly, telling the *Hollywood Reporter*, "[Donald Trump] has given me a personal directive that with the four thousand jobs we need to fill, he wants his administration to be the most diverse in history." I solicited résumés nationwide on my social media, TV, and radio appearances. I also set out to build the foundation of Trump's Office of Public Liaison, the department that engaged with veterans, faith-based groups, diverse peoples, and civil rights organizations. I hoped to be its director in good time and focused my efforts there.

"Very organized process taking place as I decide on Cabinet and many other positions. I am the only one who knows who the finalists are!" Trump tweet, November 15, 2016

It was hardly an organized process! Trump's was probably the most bizarre transition in the history of this country. He is a New York showman, and everything had to be a Broadway production. His candidates had to present themselves to him at Bedminster, his golf course in New Jersey; Mar-a-Lago in Palm Beach; or Trump Tower in Manhattan, and walk before a spray of photographers—like the Miss USA beauty pageant runway—for their audience with King Trump. The selection process for his cabinet was like an episode of *The Bachelor.* The candidates fought to win the figurative rose.

One of our campaign slogans had been "Drain the Swamp," but the cabinet quickly filled with swamp creatures, mainly white men, each new tap setting off a firestorm of criticism, as people called out the hypocrisy. Donald reveled in the headlines, and would often pretend to choose a controversial candidate just to get the attention of the press.

Let's play connect the swamp dots:

Senator Jeff Sessions for attorney general was announced on November 18, apparent payback for his support during the campaign as the first senator to come out for Donald. Trump chooses loyalty over logic; his obsession causes him to make bad decisions. If you looked at Sessions's credentials and his tremendous baggage, you would have known that that was a terrible choice. He'd been denied a federal judgeship in 1986 in part because of his alleged use of the N-word and jokes about the KKK, but Trump wanted him for attorney general? Why? Because he had been loyal to Trump when everyone was mocking him and calling his run a joke. The outrage was justified and deafening, but Trump ignored it.

Billionaire Betsy DeVos (whom Trump calls Ditzy DeVos behind her back) was selected as secretary of education. She is the sister of Erik Prince (who disclosed that he has cooperated with the Mueller investigation), the founder of Blackwater (now known as Academi), the private security firm the US government contracted to support its forces in Afghanistan and Iraq, where its mercenaries killed more than a dozen civilians. DeVos and her family members had reportedly donated tens of millions over the years to Republicans, including nearly $1 million to senators who would vote to confirm her appointment. The November 23 announcement that DeVos had been chosen to lead the Department of Education set off an explosion of anxiety, given her utter lack of experience and her advocacy for charter schools and the privatization of public education. Trump had promised to improve public education in depressed areas, but his pick here said otherwise.

ExxonMobil CEO and corporate millionaire Rex Tillerson was recommended for secretary of state by Condoleezza Rice and James Baker, two former secretaries of state, and by Robert Gates, a former secretary of defense. All three had business ties to ExxonMobil. Baker's law firm represented the company. Rice and Gates worked for Exxon via RiceHadleyGates, their consulting firm. The choice smelled swampy.

Steven Mnuchin was tapped for secretary of the treasury on November 30, which was quickly followed by derision. He was a Goldman Sachs multi-millionaire. Countless times, Trump railed against Hillary Clinton's cozy relationships with Wall Streeters. I met Mnuchin on Trump Force One when he was the head of finance for the campaign, and we worked together on my first fund-raising email blast. We talked a lot about Hollywood and the movies he'd produced, such as *The Legend of Tarzan*, *Batman v Superman: Dawn of Justice*, and *Mad Max: Fury Road*. I liked him . . . but still. He was the ultimate Wall Street type, a walking advertisement of everything we'd campaigned against.

Everybody liked to point out Donald Trump's obsession with generals. He confided to me that he thought the generals would send a message to the world that he was "badass." So we watched him bring the stars and bars into the cabinet or to cabinet-level positions: General Michael Flynn as national security adviser, who was replaced soon after by General H. R. McMaster (who has since been replaced by the non-general John Bolton), (Ret.) Lieutenant General Keith Kellogg as chief of staff and executive secretary of the National Security Council (who now serves as national security adviser to Mike Pence), General Jim Mattis as secretary of defense, and General John Kelly as secretary of homeland security. The left complained that Trump was militarizing the executive branch.

While all of this was going on, the team realized that the president-elect missed the energy, excitement, and validation of the campaign trail. They took a victory lap to swing states called the "USA Thank You Tour" from December 1 to 17, starting in Ohio and making stops in North Carolina, Iowa, Louisiana, Michigan, Wisconsin, Pennsylvania, Florida, and Alabama. This was widely mocked as well. Did the president-elect have time for even more ego stroking when he was supposed to be forming a government and leading the country? Of course not! Did that stop Team Trump? Nope!

I was invited to attend the Hershey, Pennsylvania, rally on December 15, and watched Trump's address from backstage with Steve Bannon and Pennsylvania State Director David Urban, a senior adviser on the campaign who had helped secure Pennsylvania's win. I had an interesting conversation with Bannon and asked him if the rumors of his being a racist were true. He said no. He explained, "The same way you are a proud African American woman, I am a proud white man. What's the difference between my pride and your pride?" he asked.

I said, "Hate defines white supremacy."

He didn't back down and gave an impassioned defense of the alt-right. Just as he was getting revved up, the announcer came on and said, "Ladies and gentlemen! The president-elect of the United States, Donald J. Trump!"

The crowd went crazy. I remember feeling good about being back in that campaign environment, where we'd had such success, when it was just about delivering the MAGA message, not setting policy—which we really had to get back to DC to do! I felt intense pressure to get things done, but it seemed like I was always in the air, between DC and New York and Jacksonville, not to mention here in Hershey.

On the morning of December 13, Kanye West came to Trump

Tower to meet with President-elect Trump. Kanye said he wanted to discuss "multicultural issues," and tweeted, "I feel it is important to have a direct line of communication with our future President if we truly want change." It was a sentiment I agreed with, although many of his fans weren't happy to see him with Trump. I went on cable news that night to defend the meeting, although I was growing more and more concerned about the perception of those meetings with celebrities. But that was just Trump the showman; he always met with famous people. I think his personal transition, from celebrity to president, was as stalled and mired as the larger transition push.

On January 4, I arranged my first major transition briefing with African American leadership. I invited about one hundred African American civil rights and education group leaders from the NAACP, historically black colleges (HBCUs), and black churches to Washington, DC, for a "listening session" with Trump officials Ken Blackwell, his domestic policy chairman, and eleven other senior advisers from the transition team. It was an extremely productive event, with open engagement between the leaders and the Trump team. I thought we were setting a precedent for the future and laying a foundation for moving policy forward. At its conclusion, everyone said positive things, how wonderful it was, how we should keep the dialogue going. I felt optimistic about this meeting. Finally, after a month of trying to build momentum and set a tone before the inauguration, I'd made some progress. Hilary O. Shelton, NAACP Washington Bureau director and senior vice president for advocacy and policy, said the meeting "could be a great start. What happens at this point is in the hands of the administration."

That next week, I got an email from a representative for TV host Steve Harvey, a native of Cleveland, Ohio, requesting a meeting with President-elect Trump, stating, "Mr. Harvey knows that for our country to succeed, the president-elect has to succeed."

I submitted the email and a scheduling request to the president's office and was surprised that four days later, the meeting was in motion for January 13. It was only a week away from the inauguration. I knew he had more pressing demands. I was also concerned about it. Thus far, the only black men Trump had met with had been actors, rappers, and sports stars. Optics matter. If Trump was going to look presidential and substantive on diversity issues, we had to stop the parade of black male celebrities through Trump Tower.

Steve and Trump talked about various things including golf for fifteen minutes, and then they posed for a quick photo. After Trump left, Harvey gave an interview to reporters, saying that Barack Obama had encouraged Harvey to meet with Trump to begin a dialog about how to address problems in inner cities. My eyebrow went up. That was an interesting spin on things.

Back on December 10, 2015, I had gone on Steve Harvey's TV show and he'd praised Donald, saying, "In case you're wondering where I stand on Donald Trump, I love his golf courses. I love his buildings. I like him as a guy. If he becomes president of the United States, in eight years, I'm running!" After the convention, his booking producer sent a request for candidate Trump or me, his diversity director, to appear on his show.

The fallout from his January 2017 visit to Trump Tower was immediate and far-reaching. His viewership took a severe hit, and he stated on his radio show, "Meeting with Trump was the worst mistake of my life."

Congressman John Lewis, the civil rights icon who was one of the original Freedom Riders in the 1960s, went on *Meet the Press* on January 14 and said the Trump presidency was illegitimate and that he intended to boycott the inauguration. Trump wasted no time in responding on Twitter, writing, "Congressman John Lewis should spend more time on fixing and helping his district, which is in horrible shape and falling apart (not to mention crime infested) rather than falsely complaining about the election results. All talk, talk, talk—no action or results. Sad!"

I was livid and called him to ask him, "Why are you doing this? John Lewis is one of the most respected men in America. Not to mention a civil rights icon! You have to stop this!"

"He took the first shot," said Donald. "If he hits me, I hit back."

I explained to him that acting presidential was not just talking the talk but walking the walk. Take the high road when people attack you. Almost surprised, and caught off guard by how upset I was about his attacks on Lewis, Donald simply said, "Well, he started it, Omarosa!"

I could not believe that Trump would insult a man who'd had his head bashed in for civil rights and who was attacked by police dogs and fire hoses. Also, in true Trump timing, I had been planning a meeting with Martin Luther King III, whose father had led the movement that Lewis was a part of.

Incredibly, Martin Luther King III didn't cancel, and the meeting at Trump Tower on January 16, Martin Luther King Day, turned out to be a much-needed, substantive tone-setting conversation. King concurred, telling the press in the lobby of Trump Tower, "We did have a very constructive meeting." The focus was disenfranchised voters. King presented a solution to the problem of unfair voter ID laws. "[Trump] said that he is going to represent all Americans. . . . We will continue to evaluate that. . . . I believe that is his intent. I believe we have to consistently engage with pressure, public pressure. It doesn't happen automatically." Regarding poverty and income inequality, he said, "At some point, this nation has got to move forward. When we roll up our sleeves, and work together, there's nothing we can't do."

It was reminiscent of when his father, Martin Luther King Jr., had met with President Lyndon B. Johnson about voting rights. King said of Johnson, "His approach to the problem of civil rights was not identical with mine—nor had I expected it to be. . . . But I do not doubt that the President is approaching the solution with sincerity, realism and, thus far, with wisdom. I hope his course will be straight and true. I will do everything in my power to make it so, by outspoken agreement whenever proper, and determined opposition whenever necessary."

It was exactly the tone and message I'd been trying to set since I joined the campaign and transition team, to bring people together to solve our nation's problems. I wished more black leaders would have come in and talked to Trump so we could get the dialogue started; I extended an invitation to Al Sharpton of National Action Network; Melanie Campbell, CEO of the National Coalition on Black Civic

Participation and convener of the Black Women's Roundtable; and Marc Morial of the National Urban League; but unfortunately they never committed.

While I was setting my policy agenda during the transition, I was also working with Reince throughout December to lock down when my position would be formally announced. The transition was sending out daily announcements about one appointment or another, but Reince had yet to announce mine. Like all the future senior staff, I was asked to give the president a list of the top three positions I wanted to be considered for. I wrote down only one: director of the Office of Public Liaison (OPL), a title once held by Elizabeth Dole under Ronald Reagan and Valerie Jarrett under Obama. I was so sure it was mine, I didn't even bother including two other options on my form.

I was summoned to Mar-a-Lago in mid-December to discuss my White House position with Reince. I assumed it was just a formality to button down the announcement date and to help put together quotes for my press release as director of the OPL. But then Reince blindsided me and told me there were a dozen or so people he was considering for the job, including me. He suggested that, because of my prior experience as deputy associate director of presidential personnel in the Clinton White House, I should consider taking a job in that department. I had no interest in presidential personnel! I had toiled and labored as vice chair of the National Diversity Coalition and as the director of African American outreach. The natural transition for me would be into the OPL.

He said, "We have to figure something else out because there are just so many other people being considered for the OPL. What do you know about public liaison, anyway? Have you ever organized a coalition?"

He needed to be reminded about the National Diversity Coalition? We'd built that from scratch, from the website on up, on our own dime. We organized all those events, with hundreds of groups. I ran through my entire résumé, including my run for Los Angeles school board and my military service, my fund-raising experience, and my diversity outreach. He seemed unimpressed. Reince could be very slippery.

I asked, "Reince, I'm curious about your overall plan for diversity in the White House." Even at that early stage, the cabinet was painted whiter than a picket fence (except for Ben Carson and Elaine Chao, the secretary of transportation). I added, "The cabinet needs to be diverse, as do the assistants to the president."

The highest appointees in the White House, besides the cabinet, are called assistants to the president (APs). It's actually a rank, like in the military. APs are at the top of the food chain. Most presidents have twenty to twenty-five. Trump would end up appointing thirty. Under the APs are deputy assistant (DAs), and under that, special assistants to the president (SAP).

"My top priority," I told Reince, "is to be an AP. That is a must. And I want Ashley Bell to be an AP, too." Ashley, a guy, was my colleague and friend, currently on Reince's staff as the head of African American outreach for the RNC. Reince didn't love that idea and said he'd intended to make Ashley an SAP. That felt like another slap. Ashley was extremely qualified and the only hope of having an African American male appointed to the senior staff of the White House.

Reince kept stonewalling me, but I didn't budge.

As fate would have it, just as I was about to text Keith Schiller to ask for five minutes with Trump, Reince's phone rang and, lo and behold, it was Donald himself. Reince said, "Hello, sir. Yes, I'm meeting with Omarosa right now, sir."

Trump must have said, "Put her on," because Reince passed the phone to me.

Donald and I discussed his dinner plans for that night. Katrina Campins, my *Apprentice* roommate, had come with me to Mar-a-Lago to discuss our outreach for the Latino community and would be joining us.

Bolstered by the call, I said to Reince, "I'd like to be an assistant to the president *and* the director of the OPL."

Reince gulped and said, "I'll see what I can do."

At dinner, Donald said, "Reince tells me you're taken care of."

It had been a long—but also incredibly short—month so far, of running uphill at full speed only to hit obstacle after obstacle, face outrage after outrage, in my role in public engagement. I felt reassured by Donald's comment, but I didn't hear from Reince with my official announcement for days. I continued to chip away at my workload, commuting, setting things up, putting out fires.

When Reince next called, it was to say that someone had placed a strong objection to my being put in charge of the OPL.

"Who?" I asked.

"Paula White," he said. "She wants you to go into some other position."

"What are you talking about? What does Paula White have to do with staffing decisions?"

"Exactly!" he said.

Paula White is a televangelist and spiritual adviser to Donald Trump. Her ministry was one of six that had been investigated by the Senate Committee on Finance for improprieties; the ministries teach the controversial "prosperity gospel" that equates material wealth with Christian faith, and the ministers' lavish spending, coupled with their churches' tax-exempt status, raised questions. White refused to cooperate with the investigation, and no penalties were levied against her when it concluded in 2011. I'd run into Paula at the convention and she had been very nice to me, so I was shocked to hear she was trying to stab me in the back.

Why would she feel she had the authority to tell Reince not to hire me in that position? Well, Trump had given her a role as an *outside* adviser on matters of faith. The OPL's portfolio included faith issues. I was an ordained minister, a military chaplain, and an unapologetic missionary Baptist. She was an evangelist. There had long been a power struggle between African American clergies and evangelists in Trumpworld. I made the logical leap that Paula White wanted an evangelical to have control over Trump's faith agenda.

Reince had been careless to tell me about her objection and cavalier in his delivery of the news. I immediately called Pastor Darrell Scott and Michael Cohen and learned that my fears were accurate.

Both affirmed, "Yes, she doesn't want you as the head of the OPL because you're not an evangelical."

I was incensed. I got on the phone with Paula, and we had a heated exchange. My contributions were along the lines of "How dare you? What gives you the authority or the audacity?"

She said, "You're misunderstanding me! I was just advising Donald that maybe you'd prefer to work in presidential personnel. Maybe you could be the head of presidential personnel? I'm only trying to be helpful."

Her condescension oozed.

My indignation must have struck some chords, but not quite loudly enough. Reince came back to me with the title of AP and "director of communications for the Office of Public Liaison." He argued it was so much better because I would be able to carve out my own portfolio in OPL and be an important part of the White House communications team as the spokesperson for the OPL. He said that Trump wanted me to be visible and to be free to do media when needed.

I got the AP title I had requested, but not the director of the OPL. I decided to make the best out of the situation and focus on my long list of priorities. I found out later that they were deep into negotiation with Anthony Scaramucci to be the director of the OPL at the time. This would never manifest, because Scaramucci's business came under scrutiny during his background check. The White House ethics office discovered that a deal under which he would sell his controlling interest in SkyBridge Capital, his hedge fund network, to HNA Group, a Chinese company, was under government review, creating a potential conflict of interest for Scaramucci. (More chaos, more controversy.) Eventually, George Sifakis from the RNC became the OPL director, though he lasted less than six months.

I got in a little trouble for mentioning my appointment on Fox News on New Year's Eve, and Reince called to say, "You can't talk about this yet. We have to make the official announcements." But Donald thought it was a good interview and called to tell me they had watched from Mar-a-Lago and that I had done a great job on Fox News's New Year's Eve Special representing the administration. Donald Trump, my audience of one.

Around the first of the year I got a call from the Presidential Inaugural Committee office asking if I could assist with the diversity outreach for the inauguration. My plate was already full, but after speaking with Tucker Davis, the new staffer assigned to the position, I really connected with him and offered to help him by sharing my extensive network of contacts I'd amassed over the years and on the Trump campaign, among other things.

Time barreled on, and we continued to scramble to get things done, like making the schedule for the inauguration events itself, with the ensuing controversies about some of the Rockettes refusing to perform, singers accepting and canceling. Every day, we had to wade through time-consuming craziness instead of filling jobs and setting policy. It was almost like we were moving backward, not forward.

The details about the inauguration ceremony were frontburnered. The PIC sent a list of to-dos to Trump Tower, and one item was Donald's choosing a Bible to be sworn in on.

Traditionally, the president-elect would visit the National Archives with a guide and select one from the vast collection of historical Bibles that had personal meaning to him or was previously owned by someone with a shared political philosophy or worldview, or that he had an affinity for. Barack Obama, an Illinois native and a black man, chose the same Bible that Abraham Lincoln was sworn in on, as well as the traveling Bible of Martin Luther King Jr. John Quincy Adams was sworn in on a constitutional law book because that held meaning for him. George Washington was sworn in on his own Masonic Bible, which Warren G. Harding, Dwight D. Eisenhower, and George H. W. Bush had since placed their hands upon during their inauguration ceremonies. Others chose a family Bible. Ronald Reagan used his mother's well-read and annotated Bible. JFK used the Fitzgerald family Bible.

Donald mentioned to me that he would have to make this choice, and wasn't inspired by his options. It's not mandatory that new presidents swear in on a Bible, but most have done so.

He asked me, "Omarosa, what do you think about me getting sworn in on *The Art of the Deal*?"

I said, "Instead of the Bible?"

"Yeah. *The Art of the Deal* is a bestseller! It's the greatest business book of all time. It's how I'm going to make great deals for the country. Just think how many copies I'd sell—maybe a commemorative inauguration copy?!"

"I know you're not going to be a traditional president, but that's just too crazy. Whatever you do, don't repeat that idea to anybody else," I said.

We laughed. He wanted me to believe he was kidding.

Two things to discuss here. One, Donald Trump has no knowledge of the Bible at all. It might as well be a paper brick to him. "We love the Bible. It's the best," he said during the campaign. "We love *The Art of the Deal*, but the Bible is far, far superior." How would he know? He says he never reads the Bible. When asked, he can't recite his favorite scripture or name the books (remember when he quoted from "two Corinthians" during the campaign?). I'm not saying the president has to be a biblical scholar, but he should be biblically aware. Since the Bible has little significance to him, it might have felt disingenuous to him to take an oath on it. But *The Art of the Deal* meant a lot to him. Nothing has more meaning to Donald than himself.

Also, I think that Donald—like Ivanka, who'd plugged her dress at the convention—hadn't fully made the shift from being a salesman. He was hardwired to constantly promote Trump brands, properties (which was why he worked out of Mar-a-Lago, Bedminster, and Trump Tower during the transition), and Trump products, like beverages (Trump Winery wine flowed at the convention). Why wouldn't he think of the inauguration itself as a branding opportunity?

Donald Trump had always been obsessed with ratings. He went on and on about how much the networks would make with that many eyeballs glued to their TVs. Historical ratings! He pondered how he could capitalize on that himself and whether it was feasible to do a pay-per-view event that would get him a piece of the action.

I was surprised to hear that Paula White was giving the invocation at the inauguration. At Bill Clinton's 1997 inauguration, that honor went to Pastor Billy Graham. At Barack Obama's 2009 ceremony, that honor went to Myrlie Evers-Williams, the widow of Medgar Evers, the slain civil rights leader. So why on earth would Paula White, the pastor at the New Destiny Christian Center, be given such a prominent, important platform? I asked.

A Trump family member pulled me aside and told me to back off. When I asked why, I was told she and Trump had enjoyed a special relationship.

I was not sure what to make of this. I had certainly never heard anything that made me wonder about the nature of their relationship before (or since). But I could not stop myself from contemplating whether her position as his spiritual adviser had ever been missionary.

It was of course totally credible from his side, but I really didn't know her well enough to know if it was from hers. In any event, once I'd been warned, I reeled it in.

I hadn't heard the last from Paula White, though. Six months later, after Reince Priebus was fired, Paula came to the OPL offices for meetings and we had a come-to-Jesus conversation about what had gone on during the transition. She claimed that Reince didn't want me as the director of the OPL and had lied when he'd told me Paula had intervened. She apologized in any event. And I moved on.

• • •

FOR THE INAUGURATION, the inaugural committee put my family and me at the historic Willard InterContinental hotel in a beautiful suite. The week before the inauguration, I had twisted my ankle painfully, but I was too busy to deal with it. Throughout breakfast, my foot swelled up like a balloon. I went to the medical team and got treated for what I thought was a sprained ankle. It ended up being much more serious. I had to wear a boot throughout the ceremony, and to all the balls and parties. The combination of the sprain, the fact that I didn't take care of it by resting and putting my foot up, and chronic inflammation caused nerve damage in my foot. In December 2017, I would finally get corrective surgery, but only after I had been hobbling around the White House on crutches for months.

As assistants to the president, we were introduced one by one to the nation. I was grateful to come out of the historical tunnel with Rick Dearborn, who graciously assisted me to my seat.

During the ceremony, I sat with Rhona Graff, executive assistant to Donald Trump, a woman I'd known for nearly fifteen years. She was so important to his life; I was happy to be seated with her.

As I looked around the platform, I noticed scant diversity, just Senator Tim Scott from South Carolina, Ben Carson, and a couple of others. There should have been more; I made a vow that day to work to increase diversity in Trumpworld.

After the ceremony, as I was headed to the motorcade, I stopped to watch the Obamas' helicopter take off. It was an emotional moment. Standing on the steps of the US Capitol, I thought about how my mom and I campaigned for then senator Obama in our home state of Ohio and now, I was witnessing the peaceful transfer of power that is the envy of the world. Obama's departure marked the end to his presidency and the beginning of Trump's presidency. It was cold, and I was shivering, but I was warmed with respect and gratitude for Obama's service.

We loaded into the motorcade and headed down Pennsylvania Avenue to the White House. My fiancé and I sat in front, a row ahead of Rex Tillerson and his wife. It was my first meeting with Rex, and I liked him very much. Not a single other car was out there on Pennsylvania Avenue as we rode along with the police escorts. The street was lined with servicemen standing every five feet. It was a thrilling, one-of-a-kind experience.

Once I got inside the White House, there was a team set up to process us quickly. While I went to the Roosevelt Room to receive my ID badge, laptop, and government-issued cell phone, my mom and fiancé went into the Oval Office and had a look around. I'd also been given my office assignment, the security code on a piece of paper, and a White House complex map with my office circled in red. Loaded up with my equipment and code, the three of us followed the map from the West Wing to the Eisenhower Executive Office Building (EEOB) to my new space. The walk, which I would make many hundreds of times over the next eleven months, took about five minutes.

Along the corridors, furniture was piled up against the walls. The government department that handled moving had only had time to empty the offices of Obama-era furnishings. When we got to my new office, I used the code to enter, and was pleasantly surprised by how big it was. It might have appeared enormous because it was empty, save for the desk.

"Wow!" I said.

"Yes, wow!" my mom agreed.

My fiancé said, "Let me go into the hallway and grab a few chairs."

While he went furniture shopping among the discards, my mother and I took a lap around the huge office, marveling at the high ceilings and the balcony overlooking Seventeenth Street and a circular park called the Ellipse.

John retrieved a beautiful desk chair and two antique chairs from outside the Public Affairs Office, which I kept for my entire time there. Since I was among the first to arrive, I got an early visit from one of the guys in charge of furnishings.

"What can I get for you?" he asked.

I'd been mentally decorating the room since I arrived, and would eventually fill it with a couch, a boardroom table with a telecom system, a coat rack behind the door, a small refrigerator and microwave, and a massive mirror over the fireplace. But that morning, I said, "I'll need a desk lamp, a printer, a table for the printer."

While that was going on, John had continued to poke around, and he found a sixty-inch TV abandoned in the hallway outside one of the directors' suites. I asked the government man if we could claim it, and he said, "It's all yours."

This TV was giant, and it had split-screen programming built in so I could watch CNN, Fox News, MSNBC, and C-SPAN simultaneously.

The three of us sat on the chairs, but we were too giddy to stay still. We talked for a spell, and then I suddenly remembered, "The parade! I have to see the marching band!"

I was referring to the Marching Tornadoes of Talladega College—a small HBCU founded in 1867 by former slaves in Alabama. I'd helped to raise money for them to come to DC to perform at the inauguration parade, another historic tradition that starts with the president and his family walking along Pennsylvania Avenue, later followed by a procession of marching groups, bands, and military units—some on horses, some on motorcycles—while the president watches from a viewing stand. When the Marching Tornadoes were initially invited to march, many alumni protested. The college president, Dr. Billy C. Hawkins, stood by his commitment to give these students a once-in-a-lifetime experience, and said participation was not an endorsement of the president himself. But, for the 230-member band to come to DC—which most of them had never visited before—they needed $75,000 and set up a GoFundMe page. Bill O'Reilly invited Dr. Hawkins on his show, and then I appeared, too, to direct people to the GoFundMe page. Together, we were able to help them raise more than $600,000 to pay for the trip and, in addition, scholarships.

We ran from my office at the EEOB along a walkway right to the presidential viewing stand on the parade route on Pennsylvania Avenue, just in time to see the Marching Tornadoes. I was cheering and filled with pride for them. Every one of those students was like me. They'd gone to an HBCU for experience and opportunities, and because of our efforts, they were here, and standing tall. I was just so proud of their determination and resilience. Despite all the protests and forces working against their coming to DC, they'd made it. And now the eyes of the world were on them.

That evening I was honored to give the prayer at the American Legion Veterans Inaugural Ball. That night, in front of all the living Purple Heart recipients, I prayed for our county, I prayed for peace, and I prayed for my friend, the forty-fifth president of the United States, Donald J. Trump.

Chapter Eleven

Tackled by My Teammates

The first one hundred days of most modern presidencies are fast-paced, with the incoming team ready to go, still high from their victory and with the enthusiasm of the majority of Americans behind them. Trump did not receive the majority of the popular vote, and the victory was tainted by that and Russia interference doubts. The first days of the Trump presidency were defined by chaos and conflict, not surprisingly, and a blistering pace of executive orders, controversial tweets, and nonstop outrage from Democrats, opening with the largest, most vociferous protests of the digital era.

Trump didn't waste any time dismantling Obama's legacy. Hours after he was sworn in, he signed an executive order aimed at repealing the Affordable Care Act.

On day two, January 21, I returned to the White House, this

time in an SUV. As we were coming down Seventeenth Street, all of a sudden, my vehicle was surrounded by women in pink hats. The first Women's March was in full swing. Protesters carried signs that read, "Dear GOP and Trump: Our pussies are none of your damn business," "Black Lives Matter," and "Keep your hands off of our country!" The protesters were peaceful; I saw no one who looked hostile.

As soon as I took a seat at my desk, I forgot about the crocheted hats and was filled with awe at the magnitude of the responsibility of running the government. What I would do from this desk, and beyond it, would impact many lives and make a difference for families.

My first act as an AP was to requisition basic equipment and furniture. Everyone was kind of stunned by the utter lack of tools and services we needed to do our jobs. We were all ready and excited to take up the reins of power, but first, we needed to figure out how to turn on the phones.

Despite the operational inadequacies, we *had* to hit the ground running. But we didn't have an organization in place to carry out the ambitious agenda set by the president and his senior advisers, myself included. It was one thing to say, "We're going to rewrite the tax code!" or "We need an infrastructure bill!" but without the staff to implement those goals, everything was at a standstill. Manpower was severely limited. The thousands of Schedule C staff jobs we were supposed to fill during the transition (many of which remain empty to this day) were still vacant. Not having support and operations teams stymied forward movement.

Trump started signing executive orders (EOs)—directives from the president that become law, pending judiciary review. We'd asked him to be "more presidential," and signing EOs was one way to do it. However, it might as well have been a doodle scribbled on a notepad without the people and logistics in place to implement it.

Later, still on day two, Trump spoke at the CIA headquarters in Virginia and harped on the inauguration crowd size, saying, "We had a massive field of people. You saw them. Packed. I get up this morning, I turn on one of the networks, and they show an empty field. I say, wait a minute, I made a speech! I looked out, the field was—it looked like a million, million and a half people. They showed a field where there [was] practically nobody standing there. And they said, 'Donald Trump did not draw well.' Liars! Fake news!"

When I was asked about the crowd size, I didn't want to tell him the inaugural committee had made getting tickets for the black community nearly impossible for me and Tucker Davis. There was even talk of charging people to attend. I'd spoken out in one of the committee meetings, saying emphatically that most black people would not attend the inauguration and would definitely not pay to go to Trump events. Tucker and I submitted list after list of possible names, with only half of them being approved, as if space was limited. We were frustrated and baffled about the pushback. I could have explained to the president why the attendance at the inauguration was so low, but it wouldn't have made a difference at that point.

Instead of a triumphant second day of the Trump presidency, we were drowning in exaggerations, protests, and side-by-side photos of the Washington Mall of Trump's modest inauguration draw of 306,000 next to Obama's 2009 record-breaking 1.8 million crowd. The Women's March massive turnout—at least five hundred thousand in DC; five million worldwide—rankled him, too. The president simply could not stand to be outsized by a bunch of women in pink hats or a black man, especially *that* black man.

Immediately, the comms team gathered to discuss the matter. Twenty minutes in, the lights in the room went out, and we couldn't figure out how to turn them back on.

The Obama administration had installed an energy-saving system so that the lights switched off after a certain amount of time. So if we were in a meeting that ran longer than twenty minutes, the lights would suddenly go out. Once we found out about that, someone would have to wave a hand in front of the sensors to turn them back on, and we'd start again. It was so tiresome, we'd say, "Just leave them off." Eventually, we got the engineers to come and adjust the timer. But for the first week or so, we were literally and figuratively governing in the dark.

Sean Spicer, the recently appointed press secretary, after speaking with President Trump in the Oval, came up with the solution. "We're going to back him up," he said. "If the president says there were a million and a half people, we'll reinforce that."

On day two, January 21, I attended Sean Spicer's first official press briefing. I sat next to Stephanie Grisham, Hope Hicks, Kellyanne Conway, and Sarah Huckabee Sanders. We looked on as Sean declared, "[T]he largest audience to ever witness an inauguration—period—both in person and around the globe." It was hard to keep a straight face as Sean proceeded to lie to the American people and then refused to take questions from the press corps. Kellyanne Conway went on *Meet the Press* the next day. Chuck Todd asked her why, at Sean Spicer's very first press briefing, he'd said an easily verifiable falsehood to the American people and whether lying about something small like this would mean he'd lie about bigger, more important issues as well. She dug the hole ten times deeper by saying, "Sean Spicer gave alternative facts." She then pivoted to the failures of Obamacare and the public education system. She also accused Todd of being biased against Trump, setting an adversarial tone with the media from day three.

• • •

Congrats on your appointment to serve as an Assistant to the President for our 45th President of the United States, Donald J. Trump. What an absolutely historic weekend it will be!

The President would like to host you and four guests at the White House this Sunday (1/22) for a small ceremony and private gathering to honor you and your hard work for him and our country.

Thank you!
Katie Walsh, Deputy Chief of Staff

On day four, my mother, the widow who worked two jobs and twelve hours a days to feed her four children in the Westlake projects, was there to see her daughter sworn in to serve the president at the highest level at the White House. She was joined by my friends Shannon Jackson and Aisha McClendon, who had worked in the

Clinton White House with me twenty years ago. My experience of that day was filtered through my mother's eyes and how grateful I was to her for everything she'd done for me. That I'd been able to make her proud didn't scratch the surface of what I hoped to do to repay her for her suffering and sacrifices on my behalf. We took lots of pictures with the president, the vice president, and the other APs and their families.

In our comms meeting we discussed the number one topic of the day, Kellyanne's use of the phrase *alternative facts*. Kellyanne was thrilled that her clip with Chuck Todd had been watched by millions and made headlines in every newspaper in the country. I started to get the feeling that Kellyanne was as passionately engaged with her own media presence as she was with the Trump agenda.

Meanwhile, I was still waiting for tables and chairs—and mouse-traps. The White House is a very old building and its longest living residents are mice. Every time we moved furniture we would see them scurrying into little holes in the historic walls.

Also on day four, Trump signed an EO reinstating the Global Gag Rule that banned federal funding to any international health organization that provided abortions or gave out any information to women in need. While he signed this directive about women's access to reproductive health care, he was surrounded by Mike Pence, Jared Kushner, Stephen Miller, Rob Porter, Steve Bannon, and a few other white men in dark suits. For a man who was all about optics and "central casting," it was a disaster. Because women's issues fell under the umbrella of the OPL, I had to field the calls of protest and concerns from women's constituency groups. I told the senior staff,

"We can't do anything as it relates to women, women's rights, again, ever in this administration, without first engaging women's rights groups and definitely not with a bunch of men standing behind the president."

When I mentioned it, people seemed annoyed that I pointed out Hope's rookie mistakes and Reince's unforced errors. But I felt I had to. No one else was bold enough to say it out loud.

Mike Pence's presence was particularly offensive to women's groups. His record of legislating against reproductive health rights is among the most aggressive. During his years in Congress and as the governor of Indiana he signed eight laws in less than four years to restrict abortions in his state, including the fetal anomaly bills that would have forced providers to cremate or bury fetal remains; forced women to have preabortion counseling, where they were told that they were destroying human life; and banned women from aborting fetuses that had been diagnosed with physical or mental disabilities and lethal conditions. A federal judge in Indiana later blocked the law from going into effect because it unconstitutionally limited a woman's right to an abortion. In Congress, Pence cosponsored a bill that said hospitals could refuse to give a woman an abortion, even if she would die without receiving one, with the one exception of "forcible" rape (as if all rape weren't forced); thankfully, it did not pass. He has legislated to limit women's access to birth control and has fought funding for Planned Parenthood.

Trump, Pence, and their posse were undoing any hope of connecting with women and minorities. He'd surrounded himself only with elite, wealthy, white, conservative men. I'd agreed to take on an epic responsibility to be the voice of my community and women of color in the White House, and I realized at that moment just how steep my climb was going to be.

On day six, January 25, Trump repeated his false claim that three to five million people cast ballots illegally. He was still litigating the November election, and would continue to do so over and over again, to this day. He was obsessed with the election, and he was furious when it came out that he'd lost the popular vote by millions. For his first few months in the White House, Trump kept big charts in his private dining room, in his den, in his study, that showed the electoral map color coded in red and blue. Most of the country was coded red, while the most populous urban centers were coded blue. When anyone walked in, he'd point to the chart and talked about the election results. If you walked in in the morning, he'd tell the story of his victory, with the visual aid of the chart. If you walked in in the afternoon, you'd hear the same story again, verbatim.

It was very concerning to listen to him go on and on about the election in private. He would get all worked up and get crazed about the "fake news" reports. I was worried that in his first week in office he was already cracking under the pressure.

We all had work to do, and things to discuss, but he only wanted to talk about the election. When he tweeted about things like illegally cast ballots, my concern was taken to a higher level, because now his obsession was in the public realm, which meant that we had to deal with it publicly.

I believed that if we gave him the right data, he'd talk and tweet about that verified information. We were in the White House, with every resource available to us to get the most accurate data imaginable. For days, I thought there had to be a glitch in the flow of accurate data to him. The correct information *was* delivered to him in his morning briefing folders—always with headlines from his love-to-hate newspapers the *New York Times* and the *Washington Post* on top—but he ignored it in favor of unverified info.

The question became, was he just making things up or was his intel coming from outside the White House? We quickly realized that the president, a gluttonous consumer of media, had been going on Twitter and picking things up from disreputable, random sources, taking what he read there as fact, and reposting for all the world to see. We needed fact-checkers, or at least a filter for POTUS Twitter posts.

The directive came down from Reince that our default position was to back up whatever the president said or tweeted, regardless of its accuracy. In fact, much of my days—from the first to the last—were spent strategizing and defending Trump tweets and statements to constituency groups that he may have offended on that particular day.

By day six, I'd established a daily routine:

7:00 a.m.: Arrival at the White House through the East Gate

7:30 a.m.: Morning huddle in Sean Spicer's office in the West Wing

8:00 a.m.: Senior staff meeting in Reince's office with about thirty people—the APs, Jared, Ivanka, Gary Cohn, General Kellogg, Spicer, Bannon, Kellyanne, et al.

8:45 a.m.: Breakfast at the White House Mess

9:00 a.m.: The OPL meetings in the EEOB

11:00 a.m.: Back to Sean's office for daily prep for press briefing

1:00 p.m.: Daily press briefing in the James S. Brady Press Briefing Room

2:00 p.m.: Back to the OPL for constituent calls or meetings

5:00 p.m.: The OPL staff meeting

6:00 p.m.: All-comms wrap-up meeting in Sean's office

Throughout the first one hundred days, whenever the president had a listening session in the Roosevelt Room, I was always standing nearby or seated behind him. When he signed an EO that related to diversity, women, veterans, any OPL group—from truckers to college presidents—I was in the Oval or other locations with him. Whenever I took point on an event—for example, going to the Smithsonian during Black History Month—I briefed him at least twice before each one. So in my official capacity, I saw the president three to four times a week.

As for unscheduled pop-ins—the times when the Oval door was open, he was seated inside, he saw me walking by and called me in—I saw him two or three additional times per week. That was how I met the Canadian prime minister. I'd just left a meeting in the Roosevelt Room and he yelled, "Hey, Omarosa, come meet Justin Trudeau!" Don't mind if I do. . . .

Most presidents did not do casual pop-ins. They stuck with their schedule. The Clintons were an exception. The culture of that administration was more relaxed. Betty Currie was Clinton's assistant, and she was a "Come on in!" open-door type of person. When I was a mid-level staffer there, I could walk in for a meeting or bring my family by to say hello. Perhaps that operational dynamic was too casual, allowing interns passage into the Oval's private areas, for example.

Trump was used to how he conducted business in Trump Tower, where he had an open-door policy and if anyone had a question or needed to talk, you just poked your head into his office. He hadn't made the shift yet to White House protocol. I hadn't made the shift yet, and whenever he invited me in, I'd go, scheduled or unscheduled. During our unscheduled meetings, the president led the conversation to whatever was on his mind, from the travel bans to Obamacare to what he had for lunch. Donald likes to talk, and he really likes having people around to listen. About once a week, he called me and said, "Have you been avoiding me? I haven't seen you in a while. Check my schedule and come by," even if I'd seen him the day before.

I think he was lonely and liked seeing a familiar face.

I was in the unique position of straddling two worlds throughout my year in the White House—working in comms in the West Wing, and the OPL in the EEOB—running all over the complex, from one meeting to another, all day long and deep into the evening.

On day eight, I appeared on *The View*. Beforehand, Donald prepped me for my interview and told me to be tough and not to let them push me around. He said, "Go boardroom Omarosa," meaning cool, calm, and deadly. We laughed. He said to particularly watch out for Joy Behar, who used to be a friend of his and Melania's, and he had the pictures to prove it. "But she turned on me like a snake," he said.

I asked for and received a briefing from the White House surrogate team and *The View* producers with a list of topics they wanted to discuss with me: my role in the White House, my first week in office, the Women's March. They invited my fiancé, John, to come sit in the front row for the taping, too, to talk about our upcoming wedding.

Of course, the questions they actually asked were not on the list *at all.* Hosts Joy Behar and Sunny Hostin hammered away at me about tax returns, insults to the disabled, p***y grabbing. Gretchen Carlson, a former Fox anchor, was lovely; she was the only one. I batted back the hostility point by point, until I noticed the one-minute warning sign flash. They hadn't acknowledged my fiancé at all, who had flown in from Jacksonville, or our upcoming wedding. I broke into the conversation with less than sixty seconds remaining to introduce him and close a contentious segment on something nice, as promised. My closing line went viral. I said about John, "I'm so happy that he's here with me, and he brings me such joy. And I hope that you one day, can find that kind of joy, Joy, in your life." She looked agitated.

Donald called me the next day before 5:00 a.m., and said, "Good job, good job, way to hit back. You still got it. I liked how you went off on Joy. She used to kiss our asses, and now she's anti-Trump. Fuggedaboutit."

On day nine, the "talker" of the day fell squarely on my plate. Trump had signed an EO to ban people from Iraq, Syria, Iran, Libya,

Somalia, Sudan, and Yemen to enter the United States for ninety days. The first travel ban dealt with the treatment of minority groups, so it was in my portfolio. It predominantly impacted people of color.

In the comms meeting, I argued that the travel ban had set off a panic in Democrats—and many Republicans as well—that their worst fears were true, that Trump was a monster, a racist, a persecutor of minorities. I said, "It advances the perception that the administration is discriminating against people of color from around the world."

Senior staffers countered, "Well, Muslim is not a race, it's a religion."

To my mind, that was even worse. It was a blatant ban of an entire religion!

In a senior staff meeting around this time, Stephen Miller ran through a litany of ideas on how to deter immigration, including the tactic of separating children from their parents at the border if they tried to enter the country illegally. We didn't discuss the pros and cons at the time. It was just one of many ideas on his list. I never thought in a million years that it would ever be implemented. It was the antithesis of who we are as Americans. Stephen Miller always was a fount of ideas, and some of them ran to the extreme.

In these meetings, Mike Pence defended Trump, saying, "God is telling me to support the president. God is telling me I'm here to serve." He was being directed by a higher deity to agree with Trump no matter what. When he'd been tapped for VP, people said that he'd bring a different perspective—a moral, Christian perspective—and speak out for compassion. But the only time he's spoken out with indignation since he'd been chosen as Trump's running mate was when General Michael Flynn lied to him about Russian sanctions.

The rollout of the travel ban was poorly coordinated, to say the least. Officers and customs agents at airports had no guidance about how to implement the policy. The melee at airports took some by surprise. Much of our catch-up work centered around the lack of coordination and the lack of messaging to go along with it. We had little or no warning about the details of the ban—which *was* a ban, then *wasn't*, then *was* again.

Throughout the drawn-out travel-ban litigation, whataboutism really came to the forefront. "*What about* the fact that Obama put these countries in a list himself!" "*What about* Obama's record with deportations of illegal immigrants?" In Trumpworld, the only defense for most situations was "whataboutism," mostly about Obama and Clinton.

I reckoned that Trump's push for the travel ban and mass deportations was a reaction to Barack Obama's stats on deportations. Donald Trump was trying to again one-up President Obama, who was nicknamed "deporter in chief" for his skyrocketing millions of deportations. I'm sure Miller or Homeland Secretary General Kelly had given him the numbers of how many people Obama deported within the first year, second year, and so forth. Trump wanted to be the crackdown president; he had to deliver on his campaign promises. But he also really wanted to outdo Barack. This entire episode was a sad opening to the presidency, along with being morally reprehensible.

I was responsible for organizing White House Black History

Month events, and I had been planning to kick off the program the first day of February, day twelve of the Trump presidency, with a listening session with POTUS and black leaders. I'd submitted my list of invitees for approval to Reince, and he'd slashed it in half. He also removed the names of several black Republicans who had given him problems during his time at the RNC when all of his African American staffers left in what was called "the GOP black exodus." Once we finalized and vetted the list, we buttoned down the event and had everything in place. I prepared the materials for the president's briefing book and submitted it the night before.

Anxious, I went to the Oval Office early for my briefing with the president. I wanted to go over his opening and closing remarks. Keith Schiller, with whom I had a friendship for about a decade, promised me an extra ten minutes. In presidential time, that's an eternity. In our briefings, Trump's attention was scattered. He was distracted, irritable, and short. Normally when Donald got into one of these moods, you knew to give him time and space. But in this case I could not. I was going over his speech, but he couldn't retain any of the bullet points. I went over them again and again, and what he should say to the press after the event. But he couldn't remember the key points and stumbled over large words, which we scratched out and replaced with simpler terms.

The change in him since his prime was dramatic. Back on season one of *The Apprentice*, there had been a mix-up on one of the episodes where a contestant lost money on a task, and they were discussing figures. Donald Trump repeated a lengthy numbers sequence with no notes in front of him, calculated them in his head in moments, and came to his conclusion that the math-addled contestant should be fired. That was how sharp he used to be. Now? The blade had been dulled.

For this particular speech, I begged him not to say, "What do we have to lose?" or to refer to the participants as "you people" as he had during the campaign's ministers' meeting. "*You people* is pejorative," I explained to him. He looked puzzled. I said, "It's bad. Just don't say it. *Ever.*" When he practiced the opener, he spoke only in fragments, not complete sentences. When I tried to correct him, he became frustrated and more irritable.

I left the Oval praying to God that Donald Trump didn't go off script or say something crazy or draw attention away from the fact that it was the first day of Black History Month. He knew I was concerned, and he said, "I got it. Don't worry. The blacks love me!"

As I feared, despite my spoon-feeding him short sentences and key points ad nauseam, he went off script and ad-libbed his opening speech, spending time vamping about the election; hating on the "opposition party," a.k.a, the media; giving a shout-out to coal miners in West Virginia; and saying outright ignorant things like, "Frederick Douglass is an example of someone who has done an amazing job and is being recognized more and more, I notice."

It was terrible. He didn't know who Frederick Douglass was, or that he had died decades ago, and the press mocked him relentlessly for it. This was the first of many incidents where I'd spent days (weeks and months) working on a project or event to benefit the African American community, moved logistical mountains, only to watch Trump destroy all my hard work with a comment or a slur. I called it being "tackled by your own teammate." I was trying to run the ball, and he would tackle me with his ignorance. The community would ponder, *What exactly is Omarosa doing in there if Trump keeps going off the rails? She must not be doing her job.* If only they knew the struggle I faced keeping Trump from sounding full racist on any given day.

Day thirteen, fireworks exploded in the White House when the news of an upcoming *Time* magazine with Steve Bannon on the cover broke. The cover line read, "The Great Manipulator." Donald lost his mind over this cover. He raged at Bannon at high volume in a room full of people, yelling, "He thinks he's a manipulator? Thinks he's so f**king smart? He thinks he can manipulate me? An idiot! An asshole!" Many expletives were hurled that day. His fury was from the cover alone, since he didn't read the article. I'd been on the receiving end of a Trump rage before, when there was that problem shooting *The Ultimate Merger* at Trump Las Vegas. When his temper flares, he does not—cannot—hold back, and it's terrifying to watch. If he'd spoken that way to a diplomat or head of state, it would have been disastrous.

Around this time, on Thursdays, I went to Capitol Hill for meetings at 11:00 a.m. and then a special invitation-only Bible study at noon, a very private nonpartisan prayer gathering, led by the Senate chaplain, Rear Admiral Barry Black. Other participants were Senators Kirsten Gillibrand, Cory Booker, John Thune, Tim Caper, former senator Blanche Lincoln, and Tim Scott. Those weekly sessions were key to keeping me spiritually grounded and helped me stay steady in the unrelenting storm.

On day seventeen, I convinced Reince to allow me to work with the Department of State to take a delegation to Haiti for the inauguration of President Jovenel Moïse. When I told DJT that I would be gone for a couple of days, he asked me, "Why did you choose that shitty country as your first foreign trip? You should have waited until the confirmations were done and gone to Scotland and played golf at [his course] Turnberry."

I admonished him for putting down Haiti and explained all that the country had been through recently. I also reminded him of all the promises he had made to the Haitian community during the campaign and that we had to deliver on our commitment to help build up Haiti. He didn't remember, drew a blank. I reminded him that he had talked about Haiti constantly during the campaign, especially in Miami, where Trump met with the Haitian American community members three or four times.

On day eighteen, Jeff Sessions (whom Trump called Benjamin Button behind his back) was confirmed as attorney general, despite the Democrats' attempt to stop it, led by the Congressional Black Caucus and, most vocally, Senator Al Franken. The irony of his confirmation during Black History Month was not lost on me. My policy with Sessions was to be polite but keep a distance. That's what you do as an African American professional in this country. If every black person quit his or her job because someone in the workplace was racist, not many of us would be employed. Despite their racist reputations, I was cordial with Steve Bannon, formerly of the anti-immigration alt-right Breitbart News, and Stephen Miller, a Sessions protégé, the writer of high school and college essays that railed against minorities. Unlike those "alleged" racists, Sessions had a long, well-documented track record of offensive policies: voting twice against including sexual orientation in the definition of a "hate crime"; saying that the NAACP and ACLU were "un-American" and "communist inspired"; pushing for an English-only government; and allegedly using the N-word repeatedly, to mention a few.

On day twenty, I flew to New York on Air Force Two with Vice President Mike Pence and his wife, Karen, to attend the Henry O. Flipper dinner in honor of the first African American to graduate from the United States Military Academy at West Point.

After this time with VP Pence, I became troubled about him. The first thing I noticed was that people on his staff kept slipping up and calling him president—accidentally sometimes. Jokingly, in private, I heard people say things like, "When we're in charge . . . ," or "Once you become president. . . ." I asked him explicitly if he had any ambitions for the highest office after Donald completed his two terms. Pence said, "Two terms? You think two terms? That's good, I like the way you think, Omarosa. I'm here to serve the president. I'm only loyal to the president." His walking in lockstep with the president, eerily beaming glances, and mindless compliance would, in good time, be a source of late-night comedy and political memes. Several months later, conservative columnist George Will would call Pence a "sycophant poodle." I suspected that Pence was just biding his time, looking the part of the perfect VP, until Trump resigned, was impeached, or served his term.

On day thirty-one, February 21, I arranged for the president to visit the Smithsonian National Museum of African American History and Culture on Constitution Avenue. This was the first presidential trip that I planned, start to finish. It involved a backbreaking amount of logistics. Sixty-two people—including the president, Reince Priebus, Ivanka Trump, Keith Schiller, physician to the president Ronny Jackson, Sean Spicer, Stephen Miller, Ben Carson and his entire family, activist and former state representative Alveda King, support staff, honored guests, fifteen reporters—into a motorcade of *eleven* vehicles to leave the South Portico of the White House promptly at 8:20 a.m. to drive five minutes to the museum. To make that drive, Secret Service had to organize the shutting down of every street between the two locations.

I briefed Donald the day before the event. I briefed him before we left the White House. I briefed him when we arrived at the museum. Even as we were walking and touring, I gave him little lines to say. For his short remarks, I requested for the White House Communications Agency (WHCA) to supply a teleprompter, which they couldn't because of time constraints. Donald read his remarks from a piece of paper, which didn't play so well, but at least it was better than the Frederick Douglass gaffe.

As the lead staffer on the event, I didn't leave Donald's side, and ticked off every instruction, movement, and introduction that had been painstakingly mapped and planned for weeks. Everything went off without a hitch, except for the *Today* show interview that I set up on site at the museum. It was Trump's first one-on-one interview with a black reporter since becoming president. Although Craig Melvin had submitted topics in advance, Donald didn't stick to the script, again.

When President Trump and Craig Melvin ventured into

uncharted territory, I started to make "wrap it up" signals. Donald had something up his sleeve, too. He started talking about recent attacks on Jewish centers. They'd been in the news and his hostile rhetoric had been blamed for the rise in anti-Semitic vandalism and crimes. I kept thinking, *Why is he talking about anti-Semitism at the National Museum of African American History and Culture?*

I was relieved as we headed for the motorcade. Donald was impressed. He said, "Good job, kiddo. Good event."

Day forty, I'd teamed up the domestic policy team to invite seventy-five presidents of historically black colleges (HBCUs) to meet with the White House senior staff, Secretary Betsy DeVos and VP Mike Pence. I'd hoped that the president might do a drop by and had checked in to ask about his availability. Jared Kushner called back and said, "Bring the group over." The invitation was a surprise, and I asked them if they'd like to go over to the West Wing. It was an offer, not a requirement. They all said yes, and our massive group made the five-minute walk, flanked by Secret Service. Once in the Roosevelt Room I asked again if they wanted to come. If not, they could stay in the Roosevelt Room and talk to some of the senior advisers. All of them accepted. They had a few minutes to shake hands with the president. Trump suggested a photo, and the president's photographer had to climb up a ladder to get the whole group. Then the press pool entered and started taking pictures as well.

Kellyanne wanted to snap pictures of the group, too, and decided to stand on the couch to get her shot. The press took a photo of Kellyanne kneeling on the couch after taking her picture. The next day the headline was about Kellyanne barefoot in the

Oval and *not* about the historic meeting with HBCU presidents in the Oval Office. It was historic because in his eight years in office Obama had never invited all the presidents to the White House. But that point was lost because of Kellyanne. This time I'd been tackled by my own teammate at the one-yard line.

This same day, Trump signed an EO that I'd pushed for since day one, the Presidential Executive Order on the White House Initiative to Promote Excellence and Innovation at Historically Black Colleges and Universities. The EO was important, as it would move the initiative for HBCUs from the Department of Education to the White House. Additionally, we could pursue funding for the colleges through the private sector. The Thurgood Marshall College Fund as well as the National Association for Equal Opportunity (NAFEO) and the United Negro College Fund (UNCF) endorsed the EO and called for an increase in the federal budget for HBCUs. I'd attended two HBCUs, Central State University and Howard University. I also attended Payne Theological Seminary before the death of my fiancé Michael Clarke Duncan. That executive order was my top policy priority within the first forty days of the administration. Donald supported me in my efforts. We got it done just in the nick of time, on the twenty-eighth of February. He had repeatedly said that funding for HBCUs was one of his priorities, and he was proving that.

Also on that long day, Donald made his first major speech, the joint address to Congress. I worked with speech writer Stephen Miller behind the scenes to get diversity acknowledgments into it, starting with the first line: "Tonight, as we mark the conclusion of our celebration of Black History Month, we are reminded of our nation's path towards civil rights and the work that still remains to be done." Later on, he talked about the EO and about working to ensure government funding and grants for HBCUs: "We must enrich the mind and the souls of every American child. Education is the civil rights issue of our time. I am calling upon members of both parties to pass an education bill that funds school choice for disadvantaged youth, including millions of African American and Latino children."

One thing that I found disturbing during the address to the joint session of Congress was how Mike Pence gazed worshipfully at the back of Trump's head for an hour straight. Every one in the senior staff thought that Mike Pence was a Stepford Veep. It seemed obvious that he was too perfect to be genuine. His and Trump's personalities and worldviews were diametrically opposed. And yet, Pence agreed with everything Trump said or did. In real life, no one beams worshipfully at you all the time like that. If someone looked at you that way, you'd be disturbed and think about a restraining order. But Trump was not normal and he liked Pence's apparent worship of him so much that they established a weekly lunch together. Perhaps his attraction to Pence was another sign of his loneliness. No one else in his life gazed at him with such adoration, certainly not his wife anymore. (Maybe Ivanka?)

Critics praised Donald for being "presidential" in his delivery of the speech, which was the objective. Some also noticed that he read off the teleprompters *very . . . very . . . slowly*. I knew from *The Apprentice* days that Donald is not a big reader. While working with him side by side on my own briefings, I'd come to understand that he read at an eighth- or ninth-grade level. That's fine for some, but for the leader of the free world? We went from Barack Obama, a scholar, an academic, to Donald Trump, who was just this side of functionally literate.

Donald is very street-smart and is talented at making quick adjustments. His adaptability has been a skill that benefited him as a businessman. But for the job he had now, he needed to be able to read, and he struggled. I'll go on the record and say that Donald Trump has never read from beginning to end any of the major pieces of legislation, policies, or even some of these executive orders that he has signed. Senior advisers spoon-feed him five to ten bullet points about the legislation and forgo any discussion of the complexities. To this day, his team pushes through Trump's EOs and bills, and Donald has only a surface-level understanding of the content he's signing into law.

When Donald once said he wanted to have an IQ-test competition with Rex Tillerson, I thought, *Oh no, you don't want to do that.* I know people will point to his wealth and say, "Well, how can you say he can barely read, if he's such a great businessman?" Donald has always relied on his charisma, his street smarts, and trusted advisers to tell him what was in the paperwork.

Everyone at the highest levels of the White House knows that he struggles with large documents or complex briefings. They make excuses for his faults and justify their own complicity, as loyal cult followers do. They believe he is the messenger, not the writer (or reader) of the message. Trump's charisma is all that matters. He has an ability to convince you that he's right, and that everything is going to be fine. You choose to believe because the alternative is terrifying, that he's not equipped with the basic skills to make crucial decisions that will impact the lives of millions of Americans and billions of people around the world.

Day forty-one, I was asked to fall on the sword this time and issue a statement that I'd been the one who insisted Kellyanne take the barefoot photo, and that the offensive image—considered disrespectful to the college presidents in the room—was actually somehow my fault. Not that it made any difference. The backlash was swift and severe. The students at HBCUs were furious that their presidents had allowed themselves to be used for a photo op by a racist. At Howard University, my alma mater, students spray-painted on a campus sidewalk, "Welcome to the Trump Plantation. Overseer: [President] Wayne A. I. Frederick." Some of the attendees of what I'd hoped would be a bridge-building event immediately stopped talking to me and told the press they'd been forced into the Oval.

On day forty-two, March 2, Jeff Sessions, the not-so-loyal follower, recused himself from the Department of Justice's investigation into the administration's involvement with Russia during the campaign. Trump was furious! That set off a vitriolic Benjamin Button rant for days.

"How low has President Obama gone to tapp [sic] *my phones during the very sacred election process. This is Nixon/ Watergate. Bad (or sick) guy!"* Trump tweet, March 4, 2017, 4:02 a.m.

On day forty-three, paranoia had set in in the Oval Office. Every day, when I'd get the daily tweet alert, I'd think, *Does he even realize he sent it?* Because of his poor impulse control, he never paused to evaluate or consider the consequences on a global scale of sending a tweet. The Donald Trump of 2005 would have sought counsel and advice. He wrote in *The Art of the Deal* about the good of consulting experts before he made a decision. Back then, he could process complex information, differences of opinion, and weigh the consequences. The Donald Trump of 2017 just went with his gut, based on a predawn call or on something he saw on TV or read online.

He tweeted, and we scrambled to prepare to explain it to the press in the famous James S. Brady briefing room. I was a fixture there. In the beginning, it was exciting sitting in that historic room watching the back and forth between the press corps and the press secretary. But over time, the excitement dimmed.

At first, Sean Spicer's press briefings were Must See TV, and the president directed them from the Oval like he was producing an episode of *The Apprentice*. We'd start the day very early with a morning huddle in Sean's office. Then Sean, Hope, Kellyanne, and I would dash to Reince's for a senior staff meeting. Sometimes, we'd have all-comms meetings in the Roosevelt Room after that. All of these meetings were devoted to finding data to support Trump's tweets and comments and getting the story straight to prep Sean at *another* meeting at 11:30 before his press briefing. Each departmental comms director would have to submit possible questions on the issues of the day that might be asked by the press corps. As the comms director for OPL, I had issues nearly every day, related to race, veterans, women, or African Americans. I learned to work very closely with Adam Kennedy, the person charged with putting the briefing book together.

Once the top issues were selected, we would drill Sean on the questions, pretending to be particular reporters. Very often, we would have to submit the questions and responses to counsel to see what could legally be addressed and how it could or should be worded. On other occasions, Sean would go directly to the Oval Office and ask Trump how he wanted Sean to address an issue. Sean had difficulty pronouncing certain words, so we would have to go through each one phonetically with him. He also stuttered a lot when he got really nervous, which could make him appear to be lying when he was not. He was just nervous.

Trump didn't help calm him down. He was, as usual, highly critical and mocking, to Sean's face and behind his back. I remember watching a clip of the press briefing with the president and he said of Sean, "He looks like a spokesman from Men's Warehouse. Cheap and tacky."

Walking into the briefing was like coming through the tunnel of a visiting team's field, with the lights, the cameras, the microphones, and the knowledge that people were watching from all around the world. Every single word, gesture, and statement would be dissected and analyzed in the twenty-four-hour news cycle ad nauseum.

All this effort to respond to and support a disastrous tweet was often a waste of time. While we were scrambling to manage the fallout of one tweet, Trump would tweet a reversal without telling anyone about it beforehand. The public would know about it at the same time we did, and we were completely exposed.

A friend of mine said, "You have to be the guardrails for the Trump train, trying to make sure the recklessly speeding train does not jump the tracks." The thing about guardrails: no matter how sturdy they are, they still get banged up.

Melania came down from New York to host her first White House event, an invite-only luncheon for International Women's Day on March 8. I received my invite, along with Ivanka, Maine Senator Susan Collins, Betsy DeVos, and Karen Pence and her daughter Charlotte. The event was in the beautifully decorated State Dining Room, with Melania giving an impassioned speech about equality and the atrocious treatment of women around the world.

I kept one eye on Melania throughout the event. It was always a challenge to read her moods with her permanent wall up. Melania and Ivanka seemed to be getting along well. Like most stepmother/ stepdaughter relationships, theirs had their ups and downs, but for the most part, the women accepted each other.

Throughout the lunch, Melania seemed to be in good spirits— until two men crashed the ladies-only event.

Donald and Mike Pence appeared. Donald greeted Melania, but it was a chilly reception, if they touched or kissed at all, it seemed perfunctory. She kept her distance from him for the few minutes he was at the event. I noticed that, while he spoke briefly to the room, she stared at him with a rictus half-smile and flashing eyes, like she could barely stand his being at her event and couldn't wait for him to leave.

I'd been watching Melania watch Donald for years. Before he won the presidency, she always wore a placid mask. She had no power to change his behavior, so she appeared to tolerate it. As a protective barrier, Melania erected a wall of indifference between herself and any curious onlookers. During the campaign, Melania's wall stayed in place, because she was rarely seen with her husband or in public at all. The media spotlight couldn't find her.

That all changed when Trump won the election. Now, the media spotlight caught her every moment. On inauguration day, Trump embarrassed her by not waiting for her when they got out of their limo at the White House to greet Barack and Michelle Obama, leaving her to climb the steps unescorted, a stinging contrast to other presidential couples who traditionally make this walk together. Later, during the inauguration ceremony, a video caught her smiling at Trump, and then, as soon as he turned his back, the smile melted into a bitter scowl. At the inaugural ball that night, when the couple danced awkwardly, Melania seemed, to all the world, to respond to her husband's touch with revulsion. The hashtag FreeMelania was the result.

It's possible that her decision to stay in New York until Barron finished the school year before moving to the White House was a result of her discomfort with losing her privacy and how the cracks in their twelve-year (at the time) marriage were being pried open by the media.

But, what she was coming to realize, in my opinion, beginning with her International Women's Day event by not bothering to mask her irritation with her husband, was that the glare of the spotlight could have its advantages. Being First Lady allowed Melania to find her "voice," albeit, not with actual words. She would never be comfortable speaking in public again, not after the RNC convention humiliation. She *could* use her facial expressions, her body language, and her style to make statements, however, and gain a measure of power and control in her marriage. I was curious to see how this change in Melania—small to some, seismic from my perspective— would unfold.

On day fifty-one, *Saturday Night Live* skewered Ivanka Trump with expert precision in an advertising parody with Scarlett Johansson as Ivanka selling a fragrance called Complicit. At the senior staff meeting, Ivanka couldn't stop bemoaning it, how offensive it was, how ridiculous it was. We'd *all* been subject to *SNL* attacks. I've been characterized by three different performers, Maya Rudolph, Sasheer Zamata, and Leslie Jones, during my time in Trumpworld. Bannon was portrayed as Death. Kellyanne had been skewered by Kate McKinnon. Sean Spicer was destroyed week after week by Melissa McCarthy (she would go on to win an Emmy for it). We'd all been hit, many of us in that same week's show. But Ivanka would not stop talking about being ribbed. Like her father, Ivanka was thin-skinned and could not seem to take a joke.

Donald said to Ivanka, "Honey, you're getting hit so hard! Why are you taking this? Just go back, run the company. I can't protect you here. I don't like how hard they're hitting you." He wanted Jared and Ivanka out of the White House. It hurt him when people attacked her. They were doing it to get to him, and it was working. When she was going to important meetings—like the visit to meet the pope, in Israel, or the G7—people were snickering all over the world about her. He knew it because of his voracious consumption of cable news. All the advisers knew it, but nobody had the heart to suggest an alternative. He also felt impotent in his inability to protect her. Ivanka, his treasured, beautiful daughter, and her family were being destroyed by the press, and there was nothing he could do about it.

On day sixty-three, March 23, the OPL was responsible for organizing a roundtable event with members of American Trucking Associations, truckers, and CEOs, to discuss health care. To welcome the group, Trump climbed into the cab of a semitruck and made tough-guy faces, miming driving the truck. Within *minutes*, the photos turned into hundreds of memes.

Day sixty-nine, Ivanka officially became an assistant to the president. The external outrage about nepotism and the press's questioning of her credentials aside, I was comforted by her new title. I'd been watching Donald for two months day to day in the White House with growing concern about his mental state. He seemed to be showing signs of deterioration. I chalked it up, mainly, to his being out of his comfort zone in unfamiliar settings and the immense pressure of the job, after having operated at the helm of the Trump Organization at Trump Tower for decades.

His forgetfulness and frustration were getting worse. Any time somebody new came in to brief him, he'd get angry and say, "Who's that guy? What's he want?" He would rail against the fact that he had a terrible team. He hated the staff because of the tsunami of leaks. He was paranoid and constantly irritable. I thought that Ivanka's promotion from adviser to assistant would give him a measure of emotional comfort and support that he needed. While the media decried her promotion, I welcomed it. Having known her for fourteen years and worked with her on *The Celebrity Apprentice*, I knew she was competent and sharp. I made a note to set up a meeting to share with her my concerns about her father's forgetfulness and strange behavior. I would often say, "He needs you. I'm glad you're here."

I came up with the idea to hold a Women's Empowerment Panel at the tail end of Women's History Month in March and brought it up at a senior staff meeting.

Kellyanne said, "Great idea! I'll host it!"

I was in favor of her moderating the panel and began planning it. Soon after, Reince called me into his office and said, "Drop Kellyanne from that panel. We want Pam Bondi instead." Pam Bondi was the attorney general of the state of Florida, a longtime Trump ally. I asked Reince why they wanted Bondi over Kellyanne, and he shrugged. "We just think she'd be a better choice to be mistress of ceremonies."

It was my job to break the bad news to Kellyanne. I went to her office and told her straight up, "Hey, can we talk? I just came from Reince's office and he told me they don't want you for the Women's Empowerment panel."

She opened her mouth in disbelief. "Why?"

"I don't know."

"What gives Reince the right to decide who moderates the women's panel?"

Good question. It might have to do with the ongoing tension between the RNC people (Reince, et. al.) and the Trump campaign people, of which Kellyanne was one. It might have to do with Reince or Trump owing Bondi a favor. It might be because Bondi was an elected attorney general, a fresh face around the White House.

In any case, Kellyanne was angry about it. She sulked for days about the slight. But, ever the calculating creature, she knew when to choose her battles. At the event—which Bondi hosted beautifully—Kellyanne sat in the front row, hugged all the panelists, and acted like the belle of the ball. She knew how to put on appearances, no matter how insulted and ignored she felt.

On day seventy-eight, on April 7, Neil M. Gorsuch was confirmed by the Senate to become a Supreme Court justice for life. This was a huge victory for Trump. He was, and is, obsessed with appointing judges to the bench who agree with his views. Someone told him that appointing Trump-like federal judges was the best way to extend the reach of his presidency far beyond his years in office. He might joke about getting rid of presidential term limits, but his real agenda is to ensure his legacy for decades to come in the judiciary. And if that doesn't scare you, it should. He's quietly succeeding at this.

On day seventy-nine, I got married!

Things in my professional life were hectic, but things in my personal life balanced them out. I was scheduled to get married to my handsome fiancé Reverend John Allen Newman, pastor of the Sanctuary @ Mt. Calvary Baptist Church in Jacksonville, Florida, in early April. Several things happened that caused us to move our wedding from Jacksonville to DC. First, in February, at my final sermon and going-away ceremony at my home church in Los Angeles, the Weller Street Missionary Baptist Church, where I had served as assistant pastor under the senior pastor K. W. Tulloss for nearly ten years, we were besieged by a crowd of protesters. They blocked the front entrance of the church and held signs critical of the Trump administration. Then we got a series of threatening calls stating that protesters would show up at John's church on our wedding day, too. I reported the issue to Secret Service and our personal security team, who advised me to consider moving the wedding to DC, where there was better jurisdiction if something should happen.

With less than two months until my wedding we made the decision to move it to DC. We chose a venue just blocks from the White House—the Trump International Hotel was more than willing to accommodate us due to the extraordinary circumstances.

The wedding was absolutely beautiful, with a cherry blossom theme to match the cherry blossom parade and festival held on the same day. One hundred and fifty guests enjoyed the seven-tier cake. Unfortunately, Donald was in Mar-a-Lago with the president of China and could not attend. Kellyanne and Sarah had thrown me a bridal party the day before at a restaurant across from the White House. It was truly the happiest day of my life. After the wedding and brunch at the hotel, we held an African-themed reception at the Park at Fourteenth. Our brunch the next day was held at the Four Seasons Hotel, where we continued to enjoy cherry blossom–themed confections. I was looking forward to our honeymoon and a much needed break. My husband chose Bellagio, Italy, on Lake Como, where George Clooney also has a home. The week in Italy flew by too quickly, and I had to get back to the swamp and to my responsibilities at the White House.

Day eighty-three, Donald dropped the "Mother of All Bombs"—the most powerful conventional bomb in the American arsenal—into a cave network in Afghanistan. He was obsessed with it. He fixated on it for weeks afterward, and his retelling of the story seemed to edge out his constant recounting of Election Night for a time. If anyone went to his offices, he'd regale them by saying, "I was sitting there with my chocolate cake and they came in and told me, 'We're going to do it!' and I gave the approval. I told them they could drop the 'mother of all bombs. . . .'" He kept repeating it, almost like he was reliving it with whomever was in his company. "Did you see that 'mother of all bombs' drop?" A day later, "Oh my God, that 'mother of all bombs!' Did you see it?"

I seriously began to suspect that the president was delusional or had a mental condition, that made him forget from one day to the next. Was Donald like Ronald Reagan, impaired while everyone around him ran the show and covered up for him? Was Mike Pence his Nancy Reagan, with the same vapid, adoring looks?

But that could not be true. It was Donald! The man I'd known forever and known to be canny and crafty. He was just overwhelmed, as we all were, by the awesome responsibility of leading the nation.

Day eighty-eight, on April 17, Melania Trump hosted the 139th annual White House Easter Egg Roll, which should have been an innocuous, nonpartisan event. Donald stood on the Truman Balcony with a man in a bunny suit. He looked stiff and uncomfortable and the memes were merciless, as was to be expected. Donald forgot to put his hand over his heart during the national anthem, and Melania had to give him a little nudge to remind him. The extended

Trump family appeared, all the men in navy suits and all the women in sleeveless, formfitting dresses. In a past event, Obama read *Where the Wild Things Are* to the kids. Trump was not going to read in public if he could help it, not even a children's book, so that duty fell on Melania, who entertained the kids by reading Kathie Lee Gifford's *Party Animals* on the South Lawn with dignity and grace.

But this was a controversial event, too. For starters, we couldn't give tickets away. Obama's last Easter Egg Roll drew a crowd of more than thirty-five thousand people to the White House. Trump's first drew about twenty thousand. Crowd size was always a bone of contention, especially when Trump was compared to Obama. Not only was demand for tickets way down, the people who did show up were predominantly white. The lack of diversity during the Easter Egg Roll was pretty remarkable.

The event was in conjunction with the social office, and the OPL was responsible for inviting different constituency groups. I spent a week trying to line up diverse groups to participate in the Easter Egg Roll, but no one wanted to come!

We were only a hundred days in. Any time now, things were going to settle down. We would stop defending tweets and work to achieve our goals. Once the protests died down, things would get back to normal.

Chapter Twelve

"I Think the President Is Losing It!"

W hen I look back at the volume, depth, and the breadth of the work I had, I see that I couldn't pause for a minute to evaluate what was going on outside the building. I couldn't come up for air. I kept getting tackled by my own teammates, always playing defense. I was working as hard and as fast as I could—my schedule during Black History Month alone exhausts me just writing about it—but the headlines were always asking, "What's she *doing* there?"

The resentment and jealousy came at me from inside and outside the White House. I was taking hits from every direction. The fact that Donald had pulled out my chair at the listening session back in February made headlines, with high-level anonymous sources asking, "Can you imagine the president of the United States pulling out a chair *for an aide*?" It was impossible not to hear the condescending and racist overtones. Would people have said that if he pulled out a chair for Hope Hicks?

The president was polite to me, and people criticized that gesture as an opportunity to put me in my place and to diminish me. And, it goes without saying, it *completely ignored the purpose of the event itself*—to build a bridge between the administration and the African American community. I was under such incredible scrutiny that I didn't have the luxury of commiserating with anyone about it.

In a *Daily Beast* article about the controversy of my being part of the Trump administration, Joy Reid noted that long knives were reaching for me. And, again, I was the only black woman, the only person inside the West Wing, who was fighting day in and day out to support HBCUs, for Pell Grants for minority students, protections for Muslims, reproductive rights for women. Yet, the hot take on me was that I was ambitious (horrors), opportunistic (the shame!), vengeful, assertive, demanding—the very qualities that helped most cabinet members and senior advisers secure their position.

Perhaps I should have just groveled gratefully.

AT THE END of April, Kellyanne and I were invited to the NRA Annual Meeting in Atlanta. She was asked to be the keynote speaker at the Women's Leadership Forum for female members. If a Republican White House official is summoned to attend an NRA convention, there is no question that you had to go. Seventy-seven percent of the gun-owning members of the five-million-strong organization were Republicans.

Although I was fascinated by the intensity of the women gun lovers, I was even more riveted by Kellyanne's performance, praising Jeff Sessions's law-and-order approach to every problem and Interior Secretary Ryan Zinke's reversal of a ban on lead ammunition in national lands. I had no idea what her position was before this event, but at that panel, she was outgunning all the other women in the room with her passionate Second Amendment zeal. Kellyanne was a chameleon, and she could change her camouflage depending on which candidate she supported or which room she was in.

Trump spoke at the main event, and recounted his election night victory, as always, and promised the crowd that as long as he was president, the NRA had a friend in the White House. As he came off stage, he said to me, "Great energy, right? Great show!" We next motorcaded to a fund-raiser less than a mile away. As White House staffers, it would have been improper for Kellyanne and me to attend the fund-raiser, so we were locked in a room for propriety's sake, and had a quick meal there.

We flew back with the President on Air Force One, my first time. It was thrilling to be on the plane, even for the less than two-hour flight. I went around taking pictures of the famous conference room and the president's Oval office.

The president and I talked about guns on that flight, and I learned that he owned a .45 caliber Heckler & Koch pistol and a .38 caliber Smith & Wesson revolver. During one of the GOP primary debates, I recalled that Trump had said, "I do carry on occasion, sometimes a lot. I like to be unpredictable." I felt a bit of a chill, putting that together with his famous claim at an Iowa rally in January 2016, "I could stand in the middle of Fifth Avenue and shoot somebody and I wouldn't lose any voters, okay?" That was certainly true of the folks I met at the NRA meeting.

Also on that flight, I spoke at length for the first time with Dr. Ronny Jackson, Trump's physician who also oversaw the White House medical program. He showed me Air Force One's mini surgical suite where open-heart surgery could be performed and said, "Come on in, I'll check your vitals."

Dr. Jackson served a function similar to concierge doctors in Hollywood. I'd seen this during my time in LA—celebrities paid a huge premium to have a doctor on call who would write them any prescription they wanted. Throughout my time in the White House, as a part of a little known program called the executive medical program, the cabinet and all APs, could get prescriptions for any ailment. They would give out anything, right from the bottle, no prescription needed. Say your back was hurting. You'd go in and complain, and walk out with a month's supply of powerful pain medication. The logic behind the free flow of meds was that the cabinet and APs had to keep ticking. We couldn't have insomnia or fatigue or be bothered by back pain. All we had to do was ask, and we would receive whatever pill we wanted.

On May 5, the head usher of the White House, Angella Reid, the first woman and second African American to hold that position was fired. Although Reid was a carryover from Obama, having held the job since 2011, it was not considered a political position and it was unusual for an incoming president to fire an usher.

I was upset because it meant one less black woman in the building, less than two months after Trump fired Shermichael Singleton, Ben Carson's senior adviser at HUD, because of an article he'd written for *The Hill* website that was critical of Trump. I made a point of asking everyone in the senior staff about Reid's firing.

"We can't keep getting rid of black people for flimsy reasons," I told a number of people. As comms director for OPL, "I need to explain why this woman was let go."

The official line: "We don't discuss personnel matters."

The unofficial line? That she wasn't very well liked and, allegedly, Trump didn't approve of her handling of his tanning bed. I'd heard he was unhappy with her efforts to procure the bed, to bring it into the East Wing securely, to find a discreet place for it, and to set it up properly. Also, apparently, Reid just hated him and didn't hide her feelings about it.

AS THE WHOLE world is well aware, the Trump presidency in May 2017 was defined by what we on the inside summed up with one phrase: *the Russian Concussion.*

On May 9, Donald fired James Comey, the director of the FBI. The public reason was that he disapproved of Comey's handling of the Hillary Clinton email investigation. Trump's famous letter to Comey included this extraordinary sentence: "While I greatly appreciate you informing me, on three separate occasions, that I am not under investigation, I nonetheless concur with the judgment of the Department of Justice that you are not able to effectively lead the bureau."

Of course, the firing was all about Comey's rejection of Trump's loyalty demand. Trump had been talking about firing Comey for weeks, but I never thought he'd go through with it.

During one of my visits he asked, "Hey, Omarosa, what do you think about Comey? I had to let him go, right? He couldn't be trusted; he was not loyal."

I appeased him by saying, "Hey, you did what you had to do."

No one—and I do mean *not a single person* in the White House—agreed with his decision. But they didn't dare tell him that. He was so all over the place at that point; anything could trigger fits of rage, and you did not want to be on the receiving end of one of those. He could get very worked up about the leaks. He wasn't happy about the staff; Ivanka and Jared were urging him to get rid of Reince and Sean. Others were bombarding him with issues he needed to deal with.

The comms team briefings on the Comey firing are incredible documents in the art of "alternative facts." The talking points will sound familiar to any news junkies, because you have heard them repeated on Fox News and by Trump spokespeople verbatim for months. For example, "Director Comey has lost the confidence and respect of the FBI rank and file" and "President Trump concluded that the only way to restore confidence in the FBI—the crown jewel of American law enforcement—was to end Director Comey's tenure." As the month went by, Donald changed public opinion of the "crown jewel of American law enforcement" quite a bit.

Hope Hicks was in charge of all the president's interviews, including the ones conducted by Lester Holt for a prime-time NBC special about the Comey firing on May 11. She and counsel prepared him to deny any collusion with Russia. It was the wisest strategy, because he could remember it. Donald thought he would get away with just saying, "There's no collusion. There's no collusion. There's no Russia. There's no Russia," that that would be enough to convince the American people that there wasn't. As time went on, his relationship with Russia would be revealed like an onion, one layer at a time.

For the Lester Holt interview, I watched it on a small TV in the upper pressroom (the lower pressroom was built on top of the old swimming pool and turned into the briefing room) by the press secretary's office. Throughout this erratic and contradictory interview, I kept thinking, *Oh no! Oh no! This is bad!*

Donald rambled. He spoke gibberish. He contradicted himself from one sentence to the next. Hope had gone over the briefing with him a dozen times, hitting the key point that he had fired Comey based on the recommendation of the DOJ, which the vice president and other surrogates had been reinforcing for days. He'd already slipped up when he'd told the Russian ambassador in the Oval Office that he'd fired Comey for doing a poor job. And then, with Lester Holt, he changed the talking point again, saying, "I decided to fire him."

Holt tried to help him. He said, "In your letter, you said that you accepted [the DOJ's] recommendation."

"But regardless of recommendation, I was going to fire Comey," said Donald. "In fact, *when I decided to just do it*, I said to myself, I said, 'You know, this Russia thing with Trump and Russia is a made-up story. It's an excuse by the Democrats for having lost an election that they should have won.'"

It was all his critics needed as proof that Trump had lied. I'd known Donald to exaggerate and boast. He'd told white lies and lies of omission, ignorance, or misunderstanding. He'd bent the truth purposefully to make himself look good. But this was different. It was like he didn't know what the truth was or couldn't remember what he'd previously stated as truth. The outrage was immediate.

While watching that interview, I realized that something real and serious was going on in Donald's brain. His mental decline could not be denied. Many in the White House didn't notice it as keenly as I did because I knew him way back when. They thought Trump was being Trump, off the cuff. But I knew something wasn't right.

But what could I do? Declare a state of mental emergency for Donald J. Trump? Should I report this insight to . . . to whom exactly? The White House doctor Ronny Jackson, whose job depended on Trump's approval of him, a man who would go on to declare an obviously obese, sleep-deprived man in excellent health? To the chief of staff, a man I didn't trust or respect? To Don Jr., Ivanka, or Eric, who had to be seeing what I saw, and had done nothing? To Melania? She was completely trapped herself. And what would I say? "I'm not a doctor, but I think the president is losing it?"

I texted Lara and said, "Hey, can we catch up? Let me know when you're in the building." When she came by in a week or so, I said, "I'm really concerned about him."

She said, "I know. The whole situation is really messed-up."

"No, I mean his language is incoherent. This is more than just a—"

"No," she said, like she didn't want to hear it.

"I think he needs to get checked."

She shook her head and said, "It's fine."

Even having the conversation with a family member was a risk. If news got out that I thought the president was delusional or mentally impaired, the impact on national and global stability could be cataclysmic. I would eventually talk to several high-level people in the White House about my concerns, and they all shut me down quickly and decisively, with warnings.

I was operating out of concern for a friend, but the friend in question was the president of the United States. And, as of May 17, that friend and his campaign and administration were under investigation by special investigator Robert Mueller for collusion with the Russians, an investigation that was spurred, to a large degree, by Trump's contradictions about the firing of James Comey.

In mid-May, Mika Brzezinski made a shocking claim about Kellyanne Conway on *Morning Joe*. "This is a woman, by the way, who came on our show during the campaign and would shill for Trump in extensive fashion, and then she would get off the air, the camera would be turned off, the microphone would be taken off, and she would say, 'Blech. I need to take a shower!' Because she disliked her candidate so much," said Mika.

Joe followed that up by saying Kellyanne described the campaign as her "summer vacay," meaning, she'd taken the job to finance a vacation to Europe. "[She said] 'I'm just doing this for the money. I'll be off this soon,'" claimed Joe.

I'd marveled at the speed with which Kellyanne's allegiance changed during the campaign. While working for the Cruz super PAC, she criticized Trump daily and called his integrity and character into question. And then, when she changed camps, she was gung-ho for him. Any sane person would look at that 180 and naturally assume she had her own reasons for taking the job, and that it had nothing to do with Trump's beliefs and vision for the nation.

The claims on *Morning Joe* fit the calculated swamp monster I took Conway for.

In our daily senior staff meetings at the White House, she agreed with whatever Trump said. Although the president never wanted anyone to disagree with him, I believe Kellyanne's "yessing" turned into white noise, a sound that didn't register on his brain.

I remember, back during the campaign, flying on Trump Force One with her, Donald, Jared and David Bossie, between events. The guys were having a heated debate about some issue or another. Kellyanne kept trying to contribute to the conversation.

From her seat across the aisle, she said, "Guys, listen . . . Well, I think . . . No, hey, what about . . ."

The men completely ignored her.

She said, "No one is listening to me!"

Not to say that the men weren't rude in how they ignored her or that she didn't have a relevant point to make, but it seemed to me that she had overestimated her status on the campaign. It was possible that she was appointed to that role for the optics. Trump had a woman problem. Lo and behold, a woman was put "in charge" of the campaign.

In another part of Trumpworld, Michael Cohen tweeted a photo of his daughter Samantha in a black bra and black tights, and captioned it, "So proud of my Ivy League daughter . . . brains and beauty channeling her Edie Sedgwick." The Twitterverse cringed *en masse* and accused Michael of following in Trump's footsteps by boasting creepily about how hot and sexy his daughter was. He responded to one critic with classic pitbull style, and said, "Beauty and brains you a-hole!" To another who wrote Cohen was posting "spank-bank material of his own daughter," he replied, "Jealous?"

I knew Samantha well. She'd been doing an internship in Melania's office, and Michael came to me and said, "They have her cutting newspaper clips all day long. Can she come to your office to finish her internship? She needs to use her brilliant brain!" I put her to work rebranding Michelle Obama's Let Girls Learn program. She did a wonderful job with her report and even presented her project to the staff at the Peace Corps. Cohen was a proud dad and just as proud of her smarts as her looks. The aggressive defense of his tweet was wrapped up in his love for her.

Also in May, Mike Pence quietly formed a PAC, the Great America Committee, run by campaign strategist Nick Ayers. It is generally unheard of for the VP of a first-term president to start a PAC. Ayers said its purpose was to support other GOP candidates, to pay for Pence's travel and other bills. Around this same time, many people were saying that Trump would soon be impeached and that President Pence had a nice ring to it. Ayers had been a Pence person for a while already. In good time, he'd become Pence's chief of staff in the White House, and Corey Lewandowski would take over the PAC.

My suspicions about Pence only increased when I learned about his PAC. Donald gave him unprecedented access and he happily accepted Pence's fawning praise and dreamy glances. If Donald wasn't careful, his second might try to stab him in the back. While in New York, I set up a meeting with Mike's nephew John Pence at the campaign office in Trump Tower. I told him of my concern about the PAC. He assured me that it was shut down and was not as nefarious as the press made it out to be.

On May 22, Donald and Melania flew on Air Force One to Tel Aviv, Israel, landing at Ben Gurion Airport where Prime Minister Benjamin Netanyahu and his wife Sara greeted their counterparts with fanfare and a red carpet laid out for the Americans on the tarmac. As usual, Donald walked ahead of Melania down the plane steps—a habit of his that the media and Twitter found rude, chauvinistic, or just mindless. After a few words were spoken to the small crowd, the two couples continued down the red carpet to waiting limos. Donald walked ahead, and then, he reached back to take Melania's hand. She swatted his hand away with a flick of her wrist and walked elegantly on.

I saw the coverage from my office in the EEOB, and watched the "hand slap" on four channels simultaneously, in super close up.

The very next day, the first couple flew to Rome, and Melania avoided hand-to-hand contact with Donald again, in full view of the waiting press spray. They stood at the top of Air Force One's staircase and waved. Then Donald tried to take her hand, and she quickly moved to brush hair out of her face to avoid him.

It was simply not possible that Melania was unaware of the tremendous reaction the world would have to these small gestures. I believe that something was going on with the two of them privately— one can only surmise that it was about the many allegations of his

sexual misconduct during their marriage, or her upcoming reloca-
tion to the White House. Unlike the past, when she had no recourse
or influence, she no longer had to accept her powerlessness. I believe
that by avoiding Donald's clasp in public, Melania was grasping the
full extent of her new power. At any time, if she so desired, she could
humiliate him in public with small, ambiguous gestures, just as he'd
openly humiliated her with his affairs and lascivious behavior for
years. And there was nothing anyone could do to stop her.

When she moved into the White House in mid-June, people on
the staff hoped that she'd be a calming influence on him, but I didn't
see how that could be possible. Their relationship did not appear to
be nurturing or intimate; it was understood long before she moved
to DC from New York that she would have a separate bedroom in
the residence, just as she had a separate bedroom at Trump Tower.

To close out the month, Trump went to a NATO summit in
Brussels, and shoved Duško Marković, the prime minister of Mon-
tenegro, out of the way so he would be standing in the center of the
group photo. Of course, he was called out for the move. I asked him,
"You came off a little aggressive. Why did you do that?"

He said, "Oh, he's just a whiny punk bitch."

We'd all been under intense stress for what felt like forever.
Around this time, I remember a handful of senior advisers were in
the Oval, and Kellyanne excused herself. As soon as she was out of
the room, Trump waved his hand under his eyes, and said, "This
place is taking a real toll on Kellyanne," meaning she wasn't looking
good. This was another classic Trump move, to insult or criticize
someone's appearance or manner as soon as they left the room.

• • •

AS I MENTIONED, Donald always took it as a personal betrayal when former friends became his enemies. He'd asked me at one point to tell him who I thought the leakers were, and I didn't miss a beat and started with, "Katie Walsh."

Donald said, "I didn't want her anyway. Reincey brought all these people in from the RNC. All disloyal, ungrateful people."

Donald set out to clean house, and he wanted to know who was loyal and who he couldn't trust. His level of paranoia was at an all-time high.

Joe Scarborough and Mika Brzezinski were people he considered to be backstabbers. When they spoke harshly of him on MSNBC's *Morning Joe*, he would often rail, "No loyalty! None!" at the screen.

"I heard poorly rated @MorningJoe speaks badly of me (don't watch anymore). Then how come low I.Q. Crazy Mika, along with Psycho Joe, came . .

. . . to Mar-a-Lago 3 nights in a row around New Year's Eve, and insisted on joining me. She was bleeding badly from a face-lift. I said no!"

Trump tweets, June 29, 2017, 5:52 and 5:58 am

He *did* watch the show, and was incensed by it. When he tweeted about Psycho Joe and low IQ Crazy Mika's face-lift, an offensive, sexist tweet to be sure, the president was not taken to task for it by his advisers.

But I was.

I was blamed for Trump's writing those tweets. News accounts accused me of setting him off, but that was just not the case. Early on, during the first one hundred days, he frequently called me and others to "pull up an article" or research and print out something he saw on cable news. He would ask for different news clippings, too. His morning press-briefing folders, prepared by Spicer and his staff, only contained positive news items about Trump. They thought that if he read just the glowing reviews, he wouldn't tweet something crazy. The strategy made no sense, since he watched TV continuously. Unless he was in a meeting or at an event, he was sitting in his private dining room off the Oval Office, in front of a wall of cable news TV with his ubiquitous Diet Coke and whatever snacks he'd summoned from the kitchen via the button on his desk.

Donald J. Trump was the president of the United States. If he asked me to print out an article and give it to him, I did it. I was not his nanny or his nurse. Nor was I his secretary or his executive assistant. He knew he could ask those people for paper. But he didn't want others to know what he was reading or researching, especially if it was gossip. Any paper that goes to the president must pass first to staff secretary Rob Porter or his executive assistant, per the Presidential Records Act, so anything he touched would be documented and archived. In early 2018, some former White House clerical staff described the laborious process of taking shreds of paper Trump tore up—an old habit from his Trump Organization days—and scotch-taping them back together to uphold the Records Act. I guess they didn't know that he would pocket sensitive notes or that once, after a meeting in the Oval with Michael Cohen, I saw him put a note in his mouth. Since Trump was ever the germaphobe, I was shocked he appeared to be chewing and swallowing the paper. It must have been something very, very sensitive.

The Mika and Joe tweets were a bridge too far for the leakers, a.k.a. "multiple sources inside the White House." They worked the phones and said that it was common practice for certain aides to sneak into the Oval and give the president intentionally distracting and infuriating coverage. I was pointed out as the "worst offender."

If that were true, it was because Donald constantly called me directly, or he sent someone to find me and tell me, "The president asked for you to stop over; he wants to ask you something." I would drop whatever I was doing and do as the president asked.

I rarely went through the front entrance that you see on *The West Wing*, with the Marines out front opening the door. There were always camera crews or press monitoring the visitors in and out of the entrance.

I took the back way, a route most are unaware of. My usual route was a walk from the EEOB, through a corridor, up a flight of stairs to another corridor, make a right by the vice president's office, walk straight past the chief of staff's office suite and his many assistants seated in the front room, around a corner by Jared's and Bannon's offices and their front rooms of assistants, to the entrance to Donald's dining room, which connected to the Oval through a private study. I would leave the document on the counter in the small kitchen nook, and then I would dash back to my office.

Unlike Reince and Sean, who tried to spoon-feed him only positive news, I didn't filter the good from the bad. He trusted me to be truthful, not to try to manipulate him (remember how he had freaked out about that Bannon "the Great Manipulator" *Time* cover?). Often, he'd reflect to me privately, nostalgically, about the good old days of the small campaign, surrounded by his loyal team— Corey, Hope, Dan, Keith—when anyone could pop into his office on the twenty-sixth floor of Trump Tower. In the White House, tucked away in his private quarters, with guards every five feet, a huge staff of swamp monsters, leakers, people collecting his trash for an archive, he felt paranoid and distrustful.

I should have protected myself. But there are no manuals about how to deal with your mentor of nearly fifteen years who becomes the president of the United States. I should have set boundaries, gone through the proper channels. But I believed that Donald would protect me if anything came up. If you made it into his inner circle, he would move heaven and earth to protect you. But there came a point when Donald could not protect me, or himself for that matter.

MY TOP LINE item for the Trump budget was the reinstatement of year-round Pell Grants. Barack Obama's administration had reduced the benefit to just the fall and spring semesters; during the summer, students were on their own. I went to Mick Mulvaney, the director of the Office of Management and Budget, and launched a campaign to get year-round Pell grants reinstated at the cost of $2 billion a year. When the budget was finalized, my request was granted. I'd successfully lobbied for and secured year-round benefits that could help about a million students nationwide, including students at all

101 HBCUs. I am very proud of that. During the same period, I was trying to get a line item budget increase for HBCUs, which had gotten level funding from the previous year. No cuts, no increases.

When Betsy DeVos, the secretary of education, decided to make her first visit to a college, she chose my alma mater Howard University. I was happy to accompany her to the campus, where I'd gotten my master's and worked on my doctorate, to meet with the HU president Wayne Fredrick. I was eager to show her around the "mecca."

After the meeting news spread on campus, students protested. They did not want her there, and called for the firing of the Howard president for even meeting with her. Earlier in the year, she'd visited Jefferson Middle School Academy in DC, and was met with protesters who blocked the door briefly. No one wanted DeVos to speak at their school, and her visits were written off as photo ops only.

But I was on a mission for increased education funding for HBCUs and wasn't ready to give up on involving the secretary of education in the pursuit. On May 10, DeVos and I went to the graduation ceremony at Bethune-Cookman University, a historically black college in Daytona Beach, Florida.

Betsy got up onstage to give her speech and was immediately, loudly booed by the entire audience. Graduating students and their families stood up and turned their backs on her. I was seated onstage watching this travesty unfold. When the booing started, she should have wrapped it up, but she went on and on for twenty minutes, talking over the booing. I was thinking, *It's not about you! Abandon your full speech! Adjust, woman!*

I love HBCUs so much, and to be on a stage with her to see the entire auditorium of students and parents booing her, in effect, booing Trump and the administration, was painful to experience.

I asked her later on how she felt about what happened. She said, "I did great!"

I must have looked stunned.

She said, "They don't get it. They don't have the capacity to understand what we're trying to accomplish." Meaning, all those black students were too stupid to understand her agenda.

I said, "Oh, no, Madam Secretary. They get it. They get it, and they aren't happy about you or your goals."

She'd issued a statement, saying that HBCUs were a form of school choice. "No, Secretary DeVos," I explained, "it was *not* always a choice to go to black colleges. Black students had to attend black colleges because most PWIs [predominately white institutions] did not accept black students as recently as the 1960s."

Her plan, in a nutshell, is to replace public education with for-profit schools. She believes it would be better for students, but the truth is, it's about profit. She's so fixated on *her* agenda, she can't give any consideration to building our public schools, providing financing for them, particularly their infrastructure needs. Schools are shutting down in depressed neighborhoods all over the country to be replaced with for-profit schools, eliminating neighborhood cultural centers, forcing kids to travel great distances, with little proof that only charter schools provide a better education. I think that it should be a parental choice. The parents should choose what is best for their children. Not Betsy DeVos.

The next day, in Florida, she was hosting an event at the Amway Center, and I was instructed to be in the hotel lobby at 8:00. I arrived at 7:52, but Betsy and her motorcade were nowhere to be found. I texted her staff repeatedly to see where everyone had gone. I got a call, and she said, "Sorry, we had to leave early. Change of plans. Take an Uber."

I did take an Uber—straight to the airport.

I was through.

We'd been booed by the entire auditorium. People were angry. There were protesters. I'd been getting death threats daily. And she'd left me completely alone with no security?

There is no way she should be the secretary of education. Once I returned and told DJT about what had happened, he shook his head in disgust. He said, "She is Ditzy DeVos, what do you expect? In a very short period of time, I will get rid of her. Believe me, believe me."

She is still serving and destroying the education system in this country. The depth and breadth of her ignorance is a travesty for the children.

In each cabinet meeting, I was seated in the row near her.

I can tell you, after a year of sitting in those meetings and observing her, that she's woefully inadequate and not equipped for her job. She is just as horrible as you suspect she is. When she recently visited New York City, she went to several schools, but not a single one that was run by the city. New York has more than one million public school students, but she did not tour one public school. Not one. She does not care about your children. Be afraid. Be very, very afraid.

"Despite the constant negative press covfefe," Trump tweet,
May 31, 2017, 12:06 a.m.

The baffling tweets never stopped coming, be they about a ban on transgenders in the military, the Russia witch hunt, Crooked Hillary (still), or fake news. Internally, in my text chains with senior advisers and members of the Trump family, we would react with groans and comments like, "Oh no. Twitter fingers attacks *again*." The mysterious "covfefe" tweet was nothing but a typo, we reasoned. He'd meant to write something else and hit "send" by accident. He deleted the tweet, but by then, it was set loose on the world, and the Internet immediately pounced.

Three hours later, loving the confusion and mystery around his ham-fingered typo, he tweeted, "Who can figure out the true meaning of 'covfefe' ??? Enjoy!" at 3:09 a.m.

Now, imagine the president, in his room in the residence, with only his tanning bed for company (Melania sleeps in her own room down the hall), enjoying himself immensely with the chaos and headlines he was creating in the middle of the night about an accidentally sent tweet. He stumped the world with a typo.

It was more power than one man should have, and definitely not a man who has the soul of an anarchist.

On June 5, the travel ban, version 2.0, was voted down once again, and Donald tweeted, "The Justice Dept. should have stayed with the original Travel Ban, not the watered down, politically correct version they submitted to S.C."

George Conway, Kellyanne's husband, a Harvard- and Yale-educated partner at a white-shoe law firm in New York, replied to that tweet with one of his own: "These tweets may make some ppl feel better, but they certainly won't help OSG get 5 votes in SCOTUS, which is what actually matters. Sad."

His writing "sad" at the end was particularly zingy. It would not be the last time Conway publicly criticized his wife's boss.

Soon after, I was in the Oval with Donald and he picked up an article about George Conway's counterpunch and ranted, "Would you look at this George Conway article? F**king FLIP! Disloyal! F**king Goo-goo."

I was told later that "Goo-goo" and "FLIP," an acronym for "f**king little island people," are racial slurs for Filipinos. George Conway is half Filipino. I had no idea what he meant when he'd said those words.

BY JUNE I'D given up on Betsy DeVos, and my priority was to get congressional support for HBCUs and overall African American policy priorities by inviting the Congressional Black Caucus (CBC) to meet with the president—*again*.

The first time hadn't gone well at all. Simply arranging it was controversial. It happened back in March, not long after I'd brought the HBCU presidents to the Oval Office and seen the ensuing memes about Kellyanne Conway with her shoes off, crouched on the couch. The chairman of the Congressional Black Caucus, Congressman Cedric Richmond of Louisiana, said during a Washington Press Club Foundation dinner that March, "I really just want to know what was going on [in that photo of Kellyanne], . . . because she really looked kind of familiar in that position there." Meaning, on her knees. He apologized in a statement a few days later.

In two weeks, Richmond and the executive board of the CBC agreed to meet with Trump, but they refused to sit on the same side of the table or be photographed with him, saying that they would not be used like those HBCU presidents had been. One hour before the meeting, Richmond's chief of staff delivered a 125-page report in a binder to a junior staffer in domestic policy called "We Have a Lot to Lose"—a reference to Trump's campaign question to black America, "What do you have to lose?" That staffer didn't pass the binder to me until ten minutes before the meeting. I had to race to log the document that was addressed to the president to the staff secretary and try to summarize the report. During that March 22 conversation—that included Mike Pence as well as the president—Cedric kept referring to the report, and I had to say, "Excuse me, just to be clear, Congressman Richmond, you just gave us that report less than an hour ago. We have not had adequate time to read it. We don't know what the contents are. What are your clear demands?"

Their last-minute submission of the report was a political maneuver designed to undermine the productivity of the meeting. Their strategy up until that point was to boycott, protest, refuse to meet with him and the team, be accusatory and aggressive. That strategy would never work with Donald Trump.

In mid-June, I sent an invitation and a follow-up letter to all forty-eight CBC members, asking for a meeting at the White House. Although individual members expressed their interest in working with the administration, the chairman declined on behalf of all of them. Cedric Richmond replied by letter: "Based on actions taken by you and your administration since [the March 22 meeting] it appears that our concerns, and your stated receptiveness to them, fell on deaf ears." He listed all the things the Trump administration had failed to do and ways its policies hurt black Americans, including the proposed cuts to Pell Grants and HBCUs, Jeff Sessions's accelerated war on drugs and the resulting mass incarceration of people of color, and the efforts to repeal and replace Obamacare. I was fighting the same battles in the White House myself; I was in agreement with the CBC and nearly all of their list of complaints. But between March 22, our first meeting, and Cedric's June 21 letter, only three months had passed. Washington moves slowly. The CBC cut us off before we'd had a chance to address their issues.

Congressman Richmond also objected to my signing my letter to him using my official title "honorable," the same title given to and used by every AP. The letter had been submitted to the White House correspondence department for approval before being sent, and they added the title. I was required to clear my letters through that department before I sent them out, per White House protocol.

I was grateful when a few people pointed out that I was attacked for using my rightful title, but when the other white assistants to the president had been addressed as 'the Honorable . . .' at a recent state dinner, no one complained. Excellent point!

The Congressional Black Caucus has not had a meeting with Donald Trump since my departure from the White House. They intend to go four to eight years without meeting with him at all. For the record, the CBC motto is "Black people have no permanent friends, no permanent enemies . . . just permanent interests." I guess that went out the window with Trump. I would later learn that President Obama also had a difficult relationship with the CBC. So I did not take it personally, even though Richmond had attacked me personally.

The president asked me, "Why do you keep trying to work with *those people*? They clearly hate me."

To my dismay, he still liked to use that phrase.

"Even if they dislike you, they represent districts with Americans who are suffering. We have to find a way to work with elected officials who may have different political agendas," I said.

He said, "But they are attacking you personally, Omarosa! Why?"

I was being attacked by the same group I was trying to fight for, as if hurting me would help to damage the president. It just didn't make sense or serve any purpose. It's sad and frustrating to think about now. I was in the right position, and when I offered my hand so we could help each other achieve our common goals, it was slapped down again and again.

THE RUSSIA INQUIRY continued to percolate all summer. On July 11, Don Jr. released the email chain about his meeting in Trump Tower with the Russian lawyer. When I saw Donald that day, I said, "I'm sorry to hear about Don."

He said, "He is such a f**kup. He screwed up again, but this time, he's screwing us all, big-time!"

On July 24, Trump spoke at the annual Boy Scouts Jamboree

in West Virginia. Despite the fact that his audience was comprised of thousands of teenagers, Trump decided to ramble on about fake news, the swamp ("Today, I said we ought to change it from the word 'swamp' to the word 'cesspool,' or perhaps to the word 'sewer'"), repealing Obamacare, a party with "the hottest people in New York," the stock market, the jobs report, the "incredible night with the maps," a.k.a., Election Day. He also told the saga of William Levitt of Levittown fame, with this snippet, "He went out and bought a big yacht, and he had a very *interesting* life. I won't go any more than that, because you're Boy Scouts, so I'm not going to tell you what he did. Should I tell you? Should I tell you? You're Boy Scouts, but you know life. You know life."

The implication was that Levitt's yacht was a WWII-era version of the Playboy Mansion. Nudge, wink. It wasn't appropriate content for the event for a few reasons, but mainly, it resounded as sexist and lascivious. Trump thought he'd done a fabulous job with that speech and was furious about the criticism of it in general and, specifically, that anecdote.

I said, "You have to be aware of whom you're talking to."

He said, "[The Scouts] are going to have to man up and grow some hair on their chests. They're not little boys. They have to man up!" He kept saying "man up!" over and over, for days.

THE OTHER DEFINING word for the Trump White House during the spring and summer of 2017 was *leaks*. Things got so bad on the comms team that Sean Spicer ambushed us in his office with a member of the counsels office. He explained that everyone on the team would have to submit their personal and government phones for inspection. He was looking for communications with a particular reporter. Spicer and the lawyer went through our phones one by one. I regret that I did not speak up. It was so clearly a violation of our privacy for them to inspect our personal devices. They told us we could not leave until the inspection was done. I didn't want to rock the boat, so I handed the phone to the White House lawyer as he swiped through my personal photos—stopping at one of my wedding photos and saying, "Congrats,"—my texts, and my emails. I felt disgusted. It was humiliating, and I felt powerless, but if I protested, everyone would think I was the leaker.

Reports have come out that allegedly many members of the senior staff were also leaking to individuals in the media. Kellyanne Conway had her list of sources. She'd been in Washington for decades, a bona fide swamp creature, and had any number of people to confide in. Bannon had his people, including, now famously, Michael Wolff. Ivanka and Jared kept open lines of communication with Joe Scarborough and Mika Brzezinski, New Yorkers who, for much of the campaign, were pro-Trump. Hope Hicks was cozy with Maggie Haberman. Even though we all suspected Ivanka was leaky, she always acted appalled about other people's leaking, especially if it was unflattering to her. Her father never suspected her, though.

The constant leaking created the mother of all hostile work environments. Everybody was paranoid about everyone else, everyone was angry with someone. Damaging leaks came at everyone daily. Trump was going nuclear daily. Different factions started warring with each other *Hunger Games*–style: Bannon versus Jared; the RNC faction of Spicer and Reince against the "original Trumpers"; the campaign people against the swamp monsters.

Trump was furious about the leaks. They set off violent mood swings and "going nuclear" outbursts. General John Kelly would report that Trump screamed at him with such violence, that he'd never been spoken to by anyone that way before. Kirstjen Nielsen, the head of Homeland Security, recently reported that he yelled at her so offensively, she contemplated quitting. Sean Spicer was Trump's personal verbal punching bag. Trump berated Reince, called him names, mocked him. It was humiliating for everyone to witness.

To protect myself and stay above the fray, I only went into meetings I absolutely had to be in. I didn't want to be exposed to certain information, because if it leaked and you were in the room, you might fall under suspicion. When people said disparaging things about Donald, even in a joking way, I would say, "Just for the record, I am going to remove myself from this conversation." It was like raising a warning flag to let them know that I didn't want to hear it and would not participate.

When they said, "I'm just joking," I would reply, "Say what you want, but I'm out of here."

Of all the senior staff, I might be among the few who was never labeled a leaker. In my capacity as spokesperson for OPL, I had to give reporters background information or quotes or context. But I never leaked. Donald Trump considered leakers to be traitors. Anyone who would violate his most sacred creed of loyalty would not be forgiven. Being disloyal meant the end—of your job and your reputation. A betrayal among his inner circle would have been far worse than what someone like Katie Walsh, Reince's deputy, did— she allegedly leaked from the very beginning, supposedly at Reince's behest, and was fired in late March 2017.

Meanwhile, Anthony Scaramucci was finally hired. He'd been chomping at the bit to get started for months. I remember soon after he joined the staff, flying with him on a trip to Ohio on Air Force One—which is a supremely cool experience—but Anthony couldn't contain himself. He walked around like he owned the place. He was cocky and arrogant . . . but oddly likable.

With Ivanka and Jared's blessing, Donald got rid of the comms director, Mike Dubke (he never liked him anyway, telling a room of people he was "irritating as hell" right after Dubke walked out), as well as Sean Spicer, "Mr. Men's Warehouse." He brought in Scar-amucci to take over. Sean was allowed to stay in the White House for several weeks, to just ramble around and use the office to find a new job. He was given the dignity of a peaceful transition—which was not afforded to me.

My personal relationship with Scaramucci took a blow on his first day, when he accused me of plotting against him to block his appointment as director of the OPL six months ago. My first thought: *He's lumping me in with the leakers; he's here to fire them; he wants to fire me.* Then I thought, *It's the paranoia. Everyone was point-ing fingers at everyone.*

I had to nip it in the bud immediately, because if you were

labeled a leaker, your days were numbered. I said, "Let's go straight to the president to discuss it." I started walking toward the Oval. After a few paces, I looked behind me and Anthony was nowhere to be seen. He knew Donald would not be happy with him picking a fight with me in his first week on the job.

To deal with hostility directed at me because of my longstanding relationship with the president (and the double whammy of being black and a woman AP)—from the press and the white men who surrounded me—I had to put on a silent mask. There were complaints about my title and my pay. "Why is she paid the same salary as the chief of staff and press secretary?" they would ask. I had to employ coping mechanisms like "shifting" and "code switching." If I had defended myself as passionately as I'd wanted to, I would be described as an "angry black woman" and be instantly discounted and accused of starting confrontations or of being hypersensitive because of my race. A white participant is given the benefit of the doubt; a black woman in the workplace never is, regardless of the circumstances.

Many of the senior white men on the White House staff spoke to me privately with open contempt that would probably shock a lot of people if they could have heard it. In public, they were cordial. But when no one else could hear? They changed their tone to demeaning and hostile. Two notable exceptions, men who treated me with kindness, dignity, and respect, were Tom Bossert, former homeland security adviser, and the president himself.

Anthony Scaramucci held his first press briefing, which I couldn't wait to attend. I sat in the staff seats against the wall next to Kellyanne, and watched with baited breath for something exciting to happen. I knew him to be a smooth talker but to also go off script, just like his idol, the president.

"I'm going to be very brief . . ." he said and we were off.

As soon as he began talking, I fixated on his hands. The gestures reminded me of someone . . . it took a beat before I realized they were a match to Trump's, down to the "cobra" pointed finger and the starfish finger flail. He thanked Sean Spicer and said, "I hope he goes on to make a tremendous amount of money." He described Reince and himself to be "like brothers" who liked to rough each other up once in a while. Other golden nuggets: The president had some of the best political instincts "in the world and perhaps in history," was "the most competitive person" he'd ever met, could throw "a dead spiral through a tire," and had no problem "hitting foul shots and swishing them." I almost burst out laughing. It was just so inappropriate, so cult of personality worshipful.

After a half an hour, Sarah tried to give him the wrap it up signal. He was only supposed to talk for seven minutes. He said, "I'm feeling the hook here, is it okay if I answer a few more questions?" He was having an absolute ball out there. He was not going to give up the podium until he was ready.

At the end, he actually blew a kiss to the press corps!

Afterwards, he asked, "How'd I do?"

It was the most unconventional presser I'd ever witnessed, but at least he hadn't flubbed words or attacked the press like Sean. I said, "You were quite entertaining, let's see what DJT thinks!"

It would be the last press briefing he'd do in the White House.

Along with his comms directorship, Scaramucci had a second-ary job. He was apparently the hired hit man. Very low-key, Ivanka went around to the original Trumpers, the loyal soldiers, and asked the team to compile a list of suspected leakers. I'd already said my piece about Katie Walsh directly to Donald, and she'd been let go. But Ivanka wanted a new list and, once she had it, she would give it to Scaramucci, so he could fire them all. The final list that was texted to me on July 22 had ten names on it: Vanessa Morrone (Spicer's secretary), Lindsay Walters (Reince's press secretary), Janet Montesi (Dubke's assistant), Raj Shah (deputy comms director), Kelly Sadler (she of the John McCain is "dying anyway" comment; live by the leak, die by the leak), Ory Rinat (a Dubke tech person), Kate Karnes and Lara Barger (RNC digital people), Michael Short (a press aide who resigned before Anthony had a chance to fire him), and Jes-sica Ditto (a deputy director of comms). Anthony would start firing them all, after a quick rally in Ohio.

The mega MAGA rally would be on July 25 in Youngstown, Ohio, my hometown. It felt like a celebration as much as a home-coming for me. I resolved to put any disquieting thoughts about the turmoil in the White House aside and just enjoy this day.

The trip started with a fourteen-vehicle motorcade from the White House to Andrews Air Force Base with dozens of senior staff-ers and cabinet members, including Energy Secretary Rick Perry, Interior Secretary Ryan Zinke, Reince, Kellyanne, Hope, and Rob Porter in one car, Corey and David Bossie in another, Anthony Scaramucci, Sarah Huckabee Sanders, Stephen Miller, director of social media Dan Scavino, political director Bill Stepien, and many more. When we pulled up to the plane on the runway, I couldn't resist taking a few snaps with Hope and Kellyanne in our fancy outfits; I wore an electric blue dress, perfect for my mood.

It was my second ride on Air Force One, but that didn't mean it was any less thrilling. We had assigned seats for take off. Mine was next to Bill Stepien and across from a military aide. But as soon as we were wheels up, I went to the plane's conference room and grabbed the phone. If you place a call while on Air Force One, the operator, when you connect, says, "I have Omarosa Manigault Newman on Air Force One, will you accept the call . . ." I wanted to give the small joy of hearing that to my mom, my husband, and a few friends.

I wasn't in there for long before it filled up with people. Kellyanne and Ryan Zinke, Hope and Rick Perry. Corey and David Bossie and I went exploring the massive plane, and I took some photos of the plane's Oval office, the president's private quarters and his bathroom—spacious and spotless.

Even though the flight was only an hour, they served a meal, the menu printed and leather bound. (FYI: If you fly on Air Force One, you will be invoiced for the meal whether you eat it or not.) After I finished eating, I went to a small work area and placed my final calls. Then I watched our landing at Youngstown–Warren Regional Airport on TV while we were making it.

We all walked off the plane, down that famous staircase, into waiting limos to take us to the Covelli Centre to greet a capacity crowd of more than five thousand people. I felt like I was going to burst with happiness at any moment after we landed in Ohio. There

I was, a kid from the Westlake projects, flying into town on Air Force One, driving through the streets where I grew up in the presidential motorcade, to be the guest of honor in the VIP box along with Lara, Eric and Melania Trump, at a rally for the man I helped get elected. There were only good vibes in the box. Of the four elder Trump children, Eric was the easiest, always kind and pleasant to be around. I believe he was Melania's favorite.

In every photo of that day, I am beaming! When I entered the stadium and waved, the crowd of people cheered for me. My aunt Evelyn McClendon and my younger cousin Darian Rushton came to see me in the green room. I missed my family so much, but this was the only time I would get to see them. I would be back in the motorcade and on the plane with the president immediately after the rally. The local headlines heralded my triumphant return. However troubled things were in the White House, this rally was like a blessed balm. It reconnected me with a purpose and reminded me of my larger goals. The optimism seemed to be shared by everyone that day. After Melania introduced Donald, the two even kissed at the podium. In some photos the next day, it looked like she was smiling. In others, she was grimacing. I'd noticed on the plane that they kept their distance and that at the rally itself, the air between them was several degrees colder than the AC in the venue.

But nothing could have upset me that day, or distracted me from how happy I was. It was the single most thrilling event of the entire year for me. I'm not embarrassed to say that I felt lucky, and special, as well as the unique satisfaction of returning home in grand style.

And then, on July 27, the day before he was going to fire everyone on the Hit List, Scaramucci talked to Ryan Lizza from *The New Yorker*, who recorded the interview. It was all about leaks, including one that said the president was getting strategic advice from Sean Hannity. Anthony boasted about heads rolling. He called Reince a "f**king paranoid schizophrenic," and made some anatomically descriptive comments about Steve Bannon, a man who, to my knowledge, does not do yoga and is not nearly as flexible as Anthony made him out to be. When I first heard the vulgar conversation, I thought the language was not becoming of someone who was going to be taking the same oath that I had taken in front of the nation.

Reince was fired the next day—literally kicked out of the presidential motorcade at an airport. To replace him, Donald hired General John Kelly as the new chief of staff. Anthony lingered for another three days, and on July 31, ten days after he was hired, Donald called him in and said, "You have to go."

Anthony walked out, made a left by the chief of staff's office, where all the assistants sat, stepped into a little cubby-like office, and started crying. One of the assistants saw and heard the whole thing. She described it as "a girly cry."

I like to think that somewhere in the West Wing, Sean Spicer was still rambling around in the final days of his grace period, heard Anthony's high-pitched, plaintive wail, and smiled.

Chapter Thirteen

The Unraveling

"John Kelly, New Chief of Staff, Is Seen as Beacon of Discipline," *The New York Times*, July 28, 2017

The senior staff meetings will now take place in the Roosevelt Room. Effective immediately.

One of General Kelly's first acts as chief of staff was to move the daily senior staff meetings from the chief of staff's office where Reince Priebus held them to the Roosevelt Room, which would comfortably hold thirty-plus senior staff members. I always sat at the table, while most of the female senior staff members sat along the wall or on the couches.

Kelly ran his senior staff meetings like a military operation. He barked each person's name and would cut them off if they got too long winded. He was particularly short with General H. R. McMaster. He would rudely cut him off midsentence and say, "Let's pick this back up at another time." He would often lament about the press and constantly reminded us that he was there to enforce discipline and order.

General Kelly wanted total control over the West Wing. In order to achieve that, he had to divide it like a battlefield and set up perimeters. He informed all the senior staff that everyone would have to stop dropping into the Oval. If you wanted to see the president or bring guests by, you now had to submit a formal scheduling request.

I welcomed the change, as I was getting exhausted with running back and forth between the West Wing and the EEOB. If the president needed anything from now on, he would go to his chief of staff. Kelly also demanded that, if by chance, the president contacted you outside the outlined protocols, you were to come to his office and debrief him on your exchange with the president, no matter how brief or trivial the topic. Most of the APs rolled their eyes at these requests. In my mind, I realized how little Kelly understood the job he was about to undertake. He also had no idea what he was in for.

When the first 5:00 a.m. call from the President came post-Kelly takeover, I told Donald that he had to curtail his communications with everyone, especially by cell phone. He asked why. I told him that Kelly wanted everything to go through official channels. And I didn't disagree. The president went back to his NYC days and said, "F**k Kelly! I will do whatever I want to do!"

I did not debrief Kelly on this conversation with the president.

I was used to talking often with Keith Schiller, whom I had known just as long as Donald. Keith confided that he was fed up with the way they were treating him. Apparently, Kelly was also trying to install boundaries between the president and his longtime body man.

I begged Keith not to leave. "If you go, DJT will really lose it."

The bright side of Kelly becoming COS: I could lobby him directly for the extension of temporary protected status (TPS) that stopped the deportation of immigrants from Haiti and other South American countries, which was set to expire.

We made a commitment to work closely with the Haitian community in particular during my visit there. This was the top priority for President Jovenel Moïse, who requested an extension of the TPS.

The new chief of staff made some dramatic and immediate changes, such as closing the door to the Oval so that President Trump could not see who was passing outside. The only way into the Oval was by passing his assistants Madeleine Westerhout, Keith Schiller, and John McEntee. This change, he reasoned, was to block pop-ins via the back entrance to Donald's dining room, and to rescind what were known as walk-in privileges to trusted advisers. Due to my Secret Service–issued "kiss pin"—so called because it allowed you to get in close proximity of the principles—I could still move freely throughout the whole complex.

Leaked reports to the press described me as Kelly's first test subject of people to keep away from the president. Ever since I'd been blamed for the Mika face-lift tweet, the prevailing opinion inside the White House was that my "dirty dossier" deliveries were the reason Donald would fly into rages and lose an entire day of productivity while in a snit.

I requested meetings with General Kelly to discuss this and other OPL concerns, but he would not give me an opportunity to meet with him. If I were put on his schedule, he canceled. From his arrival in late July until my departure in mid-December, Kelly and I spoke to each other exactly twice. The first time was in his office during a meeting where he informed me that Secretary DeVos wanted to cancel the fall HBCU conference (more on that later), and second, when he locked me in the Situation Room and threatened me with a court martial.

The idea of limiting Trump's exposure to people might have seemed wise at first. But what it actually did was cut him off from trusted friends who kept him grounded and somewhat sane. Kelly's move to isolate Trump drove him crazy; he watched even more cable news and relied on phone calls and social media—even more than before—to satisfy his deep need for positive feedback, in-person affirmation of his greatness, and an ear to vent to.

Every piece of paper that went to the president had to go through handlers first and then to Kelly to review. He couldn't prevent Donald from calling people from his private line in the residence, or from using his personal cell phone. Nor could he stop certain people whom DJT cleared to call directly through the White House switchboard. Donald sometimes called us from a nontraditional phone he borrowed from a military aide or a visitor, which was not always secure, as a reaction to Kelly's crackdown.

Kelly also sent word that APs in particular were required to brief him on any conversation that Donald and we had, per the Presidential Records Act. Failing to do so would put us in legal jeopardy, a threat meant to intimidate or dissuade us from talking to the president.

Most of our conversations at the time were of my listening to Donald rambling incoherently, speaking in random fragments, veering from thought to thought and topic to topic: the election, fake news, Clinton emails, trade, Obama tapping his phones, and all the people who'd slighted him.

Here is a snippet of one of those conversations, to the best of my recollection:

"Hey, I'm going to meet about, you know what? This guy's a good guy. China, the people, look, China is getting us. These guys are no good. But the wall, the wall." It would have been ridiculous to write a memo about each one of those conversations on substance. At the time, I was uneasy about documenting evidence of his mental impairment or decline, for all of posterity.

So Kelly limited office visits. Every document passed through him. Every phone call had to be briefed. Nothing went in or out that he didn't approve first.

Who was the president now? Kelly seemed to be setting himself up to be a Dick Cheney figure, pulling the strings, controlling the president and calling the shots.

I didn't swear an oath to serve at the pleasure of John Kelly. As miserable as things were at the White House, and outside it, I reminded myself of my commitment, and did my job to the best of my ability.

On August 11, I flew to New Orleans to speak on a panel at the National Association of Black Journalists (NABJ). The panel, moderated by Ed Gordon of Bounce TV, was called "Black and Blue: Raising Our Sons, Protecting Our Communities." I was asked to speak for the first time publicly about the murder of my father and brother and how violence had impacted my life.

I learned in coverage of the event that some panelists dropped out when they heard I was coming. Some members of the black press were not covering me objectively. About three months before the panel, I'd been invited to a luncheon for the National Action Network's annual convention in New York. After I spoke briefly about what I'd been doing to support black colleges, Al Sharpton got up and said, "You are in a very precarious position, because you represent an administration that many of us disagree with. But I would not be loyal to what I am if I did not address those issues and ask you to go back and tell them, 'Yes, they were respectful. . . . No, they would not allow me to be silenced, but they told me to tell you that we as blacks and women are, in the first 100 days, seeing a disaster in Washington, DC.'" He scolded me like a child in front of a room full of my peers at a women's luncheon. It was carried live on CNN and C-SPAN. I was disappointed with another missed opportunity to connect with the civil rights community.

I got out of there as soon as I could.

And here I was again at NABJ, right back in the lion's mouth.

Within five minutes on the panel, Ed Gordon pushed me to defend Trump about some of the inflammatory things he'd said— namely, that cops on Long Island should get "rough" with suspects who were predominantly people of color. I didn't agree with that! Not in the slightest! I stuck to my purpose, to say that I understood as well as anyone the pain of losing a family member to violence, and that I sympathized with the families of people who'd been beaten or killed by the police.

Black Lives Matter activists in the packed ballroom stood up in their seats and turned their backs. Others shouted at me and raised their fists. Some jeered and laughed as if I were a joke. This protest was different from the kind I was used to. At least Sharpton had asked me to deliver a message. Some people at the NABJ just wanted to kill the messenger. "When you have someone in the room," I said, "you don't beat the hell out of them. You inform them of what's going on in the community so they can be an advocate. You don't walk away from the table, because if you're not at the table, you're on the menu."

Gordon kept hammering at me to defend Trump. He came from behind the podium and got right up in my face. In the video posted on YouTube you can see how he looms over me, intending to be aggressive. The panel was about violence, and ironically I felt physically threatened sitting in the white leather chair on the stage. He came from behind the podium and stood over me. I tried to bring the conversation to ways to protect families, but he kept pushing me to justify Jeff Sessions's stance on immigration, for example. There was no hope of having a productive discussion, so I rose with my microphone and stood up to this bully and told him, "Don't be aggressive. Ask your question but don't lecture me . . . You can ask about the loss of my father and my brother—ask about my story. I'm not going to stand here and defend every single word or decision [of the Trump administration] . . . If you don't want to be here, don't be here, but don't disrespect the story of my father and my brother." The president of the NABJ got up to take control of the situation and ended the program. I headed for the exit.

> *"Poor @OMAROSA. Offended when asked about Trump, same day as UVA Nazi rally. She had never realized that her only relevance is as Trump's pet"*
> —Keith Olbermann tweet, August 12, 2017, 7:45 a.m.

> *"A PET? His animal? Keith! Really? These types of highly offensive inappropriate statements explain why you were dropped from TV! #FireHimGQ"*
> —My response, August 13, 2017, 4:45 a.m.

Meanwhile, in Charlottesville, Virginia, the Unite the Right rally had begun. The stated purpose was to protest the removal of the statue of Robert E. Lee, the Confederate hero, from Emancipation Park, the name of which the City Council had changed from Lee Park two months before. But that was really just an excuse to stage a full-on sheet-wearing, gun-toting, swastika-waving jamboree of white supremacists, neo-Nazis, the Ku Klux Klan, Southern militia members, and the type of people who had a Confederate flag painted on the roof of their pickup truck.

I was still in New Orleans, at a small meet-and-greet with leadership hosted by the NABJ's president. On television, we saw the images of young white men, looking furious and hateful, carrying tiki torches and chanting, "You will not replace us." "You" being any nonwhite, non-Christian person. (The chant morphed to: "Jews will not replace us," which was captured in a *VICE* documentary that went viral.)

I immediately sent a note back to the White House, asking if they were monitoring the situation. I was told that they were keeping an eye on it.

The media blamed Donald J. Trump and Stephen Bannon for the rally, citing racist rhetoric, dating back to the very first day of his campaign, that his policies and speeches gave permission to racists to crawl out from under their rocks into the light of day.

Back in the early campaign days, I went on TV and defended Donald's rhetoric, saying, "He's not racist; he's racial." I pointed out our history together the last fourteen years, and how well he'd treated me, what he'd done for me professionally, how he'd invested in my TV show and my career. Given our relationship, I couldn't believe he was a racist—but the people at this protest obviously were! The rally was attended and promoted by David Duke, white supremacist Richard Spencer, and the extremist neo-Nazi website Daily Stormer. I can find no evidence that Breitbart promoted the rally, but Bannon's news site has long been known as the foundation of the alt-right, which is how many of the Unite the Right protesters identified themselves.

The next day, I sent a message to Tom Bossert and asked, "Do you have an eye on this situation? Are you watching this?" It was a national security issue as far as I could see. Bossert and Jared were in Bedminster, New Jersey, with DJT.

When the counterprotesters—anti-fascists known as Antifa,

Black Lives Matter, church groups, socialists, and others—showed up, the situation escalated to violence, and some thirty people were injured. At about 1:45 p.m., twenty-year-old James Alex Fields Jr., a neo-Nazi from Ohio, drove into a crowd of protesters, injuring nineteen and killing Heather D. Heyer, a thirty-two-year-old paralegal.

A woman was killed on the streets in broad daylight in an American city, by a neo-Nazi. And the police in riot gear had not intervened or put a stop to this.

It was unthinkable. I called Bossert again. The protest had been raging for two days already without a comment from the president. Bossert told me that, after Fields drove into the protesters, he had gone into the room where Donald was resting at Bedminster after a round of golf and said, "Sir, you have got to wake up. This has escalated, and we have to deal with it."

While the entire nation was glued to their TVs, outraged and terrified by what they were seeing, desperate for the strong hand of leadership, the president was napping.

They discussed whether to call Governor Terry McAuliffe and offer federal assistance, but the decision was made to leave the tactical response to the local and state level and not make it a federal issue. McAuliffe did declare a state of emergency, and the Virginia State Police arrived, but the National Guard was not sent in. The White House decision on Charlottesville was to stand down and let Virginia handle it. McAuliffe praised his forces, but according to two independent evaluations, many grave errors were made by the local police. They did not intervene when protesters and counterprotesters fought on the street, and took no action to prevent the fighting. They were aware of the hostile nature of the torchlit rally but did nothing to stop it. They had no central command, which caused confusion.

As it unfolded in front of my very eyes on TV, I feared that our failed handling of the events in Charlottesville would go down as one of the bleakest stains on the Trump presidency, in terms of race relations. It defines his inability and inadequacy in dealing with the complexities of race in this country.

His first horrible mistake was to stay silent for twenty-four hours. When things go south, Trumpworld goes dark. That is their MO. Every surrogate was pulled off air. The only person to go on the Sunday news shows on August 13 was Tom Bossert. As a result, people tried to label him as an apologist for Donald, but he does not deserve that. He was the only one who had the guts to go on air and express compassion for the people who were hurting, and to discuss what was going on.

On Monday August 14, Donald issued a statement that condemned violence and said, "Racism is evil. And those who cause violence in its name are criminals and thugs, including the KKK, neo-Nazis, white supremacists, and other hate groups that are repugnant to everything we hold dear as Americans." He mentioned Heather Heyer and the two Virginia State troopers who were killed in a related helicopter crash. For many, the statement was too little, too late and didn't sound sincere.

On Tuesday, August 15, Trump was scheduled to hold a press conference at Trump Tower to announce the rollback of regulations that would be part of his infrastructure bill. I was back in

DC, watching the live press event from the White House on TV. As it was conveyed to me by someone who was there, Trump was surprised by how many press people turned up for an infrastructure discussion. He had no idea how explosive the Charlottesville situation had become over the last four days. He had not been properly briefed for the press conference, and when he got off the elevator in Trump Tower, he was faced with hundreds of press organizations from around the world.

The public fear was real and legitimate. People around the world felt deep terror at the sight of neo-Nazis beating up innocents in front of a church, Klansmen carrying torches, militia brandishing machine guns on the street in open-carry Virginia. These images conjured the worst moments in our collective consciousness about racial atrocities, our nation's shameful past dragged into the present. A dear friend of mine called me to say, "O, I'm scared for my kids and my community." I understood why she'd be afraid of white supremacists, but she said, "No, I'm scared of your boss, Trump."

I wanted to tell her not to worry, that I was there, the guardrails were in place. But, for two days, a race war had raged in the open in an American city. Until Charlottesville, I couldn't allow myself to process how bad things had become, because that would mean confronting things I'd noticed and ignored about Trump all along. My blind spot was shattered during that press conference, though. I could see with my own eyes that Trump had no idea what people were so upset about. He just did not grasp it. He was disconnected from reality.

He came down the elevator into the lobby of Trump Tower.

The doors opened, and there was a wall of press in front of him. The elevator banks were behind him. He had nowhere to go and no choice but to give his prepared talk on building regulations. He was under fire, with no means of escape, and he was irritated that this whole matter wasn't over and done with already.

After reciting his regulations speech, which was a long brag about how great his buildings were, he took questions from the press. He was asked why it'd taken him so long to condemn neo-Nazis and white supremacists. He said it was important to "take it nice and easy," and that he was waiting until he had all the information. That was BS. I knew he had all the info from Tom Bossert. He had gone dark for twenty-four hours because that is what he and Trumpworld do when faced with complicated issues or crises.

His nonverbals told the story: Trump was waving his hands aggressively, pointing his fingers with hostility. He moved like he was being attacked. A young woman was dead, and he was only thinking about his own discomfort.

He said, "How about a couple of infrastructure questions?" He had no concept of the magnitude of Charlottesville and wanted to move on to business as usual. This man did not have one ounce of empathy.

Any normal person would know that he should have been talking about what was going on from the moment the rally began. He should have instructed the National Guard to go in to establish order and better assist the local government to respond and stop the violence, not stand by and allow it to unfold. He should have calmed the fears of all the Americans who watched images that conjure up one of the darkest periods in our history, replayed by the twenty-four-hour news cycle. He should have called for a day of mourning, a day of prayer, a national symposium on race. He should have talked about the unity we desperately needed.

None of that. He wanted an infrastructure question.

When pressed, Trump mentioned Heather Heyer and said, "Her mother on Twitter thanked me for what I said." The woman's life had been destroyed, and he was bragging about a tweet? It was all about him. He had no capacity whatsoever to understand what Heather's mother was feeling. Trump's greatest character flaw is his total lack of empathy, which is itself a function of his extreme narcissism.

Trump constructs his own reality to make himself look good, even in horrible situations, and then he repeats it over and over again until his distortion becomes the only version he knows. His lies and boasts are only, always, about making him look better, e.g., "Her mother thanked me." The difference between Trump and world leaders who may be a tad bit narcissistic is that he can't function unless everything is about him. He has to be at the center of everything. If he's not in the middle of it, he'll force himself in the middle. So, it's not that a young woman died, it's that her mother liked his tweet.

While I watched, I kept thinking that the infrastructure presser should have been canceled, or they should have wrapped, or he should have been ushered away. His gestures were getting jerkier, and I could see his anger building. He was not well! He was acting impaired.

When he was asked if he had missed an opportunity to bring the country together—I yelled *YES!* at the TV—but his response was to brag about the economy. "I've created over a million jobs since I'm president. The country is booming. The stock market is setting records. We have the highest employment numbers we've ever had in the history of our country," which had nothing to do with racists driving cars into crowds of people.

When asked about senior adviser Steve Bannon, Trump said, "I like Mr. Bannon. He's a friend of mine. But Mr. Bannon came on very late. You know that. I went through seventeen senators, governors, and I won all the primaries. Mr. Bannon came on very much later than that. And I like him; he's a good man. He is not a racist, I can tell you that. He's a good person. He actually gets very unfair press in that regard." He stood there and defended Bannon, which was perceived as his apologizing for a racist. Also, he could not help but bring up the election, again, even now.

During this incredible unraveling, Trump also trashed John McCain for voting against his health care bill, called reporters fake news, pointed out that George Washington and Thomas Jefferson were slave owners, questioned the validity of removing racist symbols like Confederate statues, defended the white supremacists and neo-Nazis for having the proper permits (they didn't, actually), made a dig at Obama for not fixing race during his eight years as president, and touted that he'd brought a car factory to Wisconsin. Trump's mental decline was on full display during this press conference. I was certain everyone would see it and that it would be the headline of every paper the next day.

The most incendiary remarks were, "I think there's blame on both sides. If you look at both sides—I think there's blame on both sides. And I have no doubt about it, and you don't have any doubt about it, either. And if you reported it accurately, you would say the same. . . . You had some very bad people in that group, but you also had people that were very fine people, on both sides."

When he said those words, I could not believe that he was equivocating, not fully understanding the precarious ticking time bomb he was lobbing. I recognized by his posture and his tone that, if he'd been in private, he would have gone full DTN: "Donald Trump nuclear." He kept talking and kept digging himself into a deeper hole. Nobody protected Trump from Trump that day. When he challenged the press for not reporting "accurately," he was saying, "I'm right. You're wrong. You're all lying to make me look bad." It was a terrible example of how flawed Donald's thinking was. He was unable to see the hurt, pain, and fear his words were inflicting on the nation with his total lack of empathy.

Matt Lauer and *Today* reached out to me to come on and talk about Charlottesville. I declined the offer. I refused to defend the indefensible.

Who fell on their sword this time? On August 18, Bannon left the White House. His presence was evidence enough of Trump's racism for many people. But the only reason Bannon was there in the first place had nothing to do with ideology. Many in Trump-world suspected that it was all about money. If mega donor Rebekah Mercer insisted that Trump bring in Bannon, Kellyanne Conway, and David Bossie, Trump did it. But because Bannon's alt-right connections could have dragged down the presidency, he had to go. It worked out well for Steve. He'd felt thwarted in government and, for a while, he'd been trying to leave and return to Breitbart, where he was boss and could do and say whatever he wanted.

His exit from the White House was mutual, according to all reports. Trump tweeted, "I want to thank Steve Bannon for his service. He came to the campaign during my run against Crooked Hillary Clinton - it was great! Thanks S."

It was around this time I began to plan my own exit. After Charlottesville, I could no longer tolerate Trump's behavior. It was reprehensible. Strategically I had to find the perfect time to leave without making waves.

A few months later, after Michael Wolff's *Fire and Fury* came out and Bannon was revealed to be the author's number-one source, Trump changed his amicable tune. He made a statement on January 3, 2018, that said, "When he was fired, he not only lost his job, he lost his mind." Two days later, he tweeted, "Michael Wolff is a total loser who made up stories in order to sell this really boring and untruthful book. He used Sloppy Steve Bannon, who cried when he got fired and begged for his job. Now Sloppy Steve has been dumped like a dog by almost everyone. Too bad!"

If you leave or betray the Trump cult, you are labeled crazy and pathetic. Trump did not care that he completely contradicted himself after he'd tweeted nice things about his departed senior adviser. He changed his tone only after Bannon appeared to go against the grain. It is a pattern the White House repeats often. Lying is second nature in this administration.

Things started to settle down a little and we went a whole week scandal free, until the day of the solar eclipse. Louise Linton, the thirty-seven-year-old Scottish actress wife of Treasure Secretary Steve Mnuchin, posted a photo on Instagram of herself and her husband walking down the steps of a private government plane with the caption, "Great #daytrip to #Kentucky! #nicest #people #beautiful #countryside #rolandmouret pants #tomford sunnies #hermesscarf #valentinorockstudheels #valentino #usa."

Jenni Miller, a mother of three in Portland, Oregon, commented, "Glad we could pay for you [*sic*] little getaway. #deplorable."

And then Louise fired back: "I'm pretty sure we paid more taxes toward our day 'trip' than you did. Pretty sure the amount we sacrifice per year is a lot more than you'd be willing to sacrifice if the choice was yours. You're adorably out of touch."

Well, the entire Internet exploded, saying that Louise Linton was the one who was "out of touch." The political ramifications were that her husband was working on redoing the tax code to benefit the rich, that Trump's entire cabinet was packed with millionaires and billionaires who couldn't relate to and didn't care about the common "forgotten" men and women who'd elected him into office.

Through a mutual connection in Los Angeles, Kelly Day, Louise got in touch with me and asked me to lunch at her home in DC soon after she issued an apology to that mom in Portland. I found her to be very glamorous, very Hollywood, a far cry from the typical Washington wife.

She told me that she'd been following the advice of her publicist to tag the designers she was working with. I explained that as a representative of the US government, she was with her cabinet-member husband in front of a government plane—and she's not supposed to take gifts or use a public platform for private gain. She explained it to me in a straightforward style as a small misunderstanding and said she'd be more conscientious of "things like that" going forward. "I just don't understand how Washington works," she said sincerely.

Linton was tone-deaf but not malicious. I sympathized with her. She was being attacked by the press, and so was I, day after day. As silly as her posting was, she was suffering, and that was what I clued into during our lunch. Few people can fully understand how it feels when the whole world seems to be against you.

On August 25, Trump pardoned Arizona Sherriff Joe Arpaio, who'd been *convicted* of criminal contempt following a lawsuit against his department's racially profiling Latinos at traffic stops without cause and detaining them in concentration camp–like tent cities where Latinos were publicly humiliated, forced to labor in chain gangs, and denied basic medical care and supplies.

Trump wasn't done yet trying to convince doubters that he was definitely not a racist . . . yet bent over backward to help a man who clearly was.

For me, it was another brick in Trump's racist wall, but I was finally able to see over it. The distinction I'd made between *racial* and *racist*, with regard to Trump, was a deception I had used to convince myself. It would be a while yet before I could see the clear picture on the other side of that wall, but I was getting there.

During the campaign, I had justified his rhetoric as just political—what he resorted to in order to connect with and stir up the base. But seeing his policies and pardons, I couldn't justify his actions anymore. It hurt to see the truth about him. Imagine if you had a mentor, a friend, someone you looked up to for nearly fifteen years, someone you sacrificed a lot to stand by under fire, who suddenly revealed himself to be your worst nightmare. I didn't want to believe it. I rejected what other people said about him because they didn't know him like I did. I had to go through the pain of witnessing his racism with my own eyes, and hearing it with my own ears, many times, until I couldn't deny it any longer.

This kind of dawning does not take place in an instant. I fought it desperately, until it was impossible to do so. Part of the reason it took so long for me to come to this realization was that I don't throw around the term *racist* lightly. There is a difference between being a racist, racial, and someone who racializes. During seminary I came to read a book called *Divided by Faith*, which explains that.

But if you recognize that we live in a racialized society and label someone *racial*, you can work with that. I wanted to work with Donald to understand his broken outlook, and I believed I was teaching him about the danger of starting a cultural war, a race war, of stirring up these dark elements in our society. But when the bricks in his racist wall kept getting higher, I had to wonder if, despite everything I previously believed, he did want to start a race war. The only other explanation was that his mental state was so deteriorated that the filter between the worst impulses of his mind and his mouth was completely gone.

I wanted to leave the White House, Trumpworld, and Washington DC.

At the end of August, I was one foot out the door. I called Armstrong Williams, Ben Carson's top adviser, newspaper columnist, political commentator, conservative media and marketing empire builder, and my friend for nearly twenty years, to ask for advice.

I said to him, "That's it. Charlottesville was the last straw. I'm leaving."

Armstrong said, "It's almost September. Your HBCU conference is in three weeks. Are you going to turn your back on those students?"

The National HBCU Week Conference from September 17 to 19 was what I'd been working toward since day one. It was going to be the culmination of all my efforts, starting with pushing for the EO in the first forty days of Trump's presidency to move the HBCU office from the Department of Education back to the White House, where I could oversee it and sponsor events, like the upcoming conference. In addition to the meetings and panels of HBCU students and administrators, one hundred HBCU all-stars were visiting DC, some for the first time.

Armstrong said, "Are you really going to let down all those students? Don't let hate win. If you leave now, all those kids won't get what they need." He talked me off the ledge, but I was still ready to jump. I had to discuss it with Donald himself.

When we discussed Charlottesville, Trump was defensive and said, "Omarosa, you know what was in the report," referring to all the information about the Antifa groups who were involved in the counterprotest. There were some strident groups, but there was no moral equivalency between fascists and anti-fascists. He doesn't understand that, politically and morally, they could not be put on an equal plane.

Due to his lack of empathy and his narcissism, he did not possess the capacity to draw distinctions between angry groups of people and failed to understand what had happened in our country during that crisis. I didn't forgive him, defend him, or apologize for him. I put my head down and got to work to finalize what I needed to do for my three-day conference and hosting duties for hundreds of conference attendees.

On the last day of that long, horrible month, Secretary of the Treasury Steve Mnuchin refused to commit to the Obama-era initiative to put abolitionist Harriet Tubman on the twenty-dollar bill, replacing Andrew Jackson. His excuse was flimsy: "It's not something I'm focused on at the moment," he told CNBC. I know Trump wanted to dismantle Obama's legacy, but this, too? I quickly wrote a decision memo about the matter and gave it to Trump. While flipping through the folder, he came to the picture of Tubman, the woman who personally brought more than three hundred slaves to freedom, risking her own life every time, and said to me, "You want to put that face on the twenty-dollar bill?"

Just hold on until the conference is over, I told myself. *Just get through September, and then I'll be free.*

Chapter Fourteen

The Fall

My autumn months in the White House can only be defined as bizarre. Where the previous seasons were notorious for their crises, intensity, and conflict, my final season was just strange and full of odd surprises.

The first major crisis came in the form of hurricanes—Harvey, Irma, and Maria, one after the other.

Harvey hit Texas and Louisiana in the final days of August and did major damage. President Trump visited Texas twice in one week, on August 29 and on September 2. Within thirty days, more than $1.5 billion in federal disaster relief was paid to Texans. All told, Trump deployed more than thirty-one thousand federal and FEMA staff. FEMA delivered three million meals and three million liters of water, in addition to providing temporary shelter to more than thirty thousand people displaced in Texas and Louisiana.

Irma hit closer to home for me, battering Florida, Alabama, Georgia, South Carolina, and North Carolina on September 10. Trump visited Florida four days later. FEMA and federal staff deployed dozens of incident management assistant teams, mobile response teams, and urban search-and-rescue task forces to all five states and delivered 7.2 million meals, forty-one generators, and 5.5 million liters of water within days. The storm hit Jacksonville and caused major damage and flooding. It was difficult to concentrate when my husband and mother and our church members and community were in harm's way.

And then there was Maria. It hit Puerto Rico on September 20. Trump did not visit the US territory until October 3, two weeks later. It took FEMA a week to deliver meals, and when they did, the meals contained chocolate bars, cookies, and potato chips. They hired independent contractors to provide thirty million meals ready to eat (MRE), but after nearly a month, only fifty thousand were delivered. The electricity is still out on much of the island to this day. At a press conference, Trump said, "I hate to tell you, Puerto Rico, but you've thrown our budget out of whack." The death toll was originally reported to be sixteen, which he said was nothing compared "to a real catastrophe" like Katrina. "Sixteen people certified," Trump said. "Sixteen people versus in the thousands [with Katrina; the actual stat is 1,833]. You can be very proud of all of your people and all of our people working together. Sixteen versus literally thousands of people. You can be very proud. Everybody watching can really be very proud of what's taken place in Puerto Rico."

When Trump and Melania finally visited the island, they went to a relief distribution center near San Juan, the Calvary Chapel. He famously threw rolls of paper towels at the devastated victims who'd lost homes and didn't have enough food or water. He defended that cavalier behavior in the face of human tragedy by telling Mike Huckabee on his Trinity Broadcasting show, "They had these beautiful, soft towels. Very good towels. And I came in, and there was a crowd of a lot of people. And they were screaming, and they were loving everything. I was having fun; they were having fun. They said, 'Throw 'em to me! Throw 'em to me, Mr. President!' So, the next day they said, 'Oh, it was so disrespectful to the people.' It was just a made-up thing. And also when I walked in the cheering was incredible."

Just like Charlottesville, it was all about him. The devastated people loved him! He was unfairly persecuted by the media. Everyone was having a great ol' time! His total lack of empathy is bad enough, but I believe many of the problems and delays with getting aid to Puerto Rico were partly political. The mayor of San Juan, Carmen Yulín Cruz, was openly critical of the US response. I would not put it past Trump to punish the people of Puerto Rico to teach that woman of color a lesson.

Puerto Rico is still in complete disarray. No matter how loud the outcry, the administration was lethargic in its response. Puerto Rico will be among the worst stains on Donald Trump's presidency. And God bless Tom Bossert, who tried to get the resources, tried to fight. He and I were fighting arm in arm, hand in hand, to try to advocate for Puerto Rico to get what they needed, and John Kelly shut it down.

In the National Security meeting, he said, "Their infrastructure was already screwed up," and suggested the bankrupt government was trying to exploit the hurricane to force the United States to foot the bill to rebuild their electrical grid. Kelly, like Trump, referred to Puerto Ricans with derogatory terms many times. The death toll—immediate deaths, those due to disease or illness in the aftermath—is still unconfirmed, but a 2018 Harvard University analysis says the actual number is 4,645, due to lack of access to medical care and electricity, being cut off from aid, stress, and other hurricane-related effects.

Around the time Maria struck Puerto Rico, Trump attended the United Nations General Assembly. I also joined the delegation to attend sessions related to famine. I was pleased with the $575 billion contribution that the US made to fight hunger for twenty million Nigerians, Somalians, South Sudanese, and Yemenites, but I also pressed for more aid and asked that the US establish a famine commission. My meetings and sessions were powerful and reflected the kind of work that was an extention of my personal ministry. I made strong connections with each of the countries' delegates and was eager to continue.

During the UNGA, Trump was scheduled to give a major speech to the full body. General Kelly sat in the audience with Melania. When Trump said, "The United States has great strength and patience, but if it is forced to defend itself or its allies, we will have no choice but to totally destroy North Korea," General Kelly dropped his face into his hands, a gesture that became known as the facepalm felt around the world. However, the truth is, Kelly was not necessarily as exasperated as he appeared. Rumors circulated around the West Wing that Kelly suffers from excruciating migraines—which possibly began during his military service—and he was in the throes of one of those episodes at the assembly. According to a source close to Kelly, the stress of his new role, the noise and light in the room, and the pressure triggered the migraine and he had no choice but to sit there and suffer through it. As bad as it was to put his face in his hands, it would have looked far worse if he'd walked out. As an officer, his service is compromised by this affliction, and he doesn't talk about it and prefers to appear to be made of stone. But when he gets a headache at work, he is vicious, bordering on cruel to his staff.

"White House HBCU Conference Still On Despite Calls to Cancel Event," Associated Press, August 25, 2017

My plate was full with organizing the Trump administration's first White House Summit on HBCUs. In the wake of Charlottesville, there were calls by the CBC and other groups to cancel the HBCU conference. I immediately pushed back against these critics and continued to plan. This conference had taken place every year for twenty years. It was a campaign promise of Trump's and was mandated by the executive order he'd signed back in February. The students who had been selected to serve as HBCU all-stars were excited about making the trip to DC; I truly did not want to let down the fifteen hundred participants who were registered, especially the one hundred student representatives.

The number one driver for cancellation was none other than Secretary Betsy DeVos. Perhaps she was still reeling from being booed at Bethune-Cookman's commencement, and wasn't inclined to support the historic event. Not surprisingly, she went to John Kelly and asked him to force me to cancel it.

I was summoned to his office and told that he had something very serious to discuss. He used his best ramrod-straight military posture to intimidate me and said, "Secretary DeVos does not want to go forward with the event. So I'm going to shut it down."

I didn't flinch. "We cannot cancel the event because of her. We can't let the students down." I laid out my case and told him that it was a White House event, that she would not have to be involved if she didn't want to, and that the event should still move forward. He said he would allow me to proceed but that if it failed, I would own it solely. I heard from a member of the HBCU staff that DeVos was livid that the event was moving forward.

A week after my meeting with General Kelly, Betsy DeVos tried to shut down the event by sending out a blast notice that it was off, and then she canceled the contract with the conference's hotel. By doing so, she cost the US government $75,000 in cancellation fees. She did not care! I was angry and upset but did not let her actions destroy what I had worked for. We quickly countered her notice with a statement from the president announcing that the summit would now take place at the White House and would go three days rather than five.

The White House conference center could only hold three hundred people, so I decided on the fly to scale down and break up the conference into a series of small sessions. We'd register each session until capacity was reached, and then close it off. Hosting at the White House also solved any security concerns. To enter, you had to be vetted and cleared.

To the dismay of all the forces working against me, I had one person in my corner—President Trump. He saw me in the Roosevelt Room after a meeting and asked what I was up to. I told him I had a few minor problems with the HBCU conference. I called out no one in particular, which might have distracted him. I just let him know what I needed. He made one call, and all road blocks were removed.

Suddenly, accommodations were made, funds were available, catering fell into place, and the conference center was secured.

In a comms meetings to nail down the messaging for the conference, I had to deal with Kelly Sadler. She said, "Are you sure about doing this? You're bringing some very angry people into the White House. After Charlottesville, they might riot. They might burn the place down."

Sadler was famous for her inappropriate commentary in comms meetings. When Trump tweeted about the transgender ban in the military, she agreed on principle and said in a comms meeting that I attended, "Why should we pay for soldiers to get their d**ks cut off?"

I said to Sadler, "The students are the best and brightest in our community, who carry themselves with dignity and class. If they protest at all, they'll do so peacefully."

After all this craziness, the conference was moving forward. Sarah Sanders received questions about it in her briefing. She reinforced that I was moving forward. "It's happening, and registration is full," she said.

The same people who'd called to cancel were now begging to attend.

I turned to the president again when Secretary DeVos refused to give opening remarks to the HBCU all-stars. As a result, the head of Cabinet Affairs, Bill McGinley, told her she *had* to give the opening remarks.

It went off without another hitch, and I was relieved after the success of the conference. Much of the press commented on the reduced size and the controversy about it, but the students loved it. I considered it one of the high points of my time serving at the White House.

Right on the heels of that success, though, came bad news. Keith Schiller, Trump's bodyguard and friend of many years, left at the end of September. I knew that without Keith, the president would probably become unhinged. I spoke with my husband and a few friends, and we all agreed the best time for me to leave would be in January—what is known as the "one-year anniversary exodus"—when many staffers leave their White House positions. It would give me more time to find a possible replacement for African American outreach.

ON SEPTEMBER 22, while campaigning for Luther Strange in the Republican primary in Alabama, Trump said of NFL players who took a knee during "The Star Spangled Banner," "That's a total disrespect of our heritage. That's a total disrespect of everything that we stand for. Wouldn't you love to see one of these NFL owners, when somebody disrespects our flag, you'd say, 'Get that son of a bitch off the field right now. Out! He's fired!'"

Trump had first grabbed hold of this issue a year ago, in September 2016, during the campaign, when Colin Kaepernick began the trend to protest police violence against African Americans. When Trump mentioned it at a rally, he got a huge cheer, and that was it. He incorporated it into his greatest hits and played that tune whenever he needed to quickly rile the base. His calling black players unpatriotic was completely designed to trigger latent racial resentment in a certain population of people who were predisposed to resent wealthy black men who weren't grateful enough about their lot in life. The sentiment could be summed up as, "Shut up and play."

The Trump tactic was to reframe the issue. The players took a knee for social justice. Donald reframed it to be about patriotism, saying that if they didn't stand for the national anthem, they weren't patriotic; they were against the military.

You won't find a single player who would agree with that.

At first I thought Trump didn't understand why the players, and, in time, many of the owners, were so offended by his remarks. I put together an extensive briefing memo for the president to make sure he was properly informed on the issue. I'm certain he never read it. As long as DJT got cheers when he trashed these powerful black men, he was not going to stop.

"Trump Said 'Despicable' Racist Comments about Blacks, Jews in Taped 'Apprentice' Meetings, Claims Former Producer," *Newsweek*, October 5, 2017

In October, *Apprentice* producer Bill Pruitt started talking about the N-word tape again, this time, on the NPR podcast *Embedded* with host Kelly McEvers.

McEvers brought up Pruitt's October 2016 tweet about the Trump Tapes and his offensive language. Here is the relevant conversation.

McEVERS: Was it just about women?

PRUITT: No.

McEVERS: Mostly about women.

PRUITT: Very much a racist issue.

McEVERS: It was about race.

PRUITT: Yeah.

McEVERS: About African Americans, Jewish people, all of the above.

PRUITT: Yep. When you heard these things, there's the audible gasp that is quickly followed by a cough, kind of like (gasping), you know, and then (coughing)—yes, anyway, you know? And then you just sort of carry on.

McEVERS: Is there ever a time when you think, I wish I would have told him not to say things like that?

PRUITT: That's a really good question. It was not my place to be, hey, TV star, you know, reason we're all here, shut your [expletive] damn mouth, and don't ever, ever repeat what you just said. Of course, you know, you think that. You go back to your hotel room or your apartment that they put you up in. And you know, you do some soul-searching.

His interview must have triggered some soul-searching in the far reaches of the *Apprentice* world. Soon after, I heard more rumblings about the N-word tape. During the campaign, Mark Burnett's office had sent out reminders to everyone about their NDAs. The message was clear: forces were trying to protect DJT.

A truly unique situation came up on October 9, when Ivana Trump, the president's first wife, went on *Good Morning America* to promote her new memoir, *Raising Trump*, and said, "I'm basically first Trump wife. Okay. I'm First Lady."

She also said of Melania, "I think for her to be in Washington must be terrible."

After watching the interview, I immediately went over to the East Wing to see how Melania was taking it. She was furious. My recommendation to a member of her staff? "Melania needs to put that Ivana in her place! Those are some fighting words!" No one knew how to calm Melania down.

I didn't understand why Donald didn't step in. By not shutting Ivana down, he was empowering her to say whatever she wanted on national TV, about Melania or him! Donald should have tweeted that he had only one First Lady, Melania Trump. Personally, I think he enjoyed the *Real Housewives of the White House* spat. He loves to pit people against each other and watch them fight it out, even those closest to him. In fact, whenever Donald and Melania weren't on speaking terms—which was very often—he would call Ivana and ask her for advice. What could upset the current wife more than the husband calling up the first wife for advice?

Even then, in the comparatively halcyon pre–Stormy Daniels days of October, Melania was counting every minute until he was out of office and she could be a private citizen again.

"Wacky Congresswoman Wilson is the gift that keeps on giving for the Republican Party, a disaster for Dems. You watch her in action & vote R!" Trump tweet, October 22, 2017, 5:02 a.m.

A crisis rocked the White House, and specifically General Kelly, in mid-October. There is a bit of backstory: On October 4, four soldiers were killed in an ambush gone wrong in Niger. One of them was Army Sergeant La David Johnson, married to his childhood sweetheart, Myeshia Johnson, the mother of his two children, and pregnant with a third. Florida Congresswoman Frederica Wilson had known La David Johnson his whole life, long before her time in Congress, and had been his mentor in a special program for young men who aspired to be in the military.

After much pressure for Donald to make a condolence call to the fallen soldiers, he called Myeshia on October 17. Wilson happened to be with her at the time and listened to their conversation on speakerphone. As she recounted on CNN over two interviews, Trump showed no empathy for the widow, saying, "[Your husband] knew what he signed up for, but I guess it still hurt." Also, Trump didn't remember La David's name. As soon as the call ended, Myeshia, said Wilson, "broke down."

On October 18, Trump tweeted at 4:25 a.m., "Democrat Congresswoman totally fabricated what I said to the wife of a soldier who died in action (and I have proof). Sad!" Sarah Sanders accused Wilson of politicizing, and said her having listened in on the call was "appalling and disgusting."

In response to Trump's tweet, the fallen soldier's mother, Cowanda Jones-Johnson, who also heard the call on speakerphone, told the *Washington Post*, "President Trump did disrespect my son and my daughter and also me and my husband."

It continued to escalate. On October 19, General John Kelly held a press conference at the White House to continue to beat down this grieving widow. He explained the protocol for alerting family members of a soldier's death, and recounted the circumstances of his own son's death in Iraq. He said that he'd been the one to tell Trump what to say on his condolence calls. He then said, "I was stunned when I came to work yesterday morning, and brokenhearted at what I saw a member of Congress doing. A member of Congress who listened in on a phone call from the president of the United States to a young wife . . . It stuns me that a member of Congress would have listened in on that conversation. Absolutely stuns me. And I thought at least that was sacred."

So Trump's lack of empathy on a condolence call was being reframed by Kelly as an act of moral inferiority on the part of Congressman Wilson, whom he would not even dignify by using her name. He continued to trash Wilson, telling another story about her being "an empty barrel that makes the most noise." As he told it, at the dedication of a new FBI building in Miami to two fallen agents, the congresswoman stood up and took credit for securing the funding for the building, making the ceremony all about her. This, too, "stunned" Kelly.

The next day, the *Sun Sentinel* of Fort Lauderdale posted a video from that dedication ceremony, and showed that Congresswoman Wilson had not stood up and taken credit for the building's financing. Kelly lied, or he had a very racist memory of being offended by a black woman even when she did nothing inappropriate.

The day after that, at the daily press briefing with Sarah Sanders, reporters wanted to know if Kelly would apologize or admit he was wrong. Sanders said, "If you want to go after General Kelly, that's up to you, but I think that if you want to get into a debate with a four-star marine general, I think that that's something highly inappropriate." In other words, when a general lies to smear a black woman, it's business as usual.

Now, if you followed this story in the news, you have heard all this before. What you don't know is what was said behind the scenes. In a senior staff meeting right after Wilson came out and said the president made a war widow cry, Kelly spoke of Myeshia with such disdain, it shocked me and many others in the room. He said, "How dare she put the call on speaker? How dare she not just be grateful to receive a call at all?"

The president had waited two weeks to make that call. In the meantime, he was railing against NFL players and in a rage because

Rex Tillerson, as it came out, had called him "a moron." He was fixated on that, saying, "He's the moron! I'm a genius! My IQ is genius level. He thinks he's a big shot! I'll challenge him to an IQ test!" His rants were so repetitive and unending, I learned to tune them out as much as I could. If you engaged him on the topic, you would lose an entire day.

He only acknowledged the death of those four soldiers because the media challenged him to make the call. Just like putting out the statement about Charlottesville, he resented being forced to do the right thing. And Kelly was furious and "stunned" that two black women—a pregnant widow and a seventy-five-year-old grandmother of five—could come out of this quagmire looking far more moral and dignified than he did.

I found every aspect of this story to be disgusting and appalling, but particularly Kelly's use of his own son's death as political cover for Trump's failure and his irrational anger at the women involved. This was the man who refused to look at me in meetings, who'd refused to speak much more than a word to me in three months, who would, in good time, attempt to smear my reputation with lies. Kelly's loathing of Congressman Wilson could only be based on his hatred of black women. It was certainly not based on her actions. This is the same man who said that the Civil War was about compromise.

TRUMP MADE HEADLINES on November 15 when, during a speech in the map room, he awkwardly reached for a bottle of water and then used both hands to drink it. People made fun of him about it, but I found it worrisome. I had been concerned about his health for quite some time.

During the campaign, I had expressed concern for his medical health and what a doctor's exam would reveal. I was told by a member of the family, "Don't worry, the doctor won't let Donald down." The doctor was Harold Bornstein. He provided a glowing review of Trump's health in September 2016 that sounded too good to be true. Of course, it wasn't true. Bornstein told CNN in May 2018 that Trump "dictated that whole letter. I didn't write it. I just made it up as I went along." He also said that in February 2017, soon after Trump became president, three people had gone to his office and taken the entire Trump file, thirty-five years of medical records. The trigger for the "raid" might have been Bornstein's telling the *New York Times* about Trump's previously undisclosed use of Propecia for hair loss and a rosacea drug. As he told NBC News, "I couldn't believe anybody was making a big deal out of a drug to grow his hair." The doctor said he felt "raped, frightened and sad," and could have taken it further, but he never did. He had to have known how dangerous these people were.

Back to that awkward drinking moment in the map room: as soon as the event was over, Dr. Ronny Jackson approached the president. We were departing the room. I don't know what happened after I left, but to my untrained eye, it looked like Trump had had a small episode of some kind.

I believe that Donald Trump is physically ill. His terrible health habits have caught up with him. His refusal to exercise (except golf).

His addiction to Big Macs and fried chicken. His daily tanning bed sessions (he prefers to do it in the morning, so he "looks good" all day). Donald might brag about his superior genes, but even they can't stand up to what he puts his body through.

He is clearly obese. During the first season of *The Apprentice*, he was tall and svelte. In the ensuing seasons, Donald expanded slowly but surely. In 2007, he didn't have a belly yet or the jowl. By 2012, he'd probably put on thirty pounds eating a junk-food-only diet. His preference for steak well done with ketchup has offended many chefs all over the world. The world has yet to learn about the extent of Donald Trump's Diet Coke habit. He always had one in his hand, as far back as I've known him. He's up to eight cans a day, at least. Eight cans a day, for the last fifteen years, is 43,800 cans of Diet Coke, poured into his system.

In the White House, he just pushes a button in a wooden box on his desk. He can summon anything with that button. Whenever I went in to brief him, he'd push the button and get us Diet Cokes.

When I started to have grave concerns for his mental health, I connected the dots to his physical health and poor choices, specifically, his soda habit.

I researched it, and found a brand-new study by a team of neurologists from Boston University that linked Diet Coke consumption with dementia and increased risk of stroke.

Dementia. Not being able to remember anything, confusion, loss of vocabulary and ability to process information. Stroke. Those awkward shaking hands, struggling to bring a bottle of water to his mouth . . .

I printed out the study and put it in his stack. He never read it. Rob Porter did, and he gave me a warning. After a senior staff meeting, he said, "Stop putting articles in the president's folder. You have to go through me first. Don't do it again."

It was just like the time I had tried to talk to people at the White House about his cognitive issues. No one wanted to hear it, let alone document it. If Dr. Jackson knew what was really going on with Trump's brain and body, he did not disclose it to anyone. In January he announced that the president was in excellent health, and had excellent genes, an echo of what Trump always said about himself. His loyalty was rewarded when Donald nominated him for Secretary of Veterans Affairs, but that didn't work out. He was accused of being an unstable man who treated underlings poorly, abused alcohol, once crashed a car while drunk, banged on the hotel room door of a female colleague while drunk, and doled out prescription medications so freely he was called "Candyman."

Staff Secretary Rob Porter was another man whom Trump valued, who kept his secrets and had a very dark side.

I found Rob to be very buttoned-up, very rigid, but there was something about him that gave me pause. There was a *weird* look in his eyes. He was just not the kind of man with whom you would want to be alone in an elevator. And yet, women on the staff liked him, such as Hope Hicks, his girlfriend at that time.

I didn't challenge Porter about the study, and I steered clear of him.

Trumpworld was overpopulated with questionable men. Trump endorsed Roy Moore, a man who was accused by several women of sexual misconduct, some when they were underage. I found Trump's endorsement despicable. It was disgusting. And there was more than his alleged treatment of women. During a campaign speech, he referred to Asians as "yellows" and Native Americans as "reds." He'd compared the Koran to *Mein Kampf* and said that Congressman Keith Ellison, a Muslim, should not be permitted to serve his country. There was simply no way that Donald really wanted a person like this to be a United States senator! And yet, he supported him. January 20 could not come fast enough. I had to get out.

After Charlottesville, we needed some feel-good events. One of the ones that my office, OPL, helped to set up was a November 27 meeting to honor Navajo code talkers, veterans who'd aided the US Marines to send coded messages during World War I and II. As John McCain tweeted, "[Their] bravery, skill & tenacity helped secure our decisive victory over tyranny & oppression."

Donald spoke to the three code talkers, all of them elderly gentlemen, in the Oval. Unfortunately, the podium was right in front of a portrait of slave owner Andrew Jackson, the seventh president, a Trump favorite, who had signed the Indian Removal Act in 1830 that led to mass migration of native people along the Trail of Tears, where thousands of Cherokee died.

That was one unfortunate oversight.

Another unfortunate moment was during Trump's praising of these proud men. He said, "I just want to thank you because you're very, very special people. You were here long before any of us were here. Although we have a representative in Congress who was here a long time . . . longer than you. They call her 'Pocahontas.' "

Another unforced error. Another example of being tackled by your own team.

I was shocked. First of all, what did Massachusetts Senator Elizabeth Warren have to do with the event? Why bring her up at all? Why use a racial slur about Native Americans at a ceremony to honor Native Americans? It was unconscionable.

We had another one of our frustrating conversations immediately after that event.

I said, "Mr. President, you insulted those men. We were trying to honor them!"

He said, "I didn't insult them. I insulted Elizabeth Warren."

He couldn't make the leap, that evoking Pocahontas to belittle Warren was, in effect, insulting to native people as a whole because of Trump's intention of his usage. In my opinion, Trump didn't care that he offended those men or anyone. He thought he'd gotten in a good jab at Elizabeth Warren.

The next day, Eric Trump whataboutismed like an Olympic champion, tweeting, "The irony of an ABC reporter (whose parent company Disney has profited nearly half a billion dollars on the movie 'Pocahontas') inferring that the name is 'offensive' is truly staggering to me." The real, pressing issue wasn't that Donald insulted American heroes to their face in a White House that struggled with race. To Eric, it was that Disney made an animated film twenty-two years ago.

That tweet was beneath Eric. But to stay in the cult, followers, including Trump's children, had to compromise their own integrity to defend Donald.

I *really* had to get out of there.

It was announced in late November that Kellyanne would be the new point person on the opioid crisis. The national public health emergency fund earmarked for the crisis had shrunk to sixty thousand dollars at the same time Jeff Sessions's Justice Department pledged twelve million dollars to help prosecute drug crimes via state and local law enforcement. Kellyanne was an unusual choice for this role, since she lacked any experience or expertise in public health, drug policy, or law enforcement. Back in October, she "yessed" Trump and Sessions's view that the solution to the crisis was prevention, telling Fox News, "The best way to stop people from dying from overdoses and drug abuse is by not starting in the first place. That's a big core message for our youth." Prevention was a necessary part of any drug policy, but what about the two million people who misuse prescription pain killers, and almost six hundred thousand heroin addicts already on our streets? Was Sessions-style "round 'em up" prosecution the best strategy? I wasn't so sure about that.

Immediately, I set up a meeting with her for myself and the surgeon general, Jerome M. Adams. We walked in, sat down, and I said, "Dr. Adams and I wanted to talk to you about the impact of opioids on diverse communities."

Dr. Adams, an anesthesiologist and African American, spoke for a bit about addiction and the proliferation of opioids in African Americans.

I mentioned that, during the crack epidemic in the '90s, there was no compassionate approach to treating addiction in the inner cities. Opioids were seen as a white, suburban, and rural problem, and resources for prevention and treatment were available. "It's a major cause of death and suffering in the inner cities, too. We need to allocate resources to the minority communities, as well," I said, and presented my briefing folder with stats. Dr. Adams outlined what his prescription would be.

Kellyanne listened politely, but I could tell our passionate plea didn't sway her.

"I will look into all of this and get back to you," she said to appease us.

To this day, there has been little to no effort made to allocate opioid crisis resources to African American communities. Kelly-anne's opioid "cabinet"—which is full of political appointees—was called a "sham" by drug policy expert Congressman Patrick Kennedy in January 2018.

On December 5, Corey Lewandowski's book, *Let Trump Be Trump,* coauthored with David Bossie, came out. In an early chapter, he described how Hope Hicks would steam-press Donald's trousers while he was still wearing them. Hope was furious. It portrayed her in a servile demeaning light. It might have been a bit of revenge on Corey's part for Hope's ending their relationship to move on to a law enforcement officer. When that romance fizzled, she got involved with Rob Porter. (Incidentally, Hope was not the only female assistant to the president to have White House flings. Another highly visible assistant to the president might still be carrying on her affair right now.)

A couple of months later came the press reports of allegations that Rob Porter abused both his exes (and a third woman, a 2016 girlfriend). The ex-wives told the FBI about Porter's abuse during his security clearance, but nothing happened. He was appointed to the White House as a staff secretary to Trump anyway. For months, General Kelly kept this secret.

Incidentally, when this all came out about Porter, General Kelly didn't want him to leave. The chief of staff had known for months about Porter's history with domestic abuse but didn't seem to mind. The day of Rob's resignation, Kelly said, "Rob Porter is a man of true integrity and honor and I can't say enough good things about him. He is a friend, a confidant, and a trusted professional. I am proud to serve alongside him." So, in spite of everything that came out, Rob Porter had integrity. Kelly would later rake me over the coals about so-called "integrity issues." He has a very interesting understanding of the meaning of "integrity."

Donald called Porter's exit "very sad" and defended him by saying that Porter claimed he was innocent.

THROUGHOUT THE FALL, with all this insanity going on around me, I was miserable at the White House. Morale was at an all-time low, and the environment was toxic. I realized that Donald Trump was the biggest distraction to his own presidency. Donald Trump, the individual, the person, because of who he is and what he stands for and how he operates, would always be the biggest hindrance for us. Donald Trump, who would attack civil rights icons and professional athletes, who would go after grieving black widows, who would say there were good people on both sides, who endorsed an accused child molester; Donald Trump, and his decisions and his behavior, was harming the country. I could no longer be a part of this madness.

So, on that wintry day in December 2017, days before Christmas, what General Kelly did when he summoned me into the Situation Room—although morally bankrupt, factually wrong, and downright slimy—had a silver lining. As he executed his plan to expedite my departure from the White House that Tuesday evening, it was as if a hypnotist's assistant had snapped his fingers and the hypnosis was now over.

For the first time in nearly fifteen years, I would be free from the cult of Trumpworld.

The day *after* I left, I received a call from the president.

He said, "What's going on? I just saw on the news you're thinking about leaving. What happened?"

Did he not know I'd already left?

"General Kelly said you guys wanted me to leave," I said.

"No! No one even told me. I didn't know that. Damn it. I don't love you leaving at all." He started rambling. "It's a big operation, to tell you the truth."

He talked a little more and then said he would call me back once he spoke to Kelly. He apparently wanted to get to the bottom of this mishap.

We hung up, and I tried to make sense of that conversation.

Either he *did* know, and he was lying to me and playing me, proving his loyalty oath was completely one-sided, or he *didn't* know Kelly intended to threaten me, lock me in the Situation Room, and tell me he didn't want things to get "ugly" for me. Had he ceded all control of the White House to the general? If that were true, then Trump was powerless and that was alarming.

During the call, I heard real sadness in his voice. He seemed devastated that I was gone. He was unhappy Keith Schiller was gone. His two old friends, separated from him. In his voice, I could hear that he really did care about me. But it wasn't enough.

Ivanka and Jared called me next. She said, "I know my father spoke to you. He put out a nice tweet. I wanted to make sure you're doing okay."

"I'm hanging in there."

Ivanka said, "We've been thinking about you."

Jared added, "As we've learned, it's a brutal business."

"The reports of my exit have been insane," I replied.

He said, "We're here, and whatever you're thinking of doing next, if we can help you in any way . . ."

"Omarosa, we're here for you always," said Ivanka. "We really love you, and if we can help in any way."

"One hundred percent," said Jared. "Take care. Call us anytime, for anything."

And then, finally, I heard from Lara and Eric. During this call, Lara expressed love and concern from the whole family—"You know how much we love you, how much DJT loves you"—and offered me a position in the reelection campaign, as I've mentioned earlier.

I stalled. I had no intention of joining, but I wanted to see what they'd send me.

Lara and I discussed my plans for the holidays and when we

could finalize. I told her that I'd be going to Florida for Christmas, and we could talk after that.

"I read that *New York Times* article," she blurted. She was referring to the article I mentioned back in the Introduction, the one by Katie Rogers and Maggie Haberman that said I had "a story to tell." I hadn't seen it; I was busy recovering from foot surgery and the media attacks, and was fielding a number of offers from television, radio, and print.

I said, "What article?"

"It was on the front page, the one they wrote about you. That's not something to tell people about. If you come on board, we can't have you talking about that stuff . . . everything is positive, right? Why don't we chat on Monday?"

That's not something to tell people about . . . We can't have you talking about stuff . . .

Did she mean nearly fifteen years of Donald Trump's crazy antics that I had witnessed? Because there was *a lot*.

Within twenty-four hours, Lara sent me a contract to work on the 2020 campaign for $15,000 per month, the same salary that I'd received at the White House. The NDA attached to the email was as harsh and restrictive as any I'd seen in all my years of television. It said that I was forbidden from ever talking about the entire Trump family or the entire Pence family, to anyone in the universe, for all of eternity.

I declined the offer. I was done with Trumpworld.

However, they were not done yet with me. Two days later, I got a flurry of letters from attorneys representing the president of the United States imploring me to stay silent about Trump, or else.

• • •

FOR MONTHS AFTER my departure, I could not reach my sources about the N-word tape. And then, after I returned from my stint in Hollywood I called one of them out of the blue.

Incredibly, this person—who shall remain nameless—picked up the phone.

We spoke.

On this phone conversation, I was told exactly what Donald Trump said—yes, the N-word and others in a classic Trump-goes-nuclear rant—and when he'd said them.

During production he was miked, and there is definitely an audio track.

For over a year I'd been so afraid of hearing the specifics from someone who'd been in the room. Hearing the truth freed me from that fear. And only now that it's gone, do I realize just how heavy it's been.

Epilogue

During the telecast of the sixtieth annual Grammy Awards on CBS, I was announced as the surprise cast member of the special edition of *Celebrity Big Brother*. News of my appearance on the show went nationwide, trended on social media, and was all the talk of Washington, DC.

My decision to join the cast was simple. I wanted to get as far away from Washington and that traumatic incident in the Situation Room as I could get. The idea of being sequestered away from the world would seem daunting to most celebrities. It sounded like music to my ears. No phones, no TV, no Internet for thirty days. It sounded like just the detox I needed after spending nearly two and half years on the campaign and then the transition and time in the White House with Donald Trump. I needed a total Trump detox, and *Celebrity Big Brother* offered that unique opportunity.

During the show I got to live in total luxury and hang out with fellow celebs and just relax for a change. With my guard down, I said some things that made headlines. I wasn't aware of their effect until I got out. Some of my comments were:

"When you're in the middle of the hurricane, it's hard to see the destruction on the outer bands."

I'm sure some will see this as a rationalization, but it's just the truth. I was so embattled by negative headlines about what I was or was not really doing in the White House, by outside groups who hated the president and the administration, by other appointees, and inside the White House, getting tackled every day by my teammates. *It was difficult to process the anxiety and pain others were suffering as a result of the administration.*

When the Stormy Daniels hush money scandal broke in January and appeared on front pages around the world, I felt sorry for Michael Cohen. His biggest shortcoming was his one-hundred-percent loyalty and worship of Donald Trump. That has also become his downfall. If it weren't for Trump, Michael would be running his deals and doing other stuff, probably just as questionable, but not under a microscope. If you think about it, Cohen's side deals weren't all that different from the kind that Jared Kushner and his family make, or from Ivanka's receiving seven new trademarks for kitchenware and furniture brands from China while her father is negotiating trade deals with that country. Many people in Trumpworld are side hustling every which way to Sunday. It's what they do.

His relationship with Trump destroyed Michael Cohen. Michael was just doing what he was told to do. He was a middleman. There would be no payoff to Stormy Daniels if Trump weren't on one end of the phone line. Cohen was not the first collateral damage in Trumpworld and he is not the last. He just got caught, and as soon as he was no longer useful to Trump, he was written off. Trump loyalty, in this and other cases, was a one-way street.

Another comment I made was "As bad as you think Trump is, you should be worried about Pence. So everyone wishing for impeachment might want to reconsider it. We would be begging for the days of Trump back if Pence became president."

When the Stormy story broke, I wondered what Mike Pence had to say about it. Surely he would express indignation. Where was his outrage about the porn star, the payoff, and the president?

Pence was silent on the issue. He and his team are simply biding their time until Trump is impeached or resigns. He is definitely a swamp creature, opening the White House doors to lobbyists and being controlled by donors of his various campaigns for Congress and the governorship of Indiana.

For this reason, along with so many others I've explained in this book—the fact that our president is mentally and physically impaired, that Betsy DeVos intends to destroy public education in this country, that Jeff Sessions thinks it's okay to separate children from their parents, that dark money continues to control Washington, that the White House is packed with people who are only advancing their own interests—I told my housemate on *Big Brother*, "It's not going to be okay; it's not. It's so bad." When I implied on *The Late Show with Stephen Colbert* in February 2018 that I was only referring to immigration—and we should be very afraid about what Stephen Miller is doing on that regard—I had to edit myself a bit. I was, and still am, negotiating with John Kelly to get back my personal items that are still being held at the White House. I didn't want to poke the bear too hard . . . then.

One person who knows better than anyone just how broken and flawed Donald Trump is? Melania. She's been trying to tell the world all this time, and on June 22, 2018, she took her sartorial rebellion to the next level, by wearing a Zara jacket with the words I REALLY DON'T CARE. DO U? printed on the back, while on her way to visit detained immigrant children at a Texas border facility in the wake of the controversy about the Stephen Miller–penned "zero tolerance" family separation policy. The message on the jacket was debated in the media for days. Only Melania knows for sure what she was trying to convey, but I have a theory that no one else picked up on.

Melania's style rebellions throughout the campaign and Trump presidency have been intentionally misleading. As a student of fashion and a keenly image-conscious woman, she knows that every one of her style choices will be scrutinized and debated. Why did she wear a Gucci "pussy bow" pink blouse to the presidential debate immediately after the *Access Hollywood* bombshell? Did she purposefully wear a Hillary Clinton–esque white pantsuit to Trump's first State of the Union address? Did she mean to come off as out of touch and tone-deaf by wearing snakeskin stiletto heels to hurricane-ravaged Texas? The messages behind her style choices aren't always clear, but they are never accidental.

Taken as a whole, all of her style rebellions have served the same purpose, and not only misdirection and distraction—strategies her husband knows all too well. I believe Melania uses style to punish her husband.

It's my opinion that Melania was forced to go to the border that day in June, essentially, to mop up her husband's mess. She wore that jacket to hurt Trump, setting off a controversy that he would have to fix, prolonging the conversation about the administration's insensitivity, ruining the trip itself, and trying to make sure that no one asked her to do something like that again. Not that Melania doesn't have compassion for immigrant children; I'm sure she does. But she gladly, spitefully, wrecked her husband's directives to make him look foolish.

It was often discussed among Trumpworld intimates that Donald had something to do with Melania's obtaining a rare Einstein Visa, a.k.a. an EB-1, that gives immigrants with "extraordinary ability" or "sustained national and international acclaim" US citizenship. Many have questioned her qualifications for receiving this visa, and have speculated that Trump was able to use his networks and resources to secure it or expedite it. Since Donald is fully aware of however she acquired her permanent citizenship, he could, if there were anything fishy around it, expose the methods and somehow invalidate it. He is a vindictive man, and I would not put anything past him. If Melania were to try to pull the ultimate humiliation and leave him while he's in office, he would find a way to punish her. This is a man who has said he could pardon himself from the Mueller investigation. Why not pardon himself over an alleged visa payoff?

In my opinion, Melania is counting every minute until he is out of office and she can divorce him.

It's been several months since I said, "It's not going to be okay," and I have had time to reflect. When I first spoke those words, I was thinking short-term. My entire life for two years was about going from minute to minute, crisis to crisis, without having time to step back and see the big picture. So, in the short term, knowing what I know about the Trump administration, I couldn't see how we were going to be okay.

But now that I have been able to step back and see the long-term prospects for our country, I can provide a clearer perspective.

We are in a very critical time in history, with racial strife, class and cultural divisions, immigration issues, and economic disparities. However, I am convinced that we, as a nation, will summon the will to overcome these obstacles. Our history says that we always do. We overcame slavery and Jim Crow; we've made progress on racial and gender inequality. We will continue to improve, not that it will be simple and easy. Perfecting our nation, to borrow the words of Abraham Lincoln, is a pursuit and a process. We will take steps up, and steps back. We'll walk through peaks and valleys, but eventually, we will get to where we need to go.

Right now, I believe we are in a deep valley, and I acknowledge my role in our being here. I also have faith that we will march upward and out of it, very soon.

I believe in our country, and I believe in the people of this republic.

I believe that we will come through this period recognizing that division for political ends is vapid and empty.

Playing upon people's fears for the sake of legislative expediency is not a sustainable model for a healthy democracy, and, ultimately, we will reject it.

We will come to the conclusion that the apparent gains of division pale in comparison to the benefits of unity and the pursuit of the common good.

I cling to the indefatigable American spirit of fairness and faith. I'm a patriot and I love my country enough to criticize it when it strays from its better self, but also hold on to the belief that our greatest days are still ahead of us.

Change is coming. To bring it about we must be participants and not spectators in the pursuit of equality and unity. Together, we can make this country honor the sacrifices of our ancestors. Whether we came in on the *Mayflower*, through Ellis Island, or on slave ships, we are all in the same boat now.

Will we survive Trump?

Will the presidency ever be the same?

Is our democracy safe?

The answer is yes! We've survived wars, segregation, recessions, terrorist attacks. We will survive this, too.

As someone who knows his tricks and has seen the machine from the inside for many years, I have some suggestions on how to do it.

All we need to remember is that Trump *loves* the hate. He thrives on criticism and insults. He delights in chaos and confusion. Taking to Twitter to call him names only fuels him and riles his base. To disarm him, starve his ego: don't feed into it.

Also, the public needs to recognize that not all Trump supporters are the same. While you rail against one policy of his or another, you may not know you are speaking to a closet Trumplican. As I traveled the country, the most unsuspecting people whispered to me that they voted for him. People of all shapes, sizes, backgrounds, races, religions. It's dangerous to group all his voters into one box and insult them, when you could be listening to them and understanding their point of view, and finding common ground instead.

Rest assured that there is an army of people who oppose him and his policies. They are working silently and tirelessly to make sure he does not cause harm to the republic. Many in this silent army are in his party, his administration, and even in his own family.

We are reminded daily that Trump is still in the throes of the Mueller investigation. The special investigators are conducting interviews with subjects who have stories to tell. In early 2018, I, too, received a call from the FBI. We'll see how that goes.

But for me, fifteen years later—through *The Apprentice*, the campaign, and the White House—I can finally exhale. I've escaped from the cult of Trumpworld.

I'm free.

Acknowledgments

M om, I honor and thank you for being an incredible example of grace and beauty all my life. I am grateful for your remarkable life as a gifted artist, author, speaker, minister, confidante, and friend. You are my hero!

I wish to thank my wonderful husband, John, for loving and supporting me through this entire project. Your love, guidance, counsel, and especially prayers have sustained me throughout. As you always say, "Love is what you do." Thank you for doing exactly that, John. I love you, honey. I'd also like to thank the members of our congregation, the Sanctuary @ Mt. Calvary Church. You have been so supportive and understanding when I've had to be away while working on this book. Even from a distance, I've felt your love and support throughout this journey. Thank you from the depths of my heart.

My agent John Seitzer is awesome! Thank you, Sheva Cohen.

ACKNOWLEDGMENTS

A special thank you to my literary agent, Steve Fisher. Thank you to everyone at the Agency for the Performing Arts in Beverly Hills.

To Robert Walker and the entire American Program Bureau team, thank you for standing with me for the last ten years. Flip Porter, I'm looking forward to all that you have in store for me.

I would like to thank Leslie Moonves, Julie Chen, Kelly Kahl, Sharon Vuong, Brian Speiser, Thom Sherman, Peter Golden, Dustin Smith, Allison Grodner, and Shawn O'Neil.

Valerie Frankel, as I told you multiple times a day, I appreciate you and can't thank you enough for going through this experience with me. Considering the intense pressure we were under and the—at times—painful subject matter, we sure did laugh a lot and had way more fun than I thought possible when writing a book. Thanks again for helping me share my memories and make happy new ones.

My deep gratitude goes out to everyone at Gallery. I'm much obliged to Carolyn Reidy, Jonathan Karp, Jennifer Bergstrom, Aimee Bell, Jen Long, Jennifer Robinson, and especially Natasha Simons for all of your insightful and helpful editorial guidance. Hannah Brown and Laura Waters provided unparalleled support.

On the production and design side, a hearty thanks to Navorn Johnson, John Paul Jones, Irene Kheradi, Monica Oluwek, Caroline Pallotta, Larry Pekarek, Lisa Litwack, John Vairo, Math Monahan, Jaime Putorti, and Bryden Spevak. Much thanks for the wise counsel of Felice Javit and Elisa Rivlin.

Without researchers Beatrice Hogan and Lucy Rosenberg and transcribers Bliss Blood and Stephen Quint, this book would not have been possible. Thanks to all of you for your hard work and attention to detail.

A special thanks to Ann Billingsley for your gracious hospitality.

Pastor K.W. Tulloss and my Weller Street family, thank you for everything!

My dear friend and personal editor Bryan Monroe, thanks don't begin to cover it. Bryan is an award-winning, nationally recognized journalist, a recent author, and an educator in his own right, but for this project, he was my sounding board. Even though Bryan would regularly and aggressively challenge my positions, disagree with my politics, and push back on whatever my crazy former boss did, he was also always, I mean *always*, in my corner.

I also acknowledge the assistance of Scotton Communications Network.

Where would I be without my village: Ervin Bernard Reid, Aisha, Shannon, Esdra, Richard and Ari, Steve, MaryLove and Vivian, Damola, Lashawn, Ashley, Astrid, Betty, Mwenza, Charita, Kionna, K. W. Tullos, Jawalyn, Chris, Jackie, Kimra, Kim and Paul Long, J. Wyndal, Monique, Myran, David, Lezli, Krita, Ella, Martin, Cliff, Wayne Fredrick, Kim Wells, Dean Barron Harvey, Verna, Lynne, Jerri and Pat, Kris, Pella, Pastor H. B. Hicks, Ivan, Tom, Shirmichael, Armstrong Williams, Earl, Tucker, Joe, Harold, Najee Ali, Brandon, Natasha, Heaven, Keenan Towns, Mrs. Dabney, Stephanie, Althea, Donna, Gerry and Matt, Minyon, Hanny, Dione and Kenny, Kent and Ashlea, Carlton, Emil, Turk, Don Anthony, Ashley Bell, Bruce, Darrell, Dee, Malesa, Pam, Michael Todd, Andrew

ACKNOWLEDGMENTS

Coppa, William, Barbara, Sam, Kevin Parker, DeeDee, Derrick, Vanessa and Estee, my JCREW: Michael, Sonja, Donald, Donald, and Sherman. Jackson, Wendy and Roosevelt, Cynthia, Alexis and Max, Quentin and Terri, Craig Kirby, Qasim, Dest'n, Marcia, Kevin, Uncle Robert and Aunt Sherry, Aunt Evelyn, Darian, ReRe, Avia, Alix, Kera, Nathaniel, Justice, Melky, Wyclef, Claudinette, Cleve, Katrina Campins, Rob, Marie and Laila, Brad, Noel and Loretta, Rick, Trystin, Michelle, Nina, Joanie, Datari, John Guns and Sonjanique, Rudy, Freddy, Kyler, Keisha, Marrissa, Metta, Shannon, Mark, Wendell and Kym, Kelly Day and Robin Eisner, Dr Dea and Michelle. The Walker Family, The Manigault Family, The Niccole Family, Michael and Penny. I'm blessed to have you all in my life.

To God be the glory!

www.Omarosa.com
www.Twitter.com/Omarosa
Instagram/Omarosa
Facebook/OfficialOmarosa